KARL BARTH'S CHURCH DOGMATICS:

AN INTRODUCTION AND READER

KARL BARTH'S CHURCH DOGMATICS:

AN INTRODUCTION AND READER

R. MICHAEL ALLEN

t&t clark

Published by T&T Clark International
A Continuum Imprint
The Tower Building, 11 York Road, London SE1 7NX
80 Maiden Lane, Suite 704, New York, NY 10038

www.continuumbooks.com

British Library Cataloguing-in-Publication Data
A catalogue record for this book is available from the British Library

ISBN: 978-0-567-00356-0 (hardback)
978-0-567-15219-0 (paperback)

Typeset by Fakenham Prepress Solutions, Fakenham, Norfolk NR21 8NN
Printed and bound in India

For T. F. Torrance, G. W. Bromiley, and their band
of translators

CONTENTS

ACKNOWLEDGEMENTS

I have long desired a useful one-volume introduction and reader to *Karl Barth's Church Dogmatics*. Barth is too little read and much less understood in his classical and modern contexts. Reading through the entirety of the *Church Dogmatics* is never to be discouraged, but it is not for the faint of heart. Even the zealous probably need some macro-level orientation before attempting such an exercise. A reader seems essential. The selections published by Eerdmans and introduced by Helmut Gollwitzer cannot continue to fill this gap. Greater guidance is needed for the novice, laying Barth's statements over against his wider corpus as well as the classical dogmatic tradition and his modern interlocutors. It is hoped that this volume will serve as an entryway to deeper study: of Barth's *Church Dogmatics*, of the classical dogmatic tradition, even of modern theology, of Holy Scripture, mostly of the God whom Barth reflected upon.

Preparing this volume has been a joy. It is a pleasure to work again with Thomas Kraft, Anna Turton, and their colleagues at T & T Clark. They have committed themselves over the years to publishing the works of a number of theologians, none more sizeable than Karl Barth. I am glad to have partnered with them in this latest venture.

A number of colleagues were kind enough to read and comment on the manuscript. John Webster offered a number of decisive suggestions upon reading the entirety of the manuscript. Scott Swain used a draft of the manuscript in a course he taught on Barth, relayed the experience of the students to me, offered some concrete suggestions, and encouraged me throughout the process of writing, revising and editing (which I take as revising the revisions). Dan Treier and Wesley Hill read the manuscript and offered suggestions. My wife, Emily, was especially encouraging as she listened day by day to my reflections on the writing process. My assistant, Jason Paugh, helped with translations and formatting. My assistant, Daniel Kahr, prepared the index.

I dedicate this work to T. F. Torrance, G. W. Bromiley, and their band of translators. Far too many of us take it far too lightly that we can read theological works of great size and scope in our native tongue. The work is tedious and technical – and yet translation is so central to the task of Christian proclamation. So I rejoice in the fruit of their labours and pray that my efforts will not be found any less faithful.

CHAPTER 1

INTRODUCING KARL BARTH

Theology is work with words. Nicholas Lash goes so far as to say that theology is the practice of learning to watch our words before God. God is not embarrassed to reveal himself in words. His prophets and apostles were those who made announcements and provided testimony. Similarly Christians are called to the hard but joyous work of praise and proclamation. This means that theology involves careful study of words and texts. Theology is meant to help reorient our reading of that most crucial text, the Holy Scriptures of Israel's prophets and the church's apostles.

In the universities of the medieval era, students were schooled by Peter Lombard's *Sentences*. The Protestant Reformation involved curricular change, with Augustine's works replacing Aristotle and Aquinas as key texts. In the era of Protestant Orthodoxy, Turretin or Schmid would serve as the book of choice. Various traditions have their own resources, and different eras bring forth works of impressive significance. The most important are surely those which force the reader to grapple with the particularity of the Bible and the scandal of the gospel.

Few texts of any century prove as vital and worthy of study as Karl Barth's *Church Dogmatics* from the twentieth. To understand the power of Barth's work, we can listen to an unlikely person reflecting on the nature and need of reading. Franz Kafka once said:

> If the book we are reading does not wake us, as with a fist hammering on our skull, why then do we read it? Good God, we would also be happy if we had no books, and such books as make us happy we could, if need be, write ourselves. But what we must have are those books which come upon us like ill-fortune, and distress us deeply, like the death of one we love better than ourselves, like suicide. A book must be an ice-axe to break the sea frozen inside us.[1]

Barth's work serves as an ice-axe or, to mix metaphors, a 'bomb on the playground of theologians' (a description given in a review by Roman Catholic

---

1   A letter from Franz Kafka (cited by George Steiner, *Language and Silence* [New York: Atheneum, 1970], p. 67).

theologian Karl Adam of Barth's first book, a commentary on Paul's Epistle to the Romans). In Barth's own day, he jostled the settled conventions of a liberal intelligentsia. In the present day, he continues to force reconsideration of biblical texts, cultural ideals, even our easy practice of religion.

Of course Barth is not always right. In fact most find him to be terribly wrong (though interpreters disagree where the problems arise: in his doctrine of divine election or regarding the Spirit, about Scripture or with respect to ethics). He finds no easy home in the ecclesiastical world. He worked within the textual world of the Reformed tradition, though he proposed sweeping changes therein. He was a child of the modern world, apprenticed in its philosophies and culture, but he was something of a prodigal son.

Even when overstated or downright irritating, though, Karl Barth proves to be fruitful for thought. He forces consideration of seemingly every aspect of an issue, all the texts that relate to a doctrine, the full extent of its consideration in the tradition, the whole swathe of its relations to modern culture. In the best sense he aims at being systematic: drawing connections, seeking coherence, yet never plunging the story of God's works underneath the currents of some principle, programmeme, or alien presupposition. Reading his work, then, blesses the theologian-in-training, whether of evangelical or Roman Catholic conviction, classical or modern commitment. Barth pressures his reader to think through the implications of the gospel for all of life, portraying the intellectual task as both prayerful and difficult, joyous and awe-inspiring. He moves from analytic expression to liturgical outburst in the space of a paragraph, and he sees connections between Old Testament narratives and modern sociopolitical engagement. He does not leave his readers disengaged; he calls forth conversation and consideration of the Christian's task in the world.

Barth's Life

Barth was born on May 10, 1886 in Basel, Switzerland. His father was a pastor and teacher. His mother was the child of a minister. All things considered, they were relatively traditional in their belief and practice. Nevertheless, their son left home to study in the heart of the liberal theological world – at Berlin with Adolf von Harnack, the father of modern church history and no fan of the orthodox creedal heritage of the catholic church. Barth's education and the emerging shape of his ministry would be different from his parents. Eventually he would go to Marburg for further studies before assuming pastoral roles in Switzerland (in Geneva and then Safenwil).

In his early pastorate Barth was called the 'Red Pastor' for his political involvement and socialist ties. He had been taught by Harnack and formed by Wilhelm Herrmann, learning well their belief that Jesus came to shape social engagement. Herrmann was particularly influential in demonstrating to Barth that he must honour the uniqueness of Jesus Christ (though this is not to say that Barth had a settled notion of who Jesus was at this point). So the early Barth was a mover and a shaker: assistant editor of an important periodical (*Christliche Welt*), participant in the social democratic movement, grassroots organizer, and local church pastor.

The Great War changed it all. More specifically the establishment acquiescence to the war effort changed it all. When over a hundred leading thinkers publicly endorsed Kaiser Wilhelm's foreign policy, Barth considered the liberal project defunct. He thought their understanding of the kingdom of God as an immanent political project actually rendered them moot when placed in a position to render a prophetic word. As he later said, 'an entire world of theological exegesis, ethics, dogmatics, and preaching, which up to that point I had accepted as basically credible, was thereby shaken to the foundations, and with it everything which flowed at that time from the pens of the German theologians'.[2] A new theological approach was needed, and he could no longer look to the titans of modern liberalism (Schleiermacher, Harnack, Herrmann).

Barth turned to the Bible. He spent time with Paul's Epistle to the Romans and what he called the 'strange new world of the Bible'. He entered a period of intense study and fast-paced literary production. Alongside some powerful lectures, he published the first edition of his Romans commentary in 1919. A second edition was not far off (and he would continue to edit it time and again). He was called to serve as a professor of Reformed doctrine, owing to the success of this first book. He felt entirely unprepared for such a post and searched for doctrinal resources. In time he discovered the writings of the Reformed tradition: Calvin, the Heidelberg Catechism, Schleiermacher, Zwingli. His new post as a professor challenged him to consider the present with resources rooted before the immediate. Barth seized on the opportunity. He taught exegesis courses on various New Testament writings, lectured on key historical figures, and led seminars on pertinent texts. The theological task absorbed his impressive energies.

In this period Barth served as a lightning rod in many ways, exciting much energy and encouraging co-operation across ecclesiastical lines. He was a leading figure of a movement known as the 'dialectical theology', a gathering of relatively young theologians and

---

2 'Concluding Unscientific Postscript on Schleiermacher', in Karl Barth, *The Theology of Schleiermacher* (Edinburgh: T & T Clark, 1992), p. 264.

church leaders who were not satisfied with the way that the Protestant establishment had reduced the claims of the gospel to a sort of civil religion. Figures like Emil Brunner, Rudolf Bultmann and Dietrich Bonhoeffer also participated in this movement. Eventually Barth would have sizeable rifts with Brunner and Bultmann theologically and, of course, Bonhoeffer died tragically at a rather young age. For a time in the 1920s, though, the 'dialectical theology' was the most talked about movement in modern theology. Their journal (*Zwischen den Zeiten*, that is, 'between the times') was a major place of theological debate, and Barth regularly published there.

He was a player in the widest theological debates of the day, yet he was committed to particular churches. Indeed it is important to recognize that Barth served as a Reformed pastor and then professor of Reformed doctrine. Furthermore he did so in an ecclesiastical context that was extremely malnourished theologically. In the nineteenth century the political powers forced a merger of the Lutheran and Reformed denominations. The much larger Lutheran church dominated in the decades to come, such that the Reformed churches languished with little theological definition. In fact, Barth was called to his first teaching position, a newly created post, to try to revive Reformed theology in the area. And he admits to being thoroughly unprepared for the role: 'at that time I did not even possess the Reformed confessional writings, and had certainly never read them'.[3] That they could not find an occupant of this chair possessing familiarity with the Reformed tradition speaks volumes about the theological state of the churches at the time. The local pastor inviting Barth to take up this first professorate described Reformed theology as 'unused, forgotten, and scorned' in those days.[4] That Barth took seriously the challenge of immersing himself in this tradition says much about his theological approach. Unfortunately few critics have observed his sociological location: people to his left tend to overlook his concern to build up a vibrant orthodoxy in the modern world, while people to his right frequently fail to see how far the ecclesiastical situation had degenerated, from where he was beginning, and how far he had come.

Before too many years passed Barth turned from historical analysis to dogmatic argument, that is, to the writing of his own theological works. He made one such effort (the *Göttingen Dogmatics*), attempted another (releasing one volume of the *Christian Dogmatics*), and then began anew with his *magnum opus* (the *Church Dogmatics*). The development of the project from one title to another has often

3   Münster Faculty Album, p. 156.
4   Johann Adam Heilmann in letter to Karl Barth, January 19, 1921 (in the Barth Archives, Basel).

been categorized by interpreters (indeed even by Barth himself) as cataclysmic and crucial for grasping his theological development. Yet careful analysis reveals that the basic project remained intact (such that volume one of the *Christian Dogmatics* reads similarly to the prolegomena of the *Church Dogmatics*), and the change of title reflects, more than anything else, a concern that it be identified as a theology written in conversation with the church and not as a work identified primarily with the dialectical theology movement (which was disintegrating for political and theological reasons at this point).[5] Year after year he poured life and intellect into that sprawling work. Volume after volume appeared and ignited theological conversation in numerous countries and various church communities. Students poured into his lectures as his fame spread with the release of each volume. Almost immediately the task of translation began, rendering this German masterpiece into English. It has remained in print ever since, and a massive industry of Barth scholarship has arisen to make sense of his legacy.

One episode must be mentioned from the period in which Barth was, by and large, labouring away at his *Church Dogmatics*. A Lutheran and Reformed Christian minority believed that 1934 was a time for common confession against the hegemonic claims of Adolf Hitler and National Socialism (the Nazi Party) – Barth was very involved in this 'Confessing Church' movement against the overwhelming support for the Nazis from the state church. Barth and two Lutheran theologians were asked to prepare a statement. Their agreed statement – the 'Theological Declaration of Barmen' – was the most famous Christian confession of the twentieth century with its sharp rebuttal of the Nazi claims to enact God's will in history. Against any idea that God's ways were revealed in Nazi policy, Barmen confessed that 'Jesus Christ, as he is attested for us in Holy Scripture, is the one Word of God which we have to hear and which we have to trust and obey in life and in death'. Though the established church in Germany had caved in to the Nazi ideology, Barth believed Jesus required ultimate allegiance and demanded sharp rejection of the Nazi imperialism. Eventually Barth would be forced to leave Germany due to his stand against the Nazis (1935), and he would finish his career teaching in Basel, Switzerland.

The Barmen Declaration manifests an ongoing concern of Barth: witness to the unique nature of Jesus Christ as the revelation of God.

---

5   For analysis of the move from the *Christian Dogmatics* to the *Church Dogmatics*, see Bruce L. McCormack, *Karl Barth's Critically Realistic Dialectical Theology: Its Genesis and Development, 1909–1936* (New York: Oxford University Press, 1995), pp. 441–8.

He attempted to stamp out all forms of modern idolatry, whether ideological or theological, cultural or philosophical, by judging them against the Jesus of the Bible. Indeed some of his sharpest words regard the evil of religion; he frequently juxtaposed the practice of religion with the promise of the gospel.[6] Of course, there remains great debate about the nature of his Christology – whether he understood the actual content of the Bible's witness about Jesus (some thinking that he failed to appreciate the genuine humanity of Jesus, others suspecting that he too quickly expands Jesus' work in a universalistic way). But Barmen shows the heart of Barth's theology, observed at much greater length across the pages and volumes of his *Church Dogmatics*: reflection on the beauty and significance of Jesus Christ and him alone as our hope in life and in death. He surely aims at being not only Christ-centred but also Christ-bounded – Jesus being the grounds for and the boundary of theology's possibility. When he was asked to summarize his theology, he said, Jesus loves me. This I know, for the Bible tells me so.

What is of greatest value in Barth's theology? Many interpreters have pointed to certain patterns in his thought. He was one of the leaders of the 'dialectical theology' movement, and his use of dialectic (particularly in his doctrine of God) has been seen as a major improvement over the relatively domesticated theologies of the modern era. Dialectical theology acknowledges that God's being outspans any attempt to name God straightforwardly and, thus, must be matched by other claims. It does not simply negate knowledge of God – it locates it in a wider context spanning divine and human agents.[7] For instance, God's love is neither sentimental nor purely sanitary; thus, it must be seen as related to God's holiness (in a dialectical pairing). Only by seeing God as the one who is holy love, and whose holiness is loving, do we honour either his love or his holiness.[8] More recently, a great many theologians have pointed to Barth's actualistic ontology as his most important

---

6 See Karl Barth, *On Religion: The Revelation of God as the Sublimation of Religion* (trans. Garrett Green; London: T & T Clark, 2006). Green's introduction provides an excellent account of Barth's thoughts on religion.

7 As Terry Cross says, 'Dialectic is not just a limiter, but a helper. This aspect begins in an inchoate manner in 1927 and is more completely used in 1932. As a helper, noetic dialectic is a human tool for comprehension of God. Barth believes that God blesses our human capacities of understanding and therefore dialectic becomes useful not just as a crier against human arrogance, but as an epistemological tool to coordinate and hold in mutual reciprocity what may appear to us to be contradictory in God's nature … Therefore, analogy cannot work alone in the doctrine of God. Dialectic helps analogy to say what needs to be said about the Trinity and the perfections of God' (*Dialectic in Karl Barth's Doctrine of God* [Issues in Systematic Theology 7; New York: Peter Lang, 2001], p. 210).

8 Dialectic can be identified as 'unity-in-distinction' (a term often employed by George Hunsinger in expounding Barth's theology).

contribution to the church. Put most simply, actualism is the notion that God's being is in his act or, as George Hunsinger puts is, that God lives in a set of active relations.[9] Expressed more clearly, it is a concerted effort to acknowledge that the eternal God is manifested faithfully in temporal events.[10] Especially when engaging philosophical debates about history and faith, many find a strong actualistic approach to theology in Barth and believe it flanks some of the philosophical objections to Christianity (like Ernst Troeltsch's objection that contingent facts of history cannot be the basis for eternal truths).

These two concepts – dialectic and actualism – have actually functioned in accounts of Barth's theological development. For many years the historical reflections of Hans Urs von Balthasar dominated Barth studies.[11] Balthasar suggested that Barth's theology moved in two phases: from dialectic to analogy. That is, Barth began his move beyond liberalism by emphasizing the dialectical relation of human and divine knowledge, speaking in a shrill voice of the difference between God and creation. But Barth then shifted to appreciate the communion between God and creation (likely due to the influence of reading Anselm's natural theology in the early 1930s), so that he began speaking of an analogical relation that now emphasized the link between God and creation in Jesus Christ. A number of Barth scholars have opposed this reading, most famously Bruce McCormack.[12] McCormack has argued that both dialectic and analogy function in varying ways to emphasize what is more fundamental for Barth: his commitment to letting the gospel shape our metaphysics. Early on, he points to the way that Barth thought eschatological categories must dominate (time and eternity), but he shows how Christological categories came to

---

9   See George Hunsinger, *How to Read Karl Barth: The Shape of His Theology* (New York: Oxford University Press, 1991), p. 30. For one such example in the *CD*, see Barth's comments in II/1.264, regarding how God is 'pure act' and 'singular act'. God's being is sustained in act (in the eternally full action of God), and God's being is specifically active (in the particular history of Christ). Hunsinger employs the term 'particularism' to emphasize the specificity of God's active being (*How To Read Karl Barth*, p. 32).

10 Some will go so far as to say that God 'constitutes' himself in temporal events. Both renderings – 'manifests' and 'constitutes' – are extrapolating Barth's claims about God 'determining himself' in these events in the divine economy and about God's 'being in act' (with 'traditionalists' noting the order of 'being' logically before 'act', and 'revisionists' denying the importance of order). This debate will be addressed throughout the volume in footnotes.

11 Hans Urs von Balthasar, *The Theology of Karl Barth: Exposition and Interpretation* (trans. Edward T. Oakes; San Francisco: Ignatius, 1992).

12 Bruce L. McCormack, *Karl Barth's Critically Realistic Dialectical Theology: Its Genesis and Development, 1909–1936* (New York: Oxford University Press, 1995). Other scholars involved in this reassessment have written exclusively in German: Eberhard Jüngel, Ingrid Spieckermann, and Michael Beintker. The most sizeable pushback to McCormack's historico-genetic account has also been within the German-speaking community of Barth scholars.

shape the whole theological project in the mid to late 1920s). The decisive move, of course, comes with the revision to the doctrine of election in the mid 1930s. At this point the history of Jesus Christ is fundamental for describing God as well as humanity. Here there is not only analogical knowledge of God (because he determines to be God with us), but there is an actualistic portrayal of God (as one who has determined to be God actively relating to himself and to us).

No doubt dialectic and actualism are crucial (if not also terribly controversial and far from straightforwardly defined), and Barth is pivotal in grasping the rise of both concepts in modern theology. But I would suggest that both dialectic and actualism serve as secondary concepts doing explanatory work for what is more fundamental to his programme: key dogmatic concepts drawn from the classical and Reformed theological tradition and deployed to expound the logic of the gospel. Indeed, Barth's most important contribution is surely his deliberate retrieval of classical Protestant divinity amidst a modern theological culture that had all but forgotten such conceptualities. Actualism simply serves in an ad hoc manner to expand on his doctrine of divine election and to show its implications in varying *loci*.[13] Similarly, dialectic functions to unpack the epistemological implications of certain divine perfections (most fundamentally, the simplicity of God over against creaturely complexity). Barth really does employ dialectic and actualistic terminology – and he really does learn from philosophical resources (critically) – but he always employs such resources as handmaids to the fundamental theological task of testifying to the gospel. Much more basic to his programme – and, for my money, much more fruitful for those doing theology in his wake – are his retrievals of various bits of dogmatic teaching neglected by so many in the late modern era: the doctrine of vocation, the doctrine of Christ's heavenly session, etc. Barth studies such concepts carefully and deployed them with great power (whether by way of affirmation, negation, or modification). Such is not to say that his historiographic work was always accurate or that his constructive ressourcement was always convincing; it is simply to say that he has profoundly deepened the conversation of modern dogmatics by bringing the classical tradition back into the mix with gusto.

---

13   This example demonstrates that his retrieval is not simply reiteration of classical Protestant divinity. In fact, Barth at times radically reshapes the material content of such dogmatic concepts. But he really does invest himself in their conceptualities and demonstrate a full-throated commitment to speaking in a theological manner conversant with that tradition. He will plunder the Egyptians (philosophy), but he seeks to provide for an Israelite community (theology). Paul Nimmo agrees that actualism is rooted more fundamentally in Barth's doctrine of election (see *Being in Action: The Theological Shape of Barth's Ethical Vision* [London: T & T Clark, 2007], p. 10).

Indeed, we can make sense of the debate about Barth's theological development only if we see that dialectic and analogy are never themselves the point. For example, dialectical language appears early as well as late in his works. He employs such concepts as needed to fill out matters more consistently described with dogmatic language about the perfection of God. There need not be a sharp two-stage process, precisely because the tools (whether dialectic, analogy or actualism) are never the point in themselves. They are tools – philosophical instruments for theological work.

Barth's Work

The *Church Dogmatics* is not the easiest text to read. It is massive: its intended five volumes were not completed, though the work stands at over 9,000 pages and six million words. It is breathtaking in scope: exegeting passages from all over the biblical canon in its small-print excurses, engaging in feisty debate with classical and modern figures. It is intellectually taxing: articulating a christocentric approach to theology consistently (many would say *too* consistently), yet insisting that theology is a difficult and hard practice worthy of careful attention and lengthy consideration. For these and other reasons, it takes effort and help to get inside of Barth's theology and grasp its inner logic.

Perhaps a few comments can set the stage for reading the selections included in this reader. First, Barth structured the *Church Dogmatics* in a particular way, and readers do well to note its shape. He begins with the self-disclosure of God, believing that we can only know God as he reveals himself. Barth does this by proclaiming the name of the Trinity; thus the first volume is both an exposition of the Trinity and a reflection on theological method. Theology's method must itself be defined theologically; in other words, God determines how he will be known. Barth puts forward this method against all modern efforts to approach God via scientific methods appropriate to study of creaturely objects. God evades such efforts and calls us into question by showing up declaratively and decisively. He has done so in the history of revelation, culminating in the Incarnation of the Son. Therefore Barth moves on to consider God and the works of God: creation, reconciliation and redemption.[14] In this scheme, he planned five volumes that would appear:

Volume 1: The Doctrine of the Word of God   (Prolegomena)
Volume 2: The Doctrine of God   (Theology)

---

14   Thomas Aquinas shaped this pattern in theology of reflecting on God and the works of God. It remains an influential structuring principle in Western theology.

Volume 3: The Doctrine of Creation   (Creation)
Volume 4: The Doctrine of Reconciliation   (Salvation)
Volume 5: The Doctrine of Redemption   (Consummation)

Barth did not finish volume 4 and never began volume 5. Sadly we have but little of his explicitly eschatological material available (especially essays from the 1920s). Like so many other major theological projects (e.g. Thomas' *Summa Theologiae*), Barth's *magnum opus* remains an unfinished cathedral. But the foundation and support structure is clear – God's self-revelation shapes our thought about every aspect of life and being. The structure of his work flows from the order and shape of God's works.

Second, Barth employs three types of text in his dogmatics, each performing a different function in his work. He proposes theses in bold font at the heading of every paragraph to guide every discussion.[15] He maintains a running doctrinal exposition in large print. Every so often he launches into detailed debate about the Bible, history of doctrine, or modern philosophy in small print excurses. The main points are found big and bold, while their exposition and detailed engagement with other resources comes in smaller and even smaller packages. The wise reader should keep their eye on the big picture, even as they fix their focus on a particular smaller portion of text. This reader includes some of these small-print excurses, however, so that Barth's careful engagement of the history of doctrine and of exegetical questions can be seen. It is worth noting that many of his historical, philosophical, or exegetical excurses remain valued even by those who find his larger dogmatic proposals less than satisfying; indeed, the reverse is also true. The attuned reader will find that Barth engages issues of great detail and engagements on the largest scale alike with passion, probing insight, and joy.

Third, Barth tends to argue in a somewhat circular manner. He takes an idea, text, or question. He offers a proposal. He chews on it, unpacks it, argues it. He considers objections and counterproposals. He then circles back round to the proposal, extending it somewhat. Again he wrestles, re-engages, reconceptualizes. Over and over he extends his initial statement until he has come finally at the issue from every side. Thus Barth cannot be interpreted as if he writes in strictly linear fashion. He does not simply list a thesis and develop it bottom to top (or vice versa). Rather he moves in cascading progress onward. Each part must be viewed within the environment of the whole, or

---

15   Note that 'paragraph' here refers to a chapter-length section, not to its normal function in literature.

else it will be misleading. In reading through his work, certain patterns emerge that become helpful for reading any given part.[16] Many a reader has gone wrong in biting off a small portion of text, coming across one aspect of Barth's argument or even a hyperbolic claim and thinking this is his settled view.

The best way, then, to read Barth is to wrestle with fairly lengthy portions of his text selected from across the *Church Dogmatics*. You need to trace his argument beyond a few pages in any given place, to be sure, but you also must see how it relates to topics and texts discussed elsewhere in the massive work. This reader provides such selections, from material at the beginning to portions found at the very end.

Footnotes will explain or situate the material. Some comments will clarify the philosophical or theological notions that Barth is engaging, whether classical or modern, biblical or secular. Other notes will explain where related discussions are found in the *CD* or even in other primary sources. Finally, the best secondary sources will be mentioned where pertinent, so that the interested reader can track down the most important representatives of the ever-growing body of literature about Barth's theology. In no way are these notes comprehensive; yet they offer enough guidance to make understanding manageable and further research possible. Though there is a bustling industry of Barth scholarship in the German-speaking world, I will limit myself to English-language resources accessible to the average theological student. Fortunately the most substantial contributions of German scholars have been adopted by English-speaking scholars; many such texts have even been translated into English. In all my references to the *Church Dogmatics*, then, I will reference the English translation in its standard format.[17]

In conclusion, I should make three recommendations to the reader. First, this book works best if studied alongside a thematic introduction to the theology of Karl Barth. There are a number of these surveys available. I strongly urge readers to consider reading John Webster's *Barth* (2nd ed.; Outstanding Christian Thinkers; London: T & T Clark, 2004) as a companion volume. Webster is a matchless reader of Barth's theology and knows the larger catholic tradition well enough to read Barth within that wider context (something that cannot be said of many

---

16 George Hunsinger lists six such patterns – in addition to actualism and particularism (which we have already mentioned), he lists objectivism, personalism, realism and rationalism – which arise from and aid in interpreting the theology of Barth. For those interested in greater help in grasping the kinds of arguments that Barth makes, see his wonderful book *How to Read Karl Barth*.

17 Because the 30-volume set includes cross-references to the earlier 14-volume set, I will employ the earlier set as my baseline for references. That way every reader can find the references, whether they employ the new or the old set. However, it should be noted that this reader quotes from the newer translation, which translates all foreign-language texts.

Barth scholars).[18] Plus, this particular book of his epitomizes the two attributes that Calvin said marked any good commentary: clarity and brevity. While the present book will familiarize you with Barth's actual writing and his form of argument, Webster's study presents a broader synopsis of his theology (much more than I can offer here in the footnotes). Second, Karl Barth elsewhere offers essays that more clearly state some of his theological beliefs, serving as helpful expositions of what he does in greater detail in the *Church Dogmatics*. Three crucial essays – 'Evangelical Theology in the 19th Century', 'The Humanity of God', and 'The Gift of Freedom: Foundation of Evangelical Ethics' – are now available in a single, small volume.[19] It makes a nice complement to the selections found here and is also recommended as a way to let Barth explain Barth, specifically regarding his relationship to modernity, his doctrine of God, and his approach to ethics. Third, certain expectations are appropriate – even necessary – for being a good reader of Barth:

> [R]eading Barth nearly always involves us in *reading against* our expectations of what Christian theology ought to be like. And so, when we come to read Barth on hope, routine distinction or correlations between God's action and ours, or established arrangements of doctrine in relation to ethics, seem oddly out of place – indeed, unless we sit loose on our expectations, the texts often do not make a great deal of sense. Part of what makes Barth so demanding of his readers is the requirement that they keep alive their capacity for astonishment, for that overwhelmed sense that the gospel takes us to some very strange places and leads us to think and say very surprising things. Good readers of Barth are usually those who have not fallen into reading ruts, or (to change the image) those whose map of Barth is constantly being

18 It must be added that, for all his criticisms of Roman Catholicism as well as much in the older dogmatics of his own Reformed tradition, Barth found new ways of saying much held dear by both traditions. Appreciating such similarities – and only in light of such appreciation, being able to see the real nature of continuing differences – requires deep awareness of structures and paradigms in classical dogmatics. Barth often critiques terms and slogans, while adopting concepts and judgements in similar ways (e.g. though he consistently critiques the idea of a 'covenant of redemption' [*pactum salutis*] in the federal dogmatics of the late sixteenth and seventeenth century Reformed theologians, his doctrine of election essentially guards the same dogmatic point – namely, that God really determines to be with us and not apart from us). For surprising similarities with much in Roman Catholic ethics (regarding 'substance' metaphysics and natural law) see Matthew Rose, *Ethics with Barth: God, Metaphysics, and Morals* (Barth Studies; Surrey: Ashgate, 2011); cf. Eugene F. Rogers, *Thomas Aquinas and Karl Barth: Sacred Doctrine and the Natural Knowledge of God* (South Bend, IN: University of Notre Dame Press, 1995).

19 Karl Barth, *The Humanity of God* (trans. Thomas Wieser and John Newton Thomas; Louisville: Westminster John Knox, 1996).

redrawn. Bad readers, by contrast, are those who know what to expect, and so either make Barth say what they expect, or go away from the texts hot and cross because their labour was in vain.[20]

It is surely fitting to preface study of any text, let alone one of great profundity and depth, with prayer. We can join with that medieval master to whom Barth was so drawn. As Anselm confessed: 'I pray, O God, that I may know thee, that I may love thee, so that I may rejoice in thee. And if I cannot do this to the full in this life, at least let me go forward from day to day until that joy comes to fullness'.[21]

20 John Webster, '"Assured and Patient and Cheerful Expectation": Barth on Christian Hope as the Church's Task', in *Barth's Moral Theology: Human Action in Barth's Thought* (Edinburgh/Grand Rapids: T & T Clark/Eerdmans, 1998), p. 81.

21 Anselm, 'Proslogion', in *A Scholastic Miscellany: Anselm to Ockham* (ed. Eugene Fairweather; Library of Christian Classics; Louisville: Westminster John Knox, 1956), p. 92.

CHAPTER 2

THE WORD OF GOD IN ITS THREEFOLD FORM

As ministers we ought to speak of God. We are human, however, and so cannot speak of God. We ought therefore to recognize both our obligation and our inability and by that very recognition give God the glory.[1]

Barth begins his *Church Dogmatics* with a volume on the doctrine of the Word of God. In I/1 he offers an Introduction and then two chapters: 'The Word of God as the Criterion of Dogmatics' and 'The Revelation of God' (of which only the first of three parts is contained in this part volume). The Introduction addresses 'The Task of Dogmatics' (§1) and, more specific to this volume, 'The Task of Prolegomena to Dogmatics' (§2). The first chapter centres on the 'threefold form of the Word of God', which then serves as a framework for the rest of volume one. The three forms of God's Word include revelation itself, the testimony given to that revelation by the prophets and apostles in Holy Scripture, and the church's witness to that revelation. Thus, the following chapters address revelation, Scripture, and church proclamation.

Barth clearly has two concerns in mind in this prolegomena: liberal Protestantism and Roman Catholicism. In the preface, he mentions that he changed the title of his dogmatics from the *Christian Dogmatics* to the *Church Dogmatics* 'to show that from the very outset dogmatics is not a free science. It is bound to the sphere of the Church' (I/1: xiii). Furthermore, he determines to distinguish his approach from the existential style of his many former colleagues (e.g. Rudolf Bultmann), emphasizing that he believes the way of Friedrich Schleiermacher, Albrecht Ritschl, and Wilhelm Herrmann results in 'the plain destruction of Protestant theology and the Protestant church'. Yet he will remain Protestant, for he believes 'it is impossible ever to become a Roman Catholic'.[2] Against both approaches, Barth argues that God actively makes not only possible but actual the conditions

---

1   Karl Barth, 'The Word of God and the Task of the Ministry', in *The Word of God and the Word of Man* (trans. Douglas Horton; London: Hodder and Stoughton, 1928), p. 186.
2   Barth lists the 'analogy of being' (*analogia entis*) as the doctrine that both is 'the invention of Antichrist' and renders Roman Catholicism an impossible option. More will be said in the pages to come regarding this doctrine (see, for example, Chapters five and nine).

of theology by grace conveyed in his very Word in all its forms. So theology is *nachdenken*, a 'thinking after' the knowledge of God given in the gospel.

Bibliography

Karl Barth, 'The Word of God and the Task of the Ministry', in *The Word of God and the Word of Man* (trans. Douglas Horton; London: Hodder and Stoughton, 1928), pp. 183–217.

George Hunsinger, *How to Read Karl Barth: The Shape of His Theology* (New York: Oxford University Press, 1991), part 2.

Christoph Schwöbel, 'Theology', in *The Cambridge Companion to Karl Barth* (ed. John Webster; Cambridge: Cambridge University Press, 2000), pp. 17–36.

The Text (*CD* I/1.120–124, 132–143)

The unity of the word of God

We have been speaking of three different forms of the Word of God and not of three different Words of God. In this threefold form and not otherwise – but also as the one Word only in this threefold form – the Word of God is given to us and we must try to understand it conceptually.[3] It is one and the same whether we understand it as revelation, Bible, or proclamation. There is no distinction of degree or value between the three forms. For to the extent that proclamation really rests on recollection of the revelation attested in the Bible and is thus obedient repetition of the biblical witness, it is no less the Word of God than the Bible.[4] And to the extent that the Bible really attests revelation it is no less the Word of God than revelation itself. As the Bible and proclamation become God's Word in virtue of the actuality of revelation they are God's Word: the one Word of God within which there can be neither a more nor

---

3   The subject matter of dogmatics is given to God's people: 'Hence [dogmatics] does not have to begin by finding or inventing the standard by which it measures. It sees and recognizes that this is given with the Church' (I/1.12). Dogmatics is an activity of 'the hearing church' (I/2.797), a key theme in Reformed dogmatics that highlights the eccentric shape of Christian theology. Theology is by faith, not by sight, because it is governed by God's speech, not our own immanent reflection, aspiration, or experience. Of course, dogmatics does involve reflection and real intellectual work, but this follows the prior work of God and (if done faithfully) never puts the cart before the horse. The hopeful confidence of those who do work in dogmatics is not grounded in or sustained by an optimistic assessment of their capacities, but by the promise of God to speak sovereignly, majestically, eloquently (see I/2.867).

4   The Second Helvetic Confession affirms that 'the preaching of the Word of God is the Word of God' (i). This Reformed confession was written by Heinrich Bullinger in 1561.

a less.[5] Nor should we ever try to understand the three forms of God's Word in isolation. The first, revelation, is the form that underlies the other two.[6] But it is the very one that never meets us anywhere in abstract form. We know it only indirectly, from Scripture and proclamation. The direct Word of God meets us only in this twofold mediacy. But Scripture too, to become God's Word for us, must be proclaimed in the Church. So, to give a survey of the whole, the following brief schedule of mutual relations may be drawn up.

The revealed Word of God we know only from the Scripture adopted by Church proclamation or the proclamation of the Church based on Scripture.

The written Word of God we know only through the revelation which fulfils proclamation or through the proclamation fulfilled by revelation.

The preached Word of God we know only through the revelation attested in Scripture or the Scripture which attests revelation.

There is only one analogy to this doctrine of the Word of God. Or, more accurately, the doctrine of the Word of God is itself the only analogy to the doctrine which will be our fundamental concern as we develop the concept of revelation. This is the doctrine of the triunity of God. In the fact that we can substitute for revelation, Scripture and proclamation the names of the divine persons Father, Son and Holy Spirit and *vice versa*, that in the one case as in the other we shall encounter the same basic determinations and mutual relationships, and that the decisive difficulty and also the decisive clarity is the same in both – in all this one may see specific support for the inner necessity and correctness of our present exposition of the Word of God.

---

5   It is important to remember that Barth believes all things and persons (including God) have their 'being in becoming', though they do so in very different ways. The Bible has its being in becoming by God's free decision to make it his Word again and again. Barth's point is not to render its nature as Word dependent on the subjective experience of the reader, but the renewal of God's objective decision to speak through it. Barth has been misunderstood frequently by friend and foe alike. For helpful analysis of this point, see Bruce L. McCormack, 'The Being of Holy Scripture is in Becoming: Karl Barth in Conversation with American Evangelical Criticism', in *Evangelicals and Scripture: Tradition, Authority, and Hermeneutics* (ed. Vincent Bacote, Laura Miguélez, and Dennis Ockholm; Downers Grove, IL: InterVarsity, 2004), pp. 55–75.

6   The primacy of Jesus as the Word of God – that is, of God electing to be for us and with us in personal form – undergirds the graciousness of all human knowledge of God. The actuality of the written Word and the proclaimed Word flows from the incarnate Word and the very depths of the free Lord's eternal decision to be with us and not without us. Barth attempts here to do justice to the radical implications of 'grace alone' (*sola gratia*) in the sphere of theological knowledge (cf. I/1.168, 241.I/2.257).

The doctrine of the three forms of the Word of God in the sketch attempted here is not new. We have seen in detail how revelation, Scripture and proclamation have from the very first stamped themselves on Christian thought as special forms of God's Word. Some passages in Luther are especially relevant here. Already in the *Lectures on the Psalms* (1513–16) Luther says (on Ps. 45.1): That the word of God may be described in three ways: 1. There is a speaking by God through the external word by way of human tongues and ears, whose model Luther sees in the word of the Old Testament patriarchs and prophets under the veil of the mere letter. 2. There is a Word of God which He now speaks through His Spirit to His saints on earth, namely, in His Son, this being a word that is fulfilled and shortened compared to the prophetic Word, but still wrapped in manifold veils. 3. There is a Word that God the Father speaks in Himself and to the saints in eternal glory. So we shall hear it one day, He Himself will reveal His word to us without any medium. With His word in its single and simplest form will He then satisfy us, and the Spirit Himself will then be the one sacrament in place of all signs (*W.A.*, 3, p. 262, l. 5). That scant justice is done here to the first form, external word of preaching, and that its significance is not understood, may be seen already from the fact that Luther saw no way to carry out the Trinitarian articulation which he obviously had in mind in relation to the second and third forms, because he could not very well relate to the Holy Spirit what he then regarded as an external word. How he conceived of the advance from the first to the second form is also not clear in detail. Furthermore the separation between the Word that the Father speaks in His own person in the third form and in the Son in the second should not be made in the way it is. On the whole, however, the three forms, up to and including the eschatologically characterised third form, are very accurately perceived and described. There is an interesting variation on the theme in the already quoted sermon on Mt. 23.34f. (*W.A.*, 10^1, p. 272, l. 17), which refers to 'the three ways in which the truth may be revealed: Scripture, word, thought; Scripture by books, word by the mouth, thought by the heart. One cannot conceive the doctrine in any way save heart, mouth, and Scripture.' The last form here, called thought, is simply our 'revelation' in virtue of which Scripture and preaching reach man and touch his heart. More important is a passage in a sermon on the wise men (from the same letter of 1522). This surprises us especially by the completely new and one might almost say exaggerated value that the external word or proclamation now has in Luther. 'The oral and public sermon … the voice or word cried forth by the mouth' is now for him the light referred to in 2 Cor. 4.6; 2 Pet. 1.19. 'Now Scripture is not understood until the light ariseth.' Scripture here is primarily the prophetic word to be found in the Old Testament. At first Luther simply contrasts the New Testament with this as living, i.e., oral proclamation whose task is to open up the prophetic word which is closed in its written form. 'For through the Gospel the prophets are opened up, therefore the star must first rise and be seen. For in the New Testament preaching should be done publicly with a living voice and should bring forth to speech and hearing what was hitherto hidden in letters and secret guise. For the New Testament is nought other than an opening and revealing of the Old Testament, as is shown in Rev. 5, where the Lamb of God openeth the book with seven seals. We also see in the apostles how all their preaching was nought but bringing forth Scripture and building thereon.' And now Luther has the astonishing continuation: 'Therefore even Christ Himself wrote not down His teaching, as Moses did his, but did it orally and gave no command to write it. The apostles, too, wrote little, and not all of them that ... Even those who did write no more than point us to the ancient Scripture, as the angel pointed the shepherds to the manger and the swaddling clothes. And the star pointed the magi to Bethlehem. Therefore'tis not like the New Testament to write books about Christian doctrine, but without books there should be in all places good, learned, spiritual, diligent preachers who draw the living word out of ancient writ and unceasingly din it into the people as the apostles did. For ere they wrote they first had preached to the people and converted them by the living voice, which was their proper apostolic and New Testament work. This is likewise the right star which sheweth Christ's birth and the angelic message telling of the swaddling bands and the crib. But man's need to write books is a great injury and it is a violation of the Spirit that the need hath compelled it and is not the way of the New Testament ...' New Testament Scripture as an adjunct or interpretation of the Old Testament is regarded as a defensive measure against corruption in the Church. 'There finally had to be resort to that, and need was that some sheep should be saved from the wolves: so men began to write, and yet through writing, so far as possible, to bring Christ's little sheep into Scripture, and they prepared thereby that the sheep should be able to pasture themselves and guard themselves against the wolves when their shepherds would not pasture them or turned wolves.' But it would have been better if other books had not been written in the Church. And the star of Bethlehem, the star of the wise men, should be in every case 'the lively preaching and simple revelation of Christ as the same is hid and promised in Scripture; therefore he that seeth the star knoweth assuredly the King of the Jews, the newborn Christ; for the Gospel teacheth nought but Christ, and Scripture likewise hath nought but Christ. But whoso knoweth not Christ may hear the Gospel or hold the book right in his hands, but understanding of it he hath not yet, for to have the Gospel without understanding is to have no Gospel. And to have Scripture without the knowledge of Christ is to have no Scripture, and is none other than to let this star shine and yet not perceive it' (*W.A.*, 10¹, pp. 625–28). This exaggerated thought is by no means an isolated one in Luther at this period. For him the Old and the New Testament are related as the written word on the one side and the word preached on the other. 'Thus the books of Moses and the prophets are also Gospel, since they have preached and described beforehand the same thing about Christ as the apostles have preached and written after. Yet there is a difference between them. For if both are written on paper as regards the letter, the Gospel or the New Testament should not really be written but put in the living voice, which then soundeth forth and is heard everywhere in the world. That it is also written is surplus. But the Old Testament is put only in writing and is thus called 'a letter,' and so the apostles call it 'writ,' for it hath pointed only to the coming Christ. But the Gospel is a living sermon about Christ already come' (*W.A.*, 12, p. 275, l. 5; cf. also 259, 8; 556, 9). It need hardly be shown, of course, that in other passages Luther attached supreme importance to the written New Testament, that he did not treat it as a necessary evil, and that it is thus quite wrong to hold him systematically to this distinction. But one may still learn from the distinction how he viewed the relation between Scripture and preaching generally. Both have the same theme and content, and this in such a way that preaching takes it first from Scripture and can thus be no other than scriptural exposition, but also in such a way that it always draws from Scripture in the form of living proclamation and has thus to become God's Word to us. Allegorising on Lk. 2.12 at the same period, Luther summed up his view as follows: 'Christ is completely wrapped in Scripture as the body in the swaddling clothes. Preaching is the crib in which he lies and is set, and from it we get food and provender' (*Sermon on Lk. 2*, 1523, *W.A.*, 12, p. 418, l. 24). Protestant orthodoxy, which at the peak of its development had no liking for talk about the distinction between the forms of the Word of God and the fluidity of their mutual relations, emphasised the more zealously something which is equally true and instructive in itself, namely, their unity. With reference to the unity of the Word of God to the biblical witnesses and through them: these distinctions do not make any essential difference between the forms in which the word of God is communicated to human beings, but only describe distinct modes of communication and revelation (J. Gerhard, *Loci theol.*, 1610, *Prooem.* 18), the distinction between the unwritten and the written Word is not a difference between specific types … as though the unwritten word were another kind of thing than the written; but it is a distinction of the subject with respect to its accidental form, because it happens to the same Word that at one point it had not been written and that now it has (F. Turrettini, *Instit. theol. el.*, 1679, *Loc.* 2, *qu.* 2.4). Nor is the word of God that is from God or has inspired men of God, other than what is handed down in Scripture, or which is preached, or which is stored in human memory (Hollaz, *Ex. theol. acrom.*, 1707, III, 2, 1). All this is true. Yet in the statements of this period of transition one misses painfully the Reformers' insight into the dynamics of the mutual relationships of the three forms. Its absence comes to light in the theory of inspiration, which implies a freezing, as it were, of the relation between Scripture and revelation.[7] But it may be seen especially in the fact that the theologians of this period hardly seem to have any more a true and essential awareness of the third form of the Word of God, proclamation. Preaching is called 'God's Word' in them too, but the real connecting point between revelation and Scripture in the present is increasingly something far different from the act of Church procla-mation; it is the knowledge, faith, sanctification and blessedness of the individual. But this means that the unity of revelation and Scripture, however stiff the objectivity in which it is arrayed, takes on more and more the aspect, not of God's dealings with His Church, but rather of a private divine institution for so many private persons, preaching and the sacraments being adequate instruments of this as the so-called means of salvation. Forgetting that the correlate of revelation and Scripture is not in the first instance the saving or amending of the individual but (on the same level as revelation and Scripture) proclamation as the service of God, the Church forgot nothing less than itself. From being a place for the service of God, through which as such men are also helped, it now made itself a place for the finest service of men in which God will finally have to figure as the supremely objective and supremely miraculous means, yet only as a means. Boasting of the objectivity with which the Word of God was invested, especially in its biblical form, was only the expression of a bad conscience. It helped to conceal the fact that the men of this age no longer knew what they were really saying when they

7   Barth's concern about the doctrine of inspiration 'freezing' this relationship of the written word and the willed revelation of God impels his talk of the Bible's 'becoming the Word of God'. However, Barth's grasp of post-Reformation Protestant orthodoxy was limited by the historio-graphical material available at his time; on this and other issues, his approach to these forebears was skewed by that nineteenth-century historiography. In point of fact, there was a vibrant tradition of reflection on not just the threefold Word of God, but a fourfold Word of God by Reformed theologians in that period of reflection; see Richard A. Muller, *Post-Reformation Reformed Dogmatics: The Rise and Development of Reformed Orthodoxy, ca. 1520 to ca. 1725*, Volume Two: *Holy Scripture* (Grand Rapids: Baker, 2003), pp. 155, 194 (where he provides references to both Leonhardus Rijssen and Francis Turretin, the most influential scholastic theologian in the continental Reformed tradition).

said 'Word of God,' that they no longer knew that they were talking about the present-day action, not of man in his relation to God, but of God in His relation to man, and therefore about the Church. When they no longer knew this, was it surprising that the rising Modernism of the new age discovered that the goal of the finest service of man could be reached by a simpler and less miraculous way than that which orthodoxy still espoused with great external but not so great internal fidelity? Was it surprising if the objectivity which orthodoxy still claimed for revelation and Scripture, and theoretically for preaching and the sacraments too, struck one bright mind and thousands of bright minds and even pious hearts as more and more a superfluous idol which it could only seem to them a good work, well-pleasing to God, to smash in pieces? The catastrophic crash of orthodoxy in the 18th century, the consequences of which we still have to carry to this day, is no more puzzling than the collapse of a house whose foundations are giving way. Responsibility for the disaster must be borne, not by the philosophy of the world which had become critical, but by the theology of the Church which had become too uncritical, which no longer understood itself at the centre. For all our great respect for the work done by orthodoxy, and for all our understanding of the ultimate intentions of this work, our task to-day must be the different one of re-adopting Luther's concepts and taking proclamation seriously again as the work of the Church in and through which God is to be served and not man, and God is to speak.[8] On that basis we must then try to understand once again in what sense first the Bible, and even before that revelation, is really the Word of God. It was here that forgetfullness set in before the disaster of the 18th century. It is here obviously that new reflection must begin. Hence the direct object of dogmatics to-day must be Church proclamation.

The Word of God as the speech of God

In its form neither as proclamation, Holy Scripture, nor revelation do we know God's Word as an entity that exists or could exist merely in and for itself. We know it only as a Word that is directed to us and

8   Note that Barth's objection to the doctrine of revelation in Reformed orthodoxy involves the claim that they domesticated the Word of God, rendering human proclamation directly equivalent to the revelation of Jesus. Barth believes that human mediation of the Word is indirectly equivalent to the speech of Jesus. That indirectness implies the continuing judgement of the church's proclamation by Christ – Barth believes the distinction of Christ and the church must be maintained more strictly here to honour the Reformational principle that God's church is 'always being reformed' (*semper reformanda*) by God. The indirect nature of revelation via the Bible, however, does not negate the fact that it is revelation (see I/2.463).

applies to us.[9] The fact that it is this is not, of course, self-evident. It is not something one might deduce from a general concept of speech. It is so in fact, but it might not be. In the intertrinitarian life of God the eternal generation of the Son or Logos is, of course, the expression of God's love, of His will not to be alone. But it does not follow from this that God could not be God without speaking to us. We undoubtedly understand God's love for man, or in the first instance for any reality distinct from Himself, only when we understand it as free and unmerited love not resting on any need. God would be no less God if He had created no world and no man. The existence of the world and our own existence are in no sense vital to God, not even as the object of His love. The eternal generation of the Son by the Father tells us first and supremely that God is not at all lonely even without the world and us. His love has its object in Himself. And so one cannot say that our existence as that of the recipients of God's Word is constitutive for the concept of the Word. It could be no less what it is even without us. God could satisfy His love in Himself. For He is already an object to Himself and He is an object truly worthy of His love. God did not need to speak to us. What He says by Himself and to Himself from eternity to eternity would really be said just as well and even better without our being there, as speech which for us would be eternal silence. Only when we are clear about this can we estimate what it means that God has actually, though not necessarily, created a world and us, that His love actually, though not necessarily, applies to us, that His Word has actually, though not necessarily, been spoken to us. The purposiveness we find in proclamation, the Bible and revelation is thus a free and actual purposiveness by no means essential to God Himself. We evaluate this purposiveness correctly only if we understand it as the reality of the love of the God who does not need us but who does not will to be without us, who has directed His regard specifically on us.[10]

9   Barth believes illumination is just as crucial to our doctrine of the Word of God as is inspiration. See McCormack, 'The Being of Holy Scripture is in Becoming', pp. 62–3.

10   God speaks not out of a communicative lack, but out of his eternal communicative fullness (as Father, Son and Holy Spirit). Communication to others is an overflow of his own eternal fellowship. The Western theological tradition speaks of the processions of God (of the Son from the Father and the Spirit from the Father and the Son) sustaining or impelling the missions of God (the work of the Son and the Spirit in the economy of salvation). Barth strongly upholds the doctrine of God's aseity and this tradition of tracing the economy of salvation back to God's eternal fullness as the Triune Lord. His lengthy reflections on the metaphysics necessary to make sense of the economy of salvation veer in a direction very different from some Protestant approaches focused strictly on religious experience (e.g., Friedrich Schleiermacher), which might claim historical roots in Philip Melanchthon's radical polemic against scholastic theology and its reflection on the being of God (see, e.g., 'Loci Communes', in *Melanchthon and Bucer* [ed. Wilhelm Pauck; Library of Christian Classics; Philadelphia: Westminster, 1969], p. 21).

In this connexion it is appropriate and necessary for once to consider not what God has actually done but what He might have done, since it is only in this antithesis that we can really understand what He has done. In this light one can also see how dubious it is to set the doctrine of the Word of God in the framework of an anthropology. In that case the freedom of the divine purpose for man can be asserted only at a later stage, while it is really denied by the starting-point.

Hearing man, as the object of the purpose of the speaking God, is thus included in the concept of the Word of God as a factual necessity, but he is not essential to it. He is not, as I most astonishingly stated on p. 111 of the first edition, 'co-posited' in it in the way Schleiermacher's God is in the feeling of absolute dependence. If he is co-posited in it with factual necessity, this is God's free grace. If we think that in this sense we must see in purposiveness or relation to us a third quality of the Word of God, and if we go on to investigate the content of this purpose, the implication of this relatedness or pertinence of God's Word for its understanding, we must remember that wherever and whenever God speaks to man its content is something utterly concrete. God always has something specific to say to each man, something that applies to him and to him alone.[11] The real content of God's speech or the real will of the speaking person of God is not in any sense, then, to be construed and reproduced by us as a general truth.[12] As readers of Scripture and hearers of proclamation we can and must, of course, work with certain general conceptual materials, apparently repeating or anticipating what God has said to this or that man or will say to this or that man. There is obviously no other way in which we can remind ourselves or others of the Word of God that came then and will one day come again. We may do this in words of our own coining or in Scripture quotations. But in so doing we have always to bear in mind that these materials are our own work and are not to be confused with the concrete fullness of the Word of God itself which we recall and for which we wait, but only point to it. What God said and what God will say is always quite different from what we can and must say to ourselves and others about

---

11 On the 'utterly concrete' (*concretissimum*) and personal nature of the Word, see Paul T. Nimmo, *Being in Action: The Theological Shape of Barth's Ethical Vision* (London: T & T Clark, 2007), pp. 29–37. According to Nimmo, 'Barth's actualistic ontology therefore preserves the open possibility of a material identity of the command of God today with Scripture, but does not render it a necessity' (p. 37).

12 Barth points out that the Word of God comes to us from outside ourselves and confronts us. Thus it cannot be characterized as merely illustrative of broader principles drawn from other sources (cultural, aesthetic, intellectual, religious, etc.). This Word is God's Word that is outside us (*extra nos*), even as it is God's *Word* for us (*pro nobis*). 'God is Lord in the wording of his Word' (I/1.139).

its content. Not only the word of preaching heard as God's Word but even the word of Scripture through which God speaks to us becomes in fact quite different when it passes from God's lips to our ears and our lips.[13] It becomes the Word of God recollected and expected by us in faith, and the Word which was spoken and will be spoken again by God stands over against it afresh in strict sovereignty. But even in this strict sovereignty in which its true content remains inconceivable to us, it retains its purposiveness, it is the Word that comes to us, that is aimed at us, and as such it is a definite Word determined not by us but by God Himself as the One who aims it at us. We are not anticipating its actual content but simply noting the aspects under which we shall have to consider its actual content if we make the following points in relation to its purposiveness, in relation to the fact that it is an address to us.

(1) First, the Word of God as directed to us is a Word which we do not say to ourselves and which we could not in any circumstances say to ourselves. Every human word, including that of proclamation and even the Bible, we could and can perhaps say to ourselves as such. Encounter with the human word as such is never genuine, irrevocable encounter, nor can it be. Encounter with the Word of God is genuine, irrevocable encounter, i.e., encounter that can never be dissolved in union. The Word of God always tells us something fresh that we had never heard before from anyone. The rock of a Thou which never becomes an I is thrown in our path here. This otherness which is yet related to us and made known to us, though only in this way, stamps it fundamentally and comprehensively as the Word of God, the Word of the Lord, compared to which all other words, however profound or new or arresting, are not words of the Lord. Whatever God may say to us will at all events be said in this way; it will be said as the Word of the Lord.

(2) Secondly, the Word of God as this Word of the Lord directed to us is the Word which aims at us and smites us in our existence. No human word has the competence to aim at us in our existence and no human word has the power to smite us in our existence. The only word that may aim at us in our existence and can smite us in our existence is one which questions and answers us in just the same way as death might question and answer us at the end of our existence. But death is dumb. It neither questions nor answers. It is only the end. It

---

13   Barth insists that any human mediation of the Word (whether in Scripture or proclamation – or the humanity of the incarnate Son) is indirect revelation, over against the direct revelation of God speaking *qua* God. He will later use the paired terms veiling/unveiling to emphasize the nature of God making himself known through creaturely means – he does so, but it remains an impossibility from a creaturely vantage point. Thus, as the epigraph to this chapter states, its actuality is a gracious miracle and a cause for giving glory to God.

is not really a thing outside and above our existence which can aim at our existence and smite it. The Word of God is the Word of the Lord because it comes from the point outside and above us from which death itself would not speak to us even if it could speak at all. The Word of God applies to us as no human word as such can do, and as death does not do, because this Word is the Word of our Creator, of the One who encompasses our existence and the end of our existence, by whom it is affirmed and negated, because everything has come into being and is preserved by this Word, and without it would not exist. He who makes Himself heard here is the One to whom we belong. Whatever He may say, it will be said in this relation of the Creator to His creature.

(3) Thirdly, the Word of God as the Word of the Creator directed to us is the Word which has obviously become necessary and is necessary as a renewal of the original relation between us and Him. The fact that God speaks to us, that He reveals Himself to us, i.e., that He turns to us in a wholly new way, that as the Unknown He makes Himself known – even after creating us and although we belong to Him – all this implies on the one side a criticism of the reality of the present relation between Him and us and on the other side a declaration on His part to uphold and re-establish the relation in spite of this criticism of His. Neither of these could be the content of a human word. Only the One who has instituted the relation can confirm and renew it when it is disrupted or destroyed. Only God can pronounce the verdict and give the promise and raise the claim which all lie equally in the concept of revelation. Under this third aspect of its purposiveness the Word of God is the Word of reconciliation, i.e., the Word of the Reconciler, of the God who effects a new creation, who sets up His covenant with us afresh in judgment and grace. Whatever God may say to us, it will at all events be said in this relationship of renewal.

(4) Fourthly and finally the Word of God as the Word of reconciliation directed to us is the Word by which God announces Himself to man, i.e., by which He promises Himself as the content of man's future, as the One who meets him on his way through time as the end of all time, as the hidden Lord of all times. His presence by the Word is His presence as the coming One, coming for the fulfilment and consummation of the relation established between Him and us in creation and renewed and confirmed in reconciliation. Again this final Word cannot be a word of man. Human words are never final words. They are never the promise of a specific and definitive coming of the Other. It is proper to God's Word and to God's Word alone to be also the full and authentic presence of the Speaker even if this be as the coming One. God's Word is the Word of our Redeemer, i.e., of the Lord who will be Lord as He was and is, who in His relation to us keeps faith both with

Himself and us. In this way He is Lord indeed, the Lord of all lords. And whatever God may say to us, it will at all events be said always in this final, consummating, eschatological relation too.

Again, what God says to us specifically remains His secret which will be disclosed in the event of His actual speaking. The concrete fullness of what He has said and will say specifically to men is and remains in truth His own business.[14] We can only cling to the fact – but we must cling to it – that when He spoke it was, and when He will speak it will be, the Word of the Lord, the Word of our Creator, our Reconciler, our Redeemer. Understanding it as directed and applying to us, we are well advised to keep what we think and say about it open in at least these four directions, to be ready and vigilant from these four standpoints.

- Guard against humans making God in our image.
- This is why (one starts w/ God not theo anthro in his work. God as Liberator v. God as Reconciler

---

14   Barth's ethics of interpretation has been accurately characterized by John Webster: 'Being a reader is characterized (at the individual level) by obedient receptivity and (at the communal level) by a complex process of mutual deference and free responsibility in the interpretation and application of Scripture' (*Barth*, p. 65).

CHAPTER 3

THE TRINITY

Trinity as revelation- knowledge of God

The doctrine of the Trinity is what basically distinguishes the Christian doctrine of God as Christian, and therefore what already distinguishes the Christian concept of revelation as Christian, in contrast to all other possible doctrines of God or concepts of revelation.[1]

Theology means rational wrestling with the mystery. But all rational wrestling with this mystery, the more serious it is, can lead only to its fresh and authentic interpretation and manifestation as a mystery. For this reason it is worth our while to engage in this rational wrestling with it. If we are not prepared for this we shall not even know what we are saying when we say that what is at issue here is God's mystery.[2]

Barth intentionally addresses the doctrine of revelation and the doctrine of the Trinity in the first volume of the CD. As he puts it, 'God's Word is God Himself in His revelation. For God reveals Himself as the Lord and according to Scripture this signifies for the concept of revelation that God Himself in unimpaired unity yet also in unimpaired distinction is Revealer, Revelation, and Reveleadness' (I/1.295). He then clarifies: 'If we really want to understand revelation in terms of its subject, i.e., God, then the first thing we have to realize is that this subject, God, the Revealer, is identical with His act in revelation and also identical with its effect. It is from this fact … that we learn that we must begin the doctrine of revelation with the doctrine of the triune God' (I/1.296).

Our very knowledge of God is made real by the action of the triune God. The Father reveals (as 'Revealer'), the Son is that revelation ('Revelation'), and the Spirit makes it effectual ('Revealedness'). Barth believes that much modern theology has gone awry in severing the distinctly Christian doctrine of God from theological prolegomena, defining the method of theology on more widely accepted grounds (e.g. natural theology, against which Barth speaks: e.g. II/1.135, 175).

---

1   *CD* I/1.301.
2   *CD* I/1.368.

Doctrine of god in trinity—be careful not to be tritheism

Bibliography

David Guretzki, *Karl Barth on the Filioque* (Barth Studies; Aldershot: Ashgate, 2009).

Eberhard Jüngel, *God's Being is in Becoming: The Trinitarian Being of God in the Theology of Karl Barth* (trans. John Webster; Edinburgh/Grand Rapids: T & T Clark/Eerdmans, 2001).

Rowan Williams, 'Barth on the Triune God', in *Karl Barth: Studies of His Theological Method* (ed. Stephen Sykes; Oxford: Clarendon, 1979), pp. 147–93.

The Text (*CD* I/1: 350–361, 368)

Unity in Trinity

The idea we are excluding is that of a mere unity of kind or a mere collective unity, and the truth we are emphasising is that of the numerical unity of the essence of the 'persons,' when in the first instance we employ the concept of repetition to denote the 'persons.' It is as well to note at this early stage that what we to-day call the 'personality' of God belongs to the one unique essence of God which the doctrine of the Trinity does not seek to triple but rather to recognise in its simplicity.

This concept, too, will have to be dealt with explicitly in the doctrine of God. The concept – not what it designates but the designation, the explicit statement that God is a He and not an It – was just as foreign to the Fathers as it was to the mediaeval and post-Reformation Scholastics. From our point of view, not theirs, they always spoke much too innocently and uncritically of the deity, the divine essence, etc. as though God were a neuter. The concept of the 'personality' of God – which we are provisionally emphasising by defining God's essence as His lordship – is a product of the battle against modern naturalism and pantheism.

'Person' as used in the Church doctrine of the Trinity bears no direct relation to personality. The meaning of the doctrine is not, then, that there are three personalities in God. This would be the worst and most extreme expression of tritheism, against which we must be on guard at this stage.[3] The doctrine of the personality of God is, of course,

---

3   Barth here expresses concern that 'persons' might be equated with 'personalities' in an individuated and autonomous sense as conveyed by much modern psychology, with which he was familiar. In the modern world, 'personality' is often depicted as a unique, self-styled achievement (typified by the advice given to children: 'you can be anything you want to be'!). Were the triune 'persons' to be 'personalities' in this sense – and maximally so, because they are divine 'persons' – assumedly this would involve them having radically diverse character traits; in other words, it would involve tritheism.

connected with that of the Trinity to the extent that, in a way yet to be shown, the trinitarian repetitions of the knowledge of the lordship of God radically prevent the divine He, or rather Thou, from becoming in any respect an It. But in it we are speaking not of three divine I's, but thrice of the one divine I. The concept of equality of essence or substance (*homoousia* or *consubstantialitas*) in the Father, Son and Spirit is thus at every point to be understood also and primarily in the sense of identity of substance. Identity of substance implies the equality of substance of 'the persons.'

The claim that the Church with its doctrine of the Trinity was defending the recognition of God's unity, and therefore monotheism, against the antitrinitarians may well seem paradoxical at first, for the concern of antitrinitarians in every age has apparently been to establish the right relation between the unique significance and power of the revelation in Christ and His Spirit on the one side and the principle of monotheism on the other. It might be asked whether perhaps all one can say is that in spite of the doctrine of the Trinity the Church wanted to retain and has in fact retained the unity of God as well; that it has shaped the doctrine of the Trinity in such a way that it has attempted to do justice to Christian monotheism too, and succeeded in this attempt. But we must give an insistent No to this weaker understanding. Christian monotheism was and is also and precisely the point also and precisely in the Church doctrine of the Trinity as such. We have simply missed the point if we see here the competition between two different interests in the assertion of whose rights tensions and cleavages, etc., can easily arise. Certainly one can understand the antitrinitarian heresies from this standpoint. These all became heresies because they were answers to questions that had been wrongly put. In other words, they were attempts to reconcile falsely opposed concerns, i.e., to remove irrelevantly manufactured tensions. In contrast, the Church's line is already distinguished formally from the heretical line by the fact that what happens on it is intended and is to be understood from the very outset as responsibility to the one concern as well as the other, because in fact we do not have two concerns which are opposed to one another and then artificially reconciled. On this thin but steady line where the basic issue is not this or that principle but quite simply the interpretation of Scripture, the point from the very first and self-evidently is both the oneness of God and also the threeness of God, because our real concern is with revelation, in which the two are one. On the other hand all antitrinitarianism feels it must confess the threeness on the basis of Scripture and the oneness on the basis of reason, that it must then combine them, which it naturally cannot do because it is prevented already by the difference in the sources from which and the sense in which it speaks of the two. Inevitably – and we must see this if we are to understand the sharpness with which the Church has fought it – all antitrinitarianism is forced into the dilemma of denying either the revelation of God or the unity of God. To the degree that it maintains the unity of God it has to call revelation in question as the act of the real presence of the real God. The unity of God in which there are no distinct persons makes it impossible for it to take revelation seriously as God's authentic presence when it is so manifestly different from the invisible God who is Spirit. On the other hand – and this must be our primary concern here – to the degree that it is ready to maintain revelation but without acknowledging the substantial equality of the Son and the Spirit with the Father in heaven, the unity of God is called in question. In its concept of revelation it will not in fact be able to avoid interposing between God and man a third thing which is not God, a hypostasis which is not divine – it does not want that – but semi-divine; it cannot avoid making this the object of faith. In so far as it is not a denial of revelation, antitrinitarianism in any form is a cruder or subtler deifying of revelation.

[...]

If revelation is to be taken seriously as God's presence, if there is to be a valid belief in revelation, then in no sense can Christ and the Spirit be subordinate hypostases.[4] In the predicate and object of the concept revelation we must again have, and to no less a degree, the subject itself. Revelation and revealing must be equal to the revealer. Otherwise there is no room for them beside the revealer if this be the one God. The unity of God would render revelation and revealing impossible. Christ and the Spirit would not just be foreign to and totally unlike the Father, as Arius said in dangerous proximity to a denial of all revelation. They would have no more to do with Him than any other creatures. Only the substantial equality of Christ and the Spirit with the Father is compatible with monotheism.

Trinity in unity

The concept of the revealed unity of the revealed God, then, does not exclude but rather includes a distinction (*distinctio* or *discretio*) or order

---

4   Revelation must involve divine presence. We have been given revelation by God's 'two hands' (as Irenaeus of Lyons would put it in the second century); thus, the Son and the Spirit must be divine just as the Father is, or else their revelatory work really is not revelatory work. Barth does not believe this to be an *a priori* assumption about how a revelation from a god must proceed; rather, he seeks to unpack it by exegeting biblical texts about how God has revealed himself *a posteriori* (e.g. 1 Cor. 2: 9–16).

(*dispositio* or *oeconomia*) in the essence of God. This distinction or order
is the distinction or order of the three 'persons,' or, as we prefer to say,
the three 'modes (or ways) of being' in God.

At this point, not only we but without exception all who have studied
this matter before us enter upon the most difficult section in the investigation. What is meant here by the commonly used word 'person'?
Or, more generally, what is meant by what is distinguished or ordered
in God as Father, Son and Spirit? Under what common term are these
three to be understood? What are these three – apart from the fact that
all together as well as each individually they are the one true God?
What is the common principle of their being, now as Father, now as
Son, and now as Spirit?

We have avoided the term 'person' in the thesis at the head of the
present section. It was never adequately clarified when first introduced
into the Church's vocabulary, nor did the interpretation which it was
later given and which prevailed in mediaeval and post-Reformation
Scholasticism as a whole really bring this clarification, nor has the
injection of the modern concept of personality into the debate achieved
anything but fresh confusion. The situation would be hopeless if it were
our task here to say what is really meant by 'person' in the doctrine of
the Trinity. Fortunately this is not our task. Yet the difficulties in which
we are involved in relation to this classical concept are only a symptom
of the general difficulty of the question itself, to which some answer
must now be given.

The word person [*persona* or *prosopon*] which is supposed to have
been used first by Tertullian, originates with the controversy against
the Sabellian heresy and is thus designed to denote the being in and
for themselves of Father, Son and Spirit respectively. But did not it also
mean 'mask'? Might not the term give new support to the Sabellian
idea of three mere manifestations behind which stood a hidden fourth?
In view of this the Greek Church largely preferred to translate *persona*
by *hypostasis* rather than *prosopon*. On the other hand *hypostasis* necessarily suggested to the Westerners 'substance' in the sense of 'nature' and
'essence,' and so they saw themselves threatened here by the proximity
of tritheistic ideas. Finally, if the West clung to *persona* and the East to
hypostasis neither party could be perfectly content with the other nor
ultimately with itself.

It is something of a relief that a man of Augustine's standing openly
declared (*De trin.*, V, 9, VII, 4) that to call what is meant 'person' is
simply a necessity or protocol for speaking. A really suitable term for it
just does not exist. The reference to the three divine persons certainly
means something very different from a juxtaposition like that of three
human persons, and for this reason, that a juxtaposition of human

persons denotes a separateness of being (*diversitas essentiae*) which is completely excluded in God – in this way the possibility of the Greek objection to person is formally acknowledged. To the question: Three what? i.e., what is the general term or general concept for Father, Son and Spirit, no real answer can be given, because the supreme excellence of divinity exceeds the capacity of our customary speech. God is more truly contemplated than spoken of, and exists more truly than He can be the object of contemplation. (The more the distinction of persons is regarded as taking place in and grounded in the divine essence itself, the more inconceivable in fact becomes the inconceivability of this distinction; this distinction participates in the inconceivability of the divine essence, which would not be the essence of the revealed God if it were conceivable, i.e., apprehensible in the categories of customary speech. Hence neither person nor any other term can perform the service of making this distinction really conceivable. There is place here only for more or less fruitful and clarifying designations of the incomprehensible reality of God.) If, thinks Augustine, one still uses the expression three persons, this is done not because it has any value in itself, but simply so that we might not be altogether silent. For the excellence of an ineffable reality cannot be expressed properly by this phrase: not in order to say that the three in God are precisely persons but in order to say with the help of the term persons that there are three in God – and even the number 3 here cannot express more than the negation that Father, Son and Spirit as such are not 1. Following Augustine, Anselm of Canterbury spoke of the ineffable plurality (*Monol.*, 38) of the three … I know not what: for it is permitted that I should say 'Trinity' because of the Father and the Son and the Spirit of both, who are three; but not that I should go on to propose a single term to describe what the three are. Anselm had against the term person the soundly based objection that wherever persons are plural, they subsist separately from each other, so that it is necessary to posit as many substances as there are persons. This is true of human persons but it is not true of the divine persons. Hence he, too, will speak of persons only owing to the lack of any truly appropriate term (*ib.*, 79).

Under the influence of Aristotle the Middle Ages then tried to establish a special systematic content for the concept of person. The point of contact for the deliberations initiated here was constituted by the definition of Boethius (early 6th century, *C. Eutych. et Nest.*, 3): A person is the individual substance of a rational nature. According to Thomas Aquinas (*S. theol.*, I, *qu.* 29, *art.* 1–2) an individual substance (equivalent to a substance of a single genus or a primary substance) is an essence existing in and for itself, separate in its existence from others, unable to impart its existence to others, an individual essence. Nature

[handwritten marginal notes:]
Transcendence
self/other/other → in relationship
Trinity: at first one reality but are actually
But do they really?
Just as the persons of the Trinity seem separate but are actually one reality

denotes the general essence, the essence of the species, the secondary substance, to which such an individual essence belongs. Reasonable or rational nature is thus rational nature (including God, angels and men on the mediaeval view) as opposed to irrational nature (including all other substances from animals downwards). Person, then, is simply individual substance (which can also be called an instance of a nature, a subsisting thing or among the Greeks hypostasis) to the degree that the individual essence in view belongs to rational nature. The definition of Boethius is thus to be translated in Thomas as follows: Person is the individual rational essence. Thomas argues that this concept can be applied to God (*ib.*, *art.* 3) on the ground that person carries with it the mark of a dignity, that it even denotes indeed the most perfect quality in the whole of nature. This dignity or most perfect quality must be attributed to God in an eminent sense. Unfortunately Thomas did not say in what, according to his view, this dignity contained in the concept of person, this perfection of the person, consists. Is it the superiority of the rational individual essence over the irrational? Is it the superiority of the individual rational essence over rational nature as such? Or is it both? Be that as it may, Thomas himself recognises the objection that the principle of individuation, which is also decisive for the concept of person, is a material that exists in individuation, a something with individual existence, a potentiality, even when the reference is to rational nature. But for Thomas too, and specifically, God is immaterial, pure act. Thomas has to admit, therefore, that when the concept of person is applied to God all that remains of the element of individual essence is the attribute of the non-communicability of the existence of the essence concerned to others, so that all that remains of the concept of the individual essence is what makes it an individual essence, and the fact that it is an individual essence has been set aside (*ib.*, *art.* 3, *ad.* 4). Thomas is also familiar, of course, with the even more important objection, raised already by Augustine and Anselm, that a plurality of persons necessarily involves a plurality of essences as well, and therefore, when applied to God, a plurality of divine essences, or at least a division of the one divine essence. He has thus to state, in a way which is materially correct but which is also a threat to his concept of person, that the persons of the Trinity are subsistent entities in (i.e., in the one) divine nature. Thomas cannot help conceding that the *hypostasis* of the Greeks is in this respect nearer the facts than the Latin *persona* and that he avoids it only on account of the fatal translation *substantia*. But the subsistent entities in the divine nature are also, according to him, nothing but relations, intradivine relations (*ib.*, *qu.* 29, *art.* 4; *qu.* 30, *art.* 1). Glad as we are to follow him here, and glad as we are to agree with him methodologically when he appeals here to the uniqueness of the concept in its relation to what is meant, i.e., to what is divinely revealed – it is one thing to inquire about the meaning of this term 'person' in common usage, and another about the meaning of a divine person (*ib., qu.* 29, *art.* 4c) – we can hardly feel convinced that even a comparative aptness – there can be no question of any other – in the use of the concept of person has been explained by Thomas in such a way that we are forced to abandon the reservations in relation to it for which appeal can always be made to Augustine and Anselm. If Thomas has provided a true explanation, within the bounds of the possible, for what the three involve in triunity, he has done this, not in the form of an interpretation of the concept of person, but by means of the concept of relations.

Quite in line with Augustine and Anselm (and materially not in contradiction to Thomas) Calvin could criticise the concept of person in the words: 'The ancient doctors used the word person and said that there are three persons in God: not at all in the way that we speak in our everyday language, when we call three people three persons, or in the way that under the papacy they have the audacity to paint three mannikins and call it the Trinity. But – in Calvin's further opinion – this word 'person' in this context is used to express properties which are intrinsic to the divine essence' (*Congrégation de la divinité de Christ, C.R.,* 47, 473). Later J. Gerhard (*Loci,* 1610 L. III, 62) also spoke of an infinite qualitative distinction between the divine persons and the human ones known to us.

What is called 'personality' in the conceptual vocabulary of the 19th century is distinguished from the patristic and mediaeval *persona* by the addition of the attribute of self-consciousness.[5] This really complicates the whole issue. One was and is obviously confronted by the choice of either trying to work out the doctrine of the Trinity on the presupposition of the concept of person as thus accentuated or of clinging to the older concept which since this accentuation in usage has become completely obsolete and is now unintelligible outside monastic and a few other studies. The first possibility was chosen in the teaching of the Roman Catholic theologian Anton Günther, who was condemned by Pope Pius IX in 1857. On his view the individual persons of the Trinity are individual substances, three independently thinking and willing subjects, proceeding from one another and related to one another, and thus coming together in the unity of the absolute personality. Along the same lines on the Protestant side Richard Grützmacher

---

5   Here we see that the development of modern psychological constructs regarding 'personality' as 'self-consciousness' drives Barth's dislike for applying the term to the three members of the Godhead.

(*Der dreieinige Gott – unser Gott*, 1910) ascribed a separate I-centre with a separate consciousness and will and content to Creator, Son and Spirit respectively. As he saw it, each of the three is also absolute personality, one with the others in the fact that the essence of all three is love and holiness so that they are always experienced as working side by side and together. One can only say that it is hard not to think here of the three mannikins rejected by Calvin and that it is thus hard not to describe this doctrine as tritheism. The definition offered by Melanchthon in more than one passage (e.g., *Exam. ordinand.*, 1559, *C.R.*, 23, 2) and often quoted later: A person is a subsisting entity that is living, undivided, intelligent, incommunicable, and not upheld by anything else, has a suspicious sound in this regard, especially if one sets alongside it the fact that he could also say in the plural: three truly subsisting ... distinct or singular intelligences (*Loci*, 1559, *C.R.*, 21, 613). Life and intelligence as features in the concept of person necessarily import at least an appearance of tritheism into the doctrine of the Trinity. And the attribute of individuality when it is related to Father, Son and Spirit as such instead of the one essence of God, the idea of a threefold individuality, is scarcely possible without tritheism. 'In God, as there is one nature, so there is one knowledge, one self-consciousness' (F. Diekamp, *Kath. Dogmatik⁶*, Vol. I, 1930, p. 271).

In face of the danger which threatened at this point almost all Neo-Protestant theology obviously thought it had to seek refuge in Sabellianism. It had on the one side a desire to apply the modern concept of personality to Father, Son and Spirit, but also a justifiable fear of doing this ontologically as Günther and Grützmacher had done. It thus limited itself to a purely phenomenological doctrine of the three persons, an economic Trinity of revelation, three persons in the sense that God Himself was still in the background as absolute personality. In relation to this view it has never been clear either in ancient or modern times how far the real reference was to a Quaternity rather than a Trinity, and the more seriously revelation is taken the greater is the risk of this. One can certainly see why Schleiermacher preferred to say nothing at all about the concept of the personality of God and why D. F. Strauss (*Die christl. Glaubenslehre*, Vol. I, 1840, § 33) and A. E. Biedermann (*Christl. Dogmatik*, 1869, §§ 618 and 715 f.) went to the length of eliminating it altogether, i.e., of banishing it from the realm of truth, in which God is nothing but absolute Spirit, and assigning it to the lower sphere of an inadequate religious idea. One may still ask, of course, whether the hypothesis of a threefold divine self-consciousness is not to be described also as polytheistic if the threefoldness is described 'merely' as a matter of the economy of revelation or the religious idea. What does 'merely' really mean here if man still lives in fact with God in the power of the economy of revelation or the religious idea, but at this very point the three mannikins are nevertheless to be the final word?

The second possibility has been adopted by Roman Catholic theology, whose doctrine of the Trinity even to this day speaks of the 'persons' as though the modern concept of personality did not exist, as though the definition of Boethius still continued to be relevant and intelligible, and above all as though the meaning of the definition had been so elucidated in the Middle Ages that it is possible with its help to speak profitably of the trinitarian three.[6]

In view of the history of the term person in the doctrine of the Trinity one may well ask whether dogmatics is wise to continue using it in this connexion. It belongs to another locus, to the doctrine of God proper, and to this as a derivation from the doctrine of the Trinity. For it follows from the trinitarian understanding of the God revealed in Scripture that this one God is to be understood not just as impersonal lordship, i.e., as power, but as the Lord, not just as absolute Spirit but as person, i.e., as an I existing in and for itself with its own thought and will. This is how He meets us in His revelation. This is how He

is thrice God as Father, Son and Spirit. But is this really the concept which explains the threeness as such and which can thus be made the foundation of the doctrine of the Trinity as its hermeneutical principle? The man who wants to retain it consistently will find that in addition to ancient ecclesiastical and academic usage about the only valid argument for its venerable position is that he does not have any other or better concept with which to replace it. Yet we must always ask seriously whether the argument of piety on the one side or the technical one on the other is weighty enough to cause the dogmatician to add to the thought of the Trinity, which is difficult in any case, the extra burden of an auxiliary thought which is itself so difficult and which can be used only with so many reservations. We have no cause to want to outlaw the concept of person or to put it out of circulation. But we can apply it only in the sense of a practical abbreviation and as a reminder of the historical continuity of the problem.

The truly material determinations of the principle of threeness in the unity of God were derived neither by Augustine, Thomas nor our Protestant Fathers from an analysis of the concept of person, but from a very different source in the course of their much too labourious analyses of this concept. We prefer to let this other source rank as the

6   Barth acknowledges that one can continue using terminology, as if its modern colloquial usage did not exist. However, he finds this to be less than helpful in conveying accurate and faithful testimony to the Word the church hears (see the next paragraph).

primary one even externally, and therefore by preference we do not use the term 'person' but rather 'mode (or way) of being,' our intention being to express by this term, not absolutely, but relatively better and more simply and clearly the same thing as is meant by 'person.' The fact that God is God in a special way as Father, as Son, and as Spirit, this aspect – not that of the participation of Father, Son and Spirit in the divine essence which is identical in all and which does not, therefore, describe Father, Son and Spirit as such, nor that of the 'rational nature' of Father, Son and Spirit, which can hardly be called threefold without tritheism – is usually stressed in analysis as the first and decisive element even by those who think that they must analyse the concept of person at this point. Hence we are not introducing a new concept but simply putting in the centre an auxiliary concept which has been used from the very beginning and with great emphasis in the analysis of the concept of person. The statement that God is One in three ways of being, Father, Son and Holy Ghost, means, therefore, that the one God, i.e. the one Lord, the one personal God, is what He is not just in one mode but – we appeal in support simply to the result of our analysis of the biblical concept of revelation – in the mode of the Father, in the mode of the Son, and in the mode of the Holy Ghost.

[…]

What we have here are God's specific, different, and always very distinctive modes of being. This means that God's modes of being are not to be exchanged or confounded.[7] In all three modes of being God is the one God both in Himself and in relation to the world and man. But this one God is God three times in different ways, so different that it is only in this threefold difference that He is God, so different that this difference, this being in these three modes of being, is absolutely essential to Him, so different, then, that this difference is irremovable. Nor can there be any possibility that one of the modes of being might just as well be the other, e.g., that the Father might just as well be the Son or the Son the Spirit, nor that two of them or all three might

---

7   Barth here articulates the eternally perduring nature of these 'modes of being', thus distancing him from any modalistic heresy. In the ancient church, modalism was an attempt to resolve the tension between God's unity and his threefold revelation by considering the three persons as momentary or occasional appearances of the one true God. In other words, God was 'Father' for a time, then 'Son' for a period, and finally is 'Spirit' for a season. But Barth argues that these 'modes of being are not to be exchanged or confounded'. He and his Roman Catholic contemporary Karl Rahner both employ the term 'modes of being' to avoid the personalistic and individualistic connotations of the term 'person' in the modern era; but they equally do not intend 'modes of being' to convey modalistic meaning (see, e.g., I/1.439). However, Barth has not avoided much criticism on this very point.

coalesce and dissolve into one. In this case the modes of being would not be essential to the divine being. Because the threeness is grounded in the one essence of the revealed God; because in denying the threeness in the unity of God we should be referring at once to another God than the God revealed in Holy Scripture – for this very reason this threeness must be regarded as irremovable and the distinctiveness of the three modes of being must be regarded as ineffaceable.

Triunity

In the doctrine of the Trinity our concern is with unity in trinity and trinity in unity. We cannot advance beyond these two obviously one-sided and inadequate formulations. They are both one-sided and inadequate because a slight overemphasis on the unity is unavoidable in the first and a slight overemphasis on the trinity is unavoidable in the second. The term 'triunity' is to be regarded as a conflation of the two formulae or rather as an indication of the conflation of the two to which we cannot attain and for which, then, we have no formula, but which we can know only as the incomprehensible truth of the object itself.

[…]

In practice, however, this concept of 'triunity' can never be more than the dialectical union and distinction in the mutual relation between the two formulae that are one-sided and inadequate in themselves.[8] We see

---

8   Barth offers a hermeneutical suggestion for how to read his Trinitarian account, indeed, for how any Christian theology of God must move: doubly reflecting on God as one and as three. The Western theological tradition has used the term *redoublement* to speak of this necessary practice, and it was articulated well by an early Eastern father. Gregory of Nazianzen famously taught:

> No sooner do I conceive of the one than I am illumined by the splendour of the three; no sooner do I distinguish them than I am carried back to the one. When I think of any one of the three I think of him as the whole, and my eyes are filled, and the greater part of what I am thinking escapes me. I cannot grasp the greatness of that one so as to attribute a greater greatness to the rest. When I contemplate the three together, I see but one torch, and cannot divide or measure out the undivided light'

(Oration 40, 41).

Barth calls this double process dialectical, because each term relates directly to the other. God is one in a threefold way; God is three in an unified way. Thought of each must move (note that he terms Trinitarian thought very actively as a 'movement') back and forth, for each is 'inadequate' when considered in isolation. It is not merely that thinking of God as one and not three misses the threeness (though it will), but it will also fail to understand the oneness accurately (because the two enjoy a 'mutual relation' and are dialectically linked).

This dialectical practice shapes the structure of his Trinitarian teaching here in volume one. He addresses the 'unity in trinity' and 'trinity in unity' prior to considering the distinctive persons, in so doing emphasizing that the persons must each be understood as existing in those relations and,

on the one side how for those who hear and see revelation in the Bible the Father, Son and Spirit, or however we name the three elements in the biblical revelation, come together in the knowledge and concept of the one God. And we see on the other side how for them the source and goal of this knowledge and concept are never a sterile one but are rather the three, whatever we call them. In practice the concept of triunity is the movement of these two thoughts.

thus, understood rightly only within those relations. Here is an outline of this section, paragraph by paragraph:

§8 God in His Revelation (e.g. revelation as triune revelation)

§9 The Triunity of God (e.g. 'Unity in Trinity' and 'Trinity in Unity')

§10 God the Father (e.g. as creator and eternal Father)

§11 God the Son (e.g. as reconciler and eternal Son)

§12 God the Holy Spirit (e.g. as redeemer [or perfector] and eternal Spirit)

Note that Barth links each person (by way of appropriation) with a moment in the economy of redemption. For his thoughts on appropriation, see I/1: 137 (where he approves of Thomas Aquinas's definition of appropriation). Furthermore, he links each moment in the economy of redemption with an eternal procession in the Godhead (e.g. God creates something external to himself because God is the kind of being in eternity who generated a Son within his divine life); Western Trinitarian theology has taught this grounding of the 'divine missions' (the economic activities of God) in the 'divine processions' (the eternal life of God). See, e.g., Thomas Aquinas, *Summa Theologiae*, 1a.43; for an earlier Reformed adoption of this model, see Jonathan Edwards, 'Economy of the Trinity and Covenant of Redemption', in *The Miscellanies 833–1152* (The Works of Jonathan Edwards 20; ed. Amy Plantinga Pauw; New Haven: Yale University Press, 2002), pp. 430–43. Wary of any division of these moments in the economy to distinct persons, viewed over against or separate from the others, Barth believes the doctrine of *perichoresis* ('interpenetration') must be upheld (see I/1:369–71). For exceptional analysis of his use of *perichoresis* and appropriation, see Eberhard Jüngel, *God's Being is in Becoming: The Trinitarian Being of God in the Theology of Karl Barth* (trans. John Webster; Edinburgh: T & T Clark, 2001), pp. 42–53.

CHAPTER 4

THE WORD HEARD AND TESTIFIED

If the question what God can do forces theology to be humble, the question what is commanded of us forces it to concrete obedience. God may speak to us through Russian Communism, a flute concerto, a blossoming shrub, or a dead dog. We do well to listen to Him if He really does. But, unless we regard ourselves as the prophets and founders of a new Church, we cannot say that we are commissioned to pass on what we have heard as independent proclamation.[1]

The knowledge of God occurs in the fulfilment of the revelation of His Word by the Holy Spirit, and therefore in the reality and with the necessity of faith and its obedience. Its content is the existence of Him whom we must fear above all things because we may love Him above all things; who remains a mystery to us because He Himself has made Himself so clear and certain to us.

In this section Barth offers an introduction not only to the *Church Dogmatics* as a whole, but specifically to his prolegomena. These pages precede the two previous excerpts, though they have been placed here for rhetorical effect. Barth here describes the human action of those who hear and receive and then testify and proclaim the Word of God.

Barth begins the Church Dogmatics by offering a definition of its discipline: 'As a theological discipline dogmatics is the scientific self-examination of the Christian Church with respect to the content of its distinctive talk about God' (I/1.3). He continues in the next paragraph with a definition of prolegomena: 'Prolegomena to dogmatics is our name for the introductory part of dogmatics in which our concern is to understand its particular way of knowledge' (I/1.25). Note the emphasis on distinctiveness and particularity. Barth believes the church has been given something 'distinctive' to say about God, precisely because the church has been graced with a 'particular way of knowledge'. To begin to speak well of God, then, we must reflect on how we receive that Word.

---

1   *CD* I/1.55.
2   *CD* II/1.3.

Eventually Barth will address this topic again, when he concludes volume four with comments on the prophetic office of Jesus, the one who addresses the hearing church with his Word (see chapters 13 and 14).

Bibliography

Karl Barth, *Evangelical Theology: An Introduction* (trans. Grover Foley; Garden City, NY: Anchor, 1964).

Karl Barth, 'The Significance of the Confession in the Reformed Church', in *The Theology of the Reformed Confessions* (Columbia Series in Reformed Theology; trans. Darrell Guder and Judith Guder; Louisville: Westminster John Knox, 2002), pp. 1–37.

John Webster, 'The Theology of the Reformed Confessions', in *Barth's Earlier Theology: Four Studies* (London: T & T Clark, 2005), pp. 41–66.

The Text (*CD* I/1.56–65, 67–69)

This is what the talk about God that is to be found in the Church seeks to be when it is meant to be proclamation and is thus directed to men with the claim and expectation that it has to declare to them the Word of God. It can and should aim to be proclamation as preaching and sacrament because the Church has a commission to make such proclamation.[3]

In attempting to interpret what we have described in this way, our primary task must be to make it clear that, when man cannot regard himself as the one who gives the commission but only as the one who is commissioned, there are only two ways of establishing the factuality and meaning of a commission. Either the order must be repeated as it is thought to have been received and heard, or a fact must be created by the mere attempt to obey it. In both cases the answer given to those who ask concerning its basis is indirect. In both cases it can thus be regarded only as most unsatisfactory. In both cases the answer constitutes indeed a counter-question, and it is left to the enquirer whether, in the handing on of what has been heard as an order or in the attempt to obey the order, he perceives or recognises the will of

---

3   Barth identifies the work of the church – and, thus, of Christian men and women within her – as proclamation and declaration (in the preached Word and the sacramental Word – though it should be noted that he will have disagreements with the notion of churchly sacraments later in volume 4). The work of the church, therefore, follows from her 'commission' by God; the church is dependent and directed. Barth frequently refers to theology as 'thinking after' (*nachdenken*) to insist on this subordinate role of the church's proclamation and hence of her critical reflection on that proclamation as well. God speaks and commissions; the church listens and testifies (and does dogmatic theology so that her hearing and testimony might be conformed to that Word of God).

the one who has given the commission, the meaning of his will, and therefore the existence of a true and meaningful commission. If, then, we ask why the Church's talk about God seeks to be proclamation in the specific form of preaching and sacrament, or to what extent it thinks it has its particular commission to proclaim in this action, we can only give a twofold and either way a very simple answer. First, we can only reply that we learn from the biblical witness to revelation that Jesus Christ has given His Church not only the commandment of faith and love and hope, nor merely the commandment to call upon His name in concert and to show brotherly love, etc., but also the commission of proclamation, and indeed of proclamation by preaching and sacrament. Does He expect of His own only that they should take up their cross and follow Him? Does He desire as witness of this following only those other functions of His Church? Or does He not rather will these two things as He also and specifically and supremely wills that God's own Word should be proclaimed in and through His Church? And if so, is not the saying in Mt. 28.19 f.: 'Make disciples of all nations, baptising them – teaching them', a genuine summary of what we are told by the biblical documents with regard to this will of His, and has it not therefore to stand as His command to us? But secondly we cannot prove the existence and content of this order by referring to the convincing excellence of our obedience to it, as though the former could speak for itself in the latter. For again the question whether our act is obedience to this command is not decided by the person commissioned but by the Giver of the commission. Our talk about God may intend to be proclamation in terms of our commission. It may intend to be preaching and sacrament according to the will and command of the Lord of the Church. But we shall not find comfort in our obedience or in the uprightness of our intention to obey. We shall find it only in the actual command that we have heard – a command which must in fact speak for itself if it is to be recognisable to others as such. Once again, then, we can only ask, timidly and reluctantly enough, whether, in spite of all the concurrent disobedience, the Lord's command may not also speak, and speak for itself, in what the Church does.

Hence it is only subsequently, with reference to actual conditions, exegetically and not in the sense of demonstrating the Church's commission, that we may rightly consider whether even the thought of God's Word being revealed outside the known existing Church is possible for one who has not previously come to be acquainted with real proclamation within the Church, whether we can appeal to real parallel experiences, such as having heard the Word of God through Communism or some other reality that is thought to have existential application to us, unless we have brought a criterion to this hearing, and applied it either well or badly, on the basis of previous experience of the reality of the Word of God reaching us somehow as commissioned proclamation; above all – and this is the real point in the present context – whether the life of the Church would not lack its decisive centre, the reference point of all its other functions, without this function, the function of proclamation. We have seen indeed that all these other elements are in some sense an answer to the Word of God heard.[4] Certainly preaching and sacrament may also be put in the same category. They, too, are an answer to what man has heard. And the other elements can undoubtedly be proclamation too, and have actually been so again and again. But just as the answering elements, as we have seen, cannot try to be proclamation as such, so there must stand opposed to them an element which, while it may also be interpreted, of course, as an answer, nevertheless not only can be and time and again is proclamation as distinct from them, but also seeks to be this, and does so because it ought to do so. In this element the proclamation presupposed in the others has its proper place and distinctive position. To be sure this centre, this point of reference to which all the Church's life, including the elements of proclamation, is orientated, can only be the Word of God Himself, and proclamation will as little try to push into the place of this Word as this would be fitting for any other of the Church's functions. The question arises, however, whether the Word of God does not want representatives within the realm of man's willingness to obey, whether it does not demand a specific function in the Church, whether the Church's proclamation is not thereby made at least as much of a task as the Church's responding to God's Word, as this might take place in worship and Church nurture, in instruction and theology. Whether the answer to this question is yes is not a matter to be inferred; it is decided by the commission which must be the source of all real proclamation.

Let us assume that this commission has been issued and accepted; the next thing to be made clear will be that proclamation consists

---

4   Barth here locates all church activity as subordinate to and sustained by hearing, a posture and practice of trust in God's kind provision. The churches of the Protestant Reformation have insisted on the importance of the church as the 'creature of the word'; indeed, this is a tenet of ancient Jewish theology that was maintained by these later Christian confessions: the fundamental identity of the church is alien and extrinsic, given and gracious. Hearing emphasizes the externality of our life (in the Word), whereas sight emphasizes the possession of one's life (in the eye of the beholder). Following Luther, Barth wants to apply justification by faith alone in Christ alone (and, thus, outside of us) to theological method itself (see I/1.416–419).

significantly and precisely in preaching and sacrament.[5] That which in the form of proclamation should confront listening and answering in the Church as a representation of God's Word demands in some sense a setting apart, a special, imperious calling of the man who is to function here. Furthermore, what this man can try to say as God's Word in the discharge of preaching cannot be God's own Word as such but only the repetition of His promise, repetition of the promise: 'Lo, I am with you always!' (Mt. 28.20). Proclamation must mean announcement – announcement as distinct from the real 'I am with you' as future fulfilment. Again, if this announcement is to be the legitimate repetition of not just any promise, but of the promise given to the Church by God Himself, then it cannot be arbitrary religious discourse. It must be homily, i.e., discourse which as the exposition of Scripture is controlled and guided. But if it is to be real repetition of this promise, it cannot consist in the mere reading of Scripture or in repeating and paraphrasing the actual wording of the biblical witness. This can be only its presupposition. The concrete encounter of God and man to-day, whose actuality, of course, can be created only by the Word of God Himself, must find a counterpart in the human event of proclamation, i.e., the person called must be ready to make the promise given to the Church intelligible in his own words to the men of his own time. Calling, promise, exposition of Scripture, actuality – these are the decisive definitions of the concept of preaching. If proclamation is by commission preaching – the fact that it is so need not be proved since it cannot be proved – then these concepts are a supplementary explanation of the meaning of preaching. Obviously, however, proclamation would suffer from a palpable weakness if understood solely as preaching. Preaching is human speech in the form of words thought and expressed by men. The promise as merely preached is thus a human work both on the preacher's lips and in the hearer's ear. At best it is an 'existential' decision first made by the preacher and then to be made by the hearer. Were it no more than this, how could it be a pointer to the very Word of God? Does not man's word spoken and received, the more earnestly it is spoken and received, necessarily imply as such a total eclipse of the Word of God which it seeks to serve? The promise given to the Church and attested in Holy Scripture is itself obviously no such work of man,

---

5 Not only the content but also the contours of proclamation are given by God: the ministry of the Word and the sacraments (again, though, note that Barth will later restrict usage of 'sacramental' terminology in speaking of Christian baptism and the Lord's Supper). In terms used by sociologists of knowledge, we might say that Barth is highlighting our dependence on God not only for the message but also for the medium. We do not merely spread a message of grace and love; rather the very way in which that message is passed must always reflect its gracious and loving character (and, thus, must be both directed and empowered by God).

in contrast to the promise preached. It is the Word as the enacted divine event, as the accomplished divine action of judging and reconciling grace in which a decision is made about man prior to all his own decisions, from which alone his own decisions can be characterised as decisions of faith, from which alone, then, what the preacher and his hearer may do in human fashion can become a pointer to God's own Word. If this event is not also proclaimed, how far is the promise given to the Church really proclaimed, how far is the Church's proclamation, not a ministry of the divine word, but an insuperable obstacle placed in the path of God's own Word? Yet how is this event to be proclaimed too? How can it come about that proclamation proclaims not only truth but truth as actuality, i.e., as God's work, and thereby for the first time unequivocally grace as grace? How is this to happen inasmuch as proclamation must be unambiguously identical with preaching? We are faced here with the fundamental difficulty in the task of preaching beside which one may with a good conscience describe all others as child's play. From this standpoint it is easy enough to understand that in practice little importance is attached in the Church to the claim and expectation that preaching should speak the Word of God. It is easy to understand that on the one hand Roman Catholic preaching seems to be largely content with the level of higher instruction in religion and morals while on the other hand typical Neo-Protestant preaching does not claim to be more than the most authentic and lively possible expression of the personal piety of the speaker concerned.[6] We shall have to say more about these two aberrations. In face of the difficulty which is at the root of both, and in answer to the question how God's Word can be proclaimed as God's work, we cannot have recourse at once to what is, of course, the very true and valid reference to God Himself, to the Holy Spirit, who will confirm as His own work the work of the faith which is proclaimed in words of human thought and expression on the lips of the preacher and in the ears of the hearer, thus turning the preached promise into the event of the real promise that is given to the Church. This reference to the native power of God's own Word in and in spite of the darkness of the human word that serves it is, of course, the Alpha and Omega, the limiting case, apart from which

6   'Neo-Protestant' is a term used by Barth to describe those modern Protestants known as theological liberals. He gave a lengthy account of many such figures in his historical lectures on *Protestant Theology in the Nineteenth Century* (2nd ed.; trans. Brian Cozens and John Bowden; Grand Rapids: Eerdmans, 2002), especially part two. Barth views himself in protest against Friedrich Schleiermacher and the great liberal tradition, but he also takes them very seriously. In fact his theological seminars at the University of Basel were held in a room that contained a marble bust of Schleiermacher, to which Barth regularly gave reference as a constant theological presence to be acknowledged and engaged.

not only the concept of preaching but also that of Church proclamation generally is quite impossible. The only question is whether, in the concept of the proclamation enjoined on the Church, this reference is not represented by a second element which is not identical with preaching as such and in which proclamation might be precisely what it cannot be as preaching alone, namely, the proclamation of reality, of the promise as God's work, of the grace of the faith preached and received, of the decision taken before and beyond all our decisions, which distinguishes human speaking and hearing as worship of God in spirit and in truth. Naturally, this second element in proclamation can also be no more than human talk about God. It can seek to be no more than preaching to the degree that it, too, can only announce, i.e., announce the future revelation, reconciliation and calling, and thus be repetition of the promise, a means of grace. Nor can it seek to be independent proclamation alongside preaching. It can only seek to be its confirmation, as the seal beneath a letter confirms its authenticity but adds nothing to its contents, making no statement except under the letter and in a sense standing apart. It must be co-ordinated with preaching in the sense that, as preaching represents the promise as such, it represents the character of the promise as event and grace in contrast to all man's work on the level of human occurrence. To represent this basis of the promise it must not consist in further words; it has to be action. But to be proclamation, it cannot be arbitrarily selected action any more than preaching can. It has to be the action demanded and controlled by the biblical witness. Again, like preaching, it cannot seek to replace the Word of God itself. As preaching is a strictly representative word, so it can be only a strictly representative action. Like preaching it can only be a serving of God's Word. What in either case is more than representation, service and symbol, is the event whose subject is not the Church but God Himself. And the object which it has to represent must be the presupposition of preaching which preaching as such, as word in human thought and expression, cannot represent, for which the human word as such cannot be the symbol, namely, revelation, reconciliation and calling, which the Church can only believe, hope and proclaim that it has before it when it has it behind it as the act of divine grace, which it can only truly expect when it already owes its origin to it (as enacted once and for all in the epiphany of Jesus Christ). Promise in the form of an adjunct to preaching, action in distinction from mere word, conformity to Scripture, representative symbolical connexion with the 'once-for-all' of revelation – these are the decisive definitions of the concept of sacrament. We have not postulated this concept either, but exegeted it on the presupposition that its content is a reality in the life of the

Church on the basis of God's commission, and that to this extent it is before us as a text which can be exegeted. There can be as little question of a free establishing of the necessity of sacrament as there can of a necessity of preaching or of proclamation generally. Hence in retrospect of what has been said and in answer to the question of its final proof we should not omit to point away from the exegesis and back to the actual text before us.

In conclusion, however, this exegesis of the terms proclamation, preaching and sacrament requires an express declaration: As has been done, Evangelical dogmatics exegetes these concepts.

We may ignore at this point the fact that it is specifically Evangelical Reformed dogmatics which has done this in detail.

As regards the main concept of proclamation this exegesis stands first in antithesis to Modernist dogmatics. This, too, is acquainted with the function specified but it is not aware of its essential distinctiveness as compared with other functions in the Church – a distinctiveness which accrues to it when it rests on a commission to and for men, when as man's talk about God it has to serve God's own Word spoken from an ineffaceable antithesis to all humanity. Modernist dogmatics is finally unaware of the fact that in relation to God man has constantly to let something be said to him, has constantly to listen to something, which he constantly does not know and which in no circumstances and in no sense can he say to himself. Modernist dogmatics hears man answer when no one has called him. It hears him speak with himself.[7] For it, therefore, proclamation is a necessary expression of the life of the human community known as the 'Church,' an expression in which one man, in the name and for the spiritual advancement of a number of others, drawing from a treasure common to him and to them, offers, for the enrichment of this treasure, an interpretation of his own past and present as a witness to the reality alive in this group of men.

Even Schleiermacher's *Christian Faith* is not without a section on ministry of God's Word (§ 133 f.). But we are told at once that the 'divine Word' is simply 'the spirit in all men,' i.e., in all those united in the Church (§ 134, 3). Thus ministry of God's Word is the 'act of

---

7   Barth's fundamental concern with 'Modernist' or 'Neo-Protestant' dogmatics involves its immanent and self-referential reflection. He believes that Schleiermacher and his heirs turn theology into religious studies, an attempt to give analytic expression to our human religious experience rather than to the judging and life-giving Word of God from outside of ourselves. Thus, he believes the 'modernist' tradition does not allow God to address humanity and to challenge humanity; too often and too easily human projects – be they ideological and political or pious and religious – wag the tail of 'modernist' dogmatics. In the following small print section, Barth shows how Schleiermacher interprets the 'Word of God' as the 'spirit of all men,' an immanent voice that is incapable of challenging or promising anything beyond itself.

the community as such' (§ 135, 2), or, concretely, the 'relation of the active toward the receptive' (§ 133, 1), or the 'influence of the stronger on the weaker' (§ 113, 2) through the medium of self-impartation, i.e., a 'self-display with a stimulating effect, in which the emotion of the displayer, taken up by imitation, becomes in the receptively stimulated person who takes it up a power which calls forth the same emotion' (§ 133, 1). It embraces the 'whole Christian life' and only needs special 'management' for the sake of good order and preservation of the common consciousness (§ 134, 3; 135). We are only at the other, realistic end of the same path which Schleiermacher entered upon idealistically when, a century later, P. Tillich argues that 'a new sacramental situation' will have to be 'created' to save Protestantism (Relig. Verwirkl., 1930, p. 166) by our 'successfully reaching the depths of our own undivided, pre-objective being' (op. cit., p. 154) and thus gaining an understanding of the fact that there is a mastery over natural things and situations, and hence over the Word among other things, that this is experienced in the 'historical destiny' of reciprocal apprehending and being apprehended, and that in virtue of it these things can become the vehicles of 'sacramental mastery' for believers (p. 176). If by 'sacramental situation' Tillich means the same as what we call proclamation, and if the way to this 'sacramental situation,' i.e., the historical destiny by which it is created, is really the relation between a deepened understanding of self and a deepened understanding of the world, and vice versa, then we are forced to conjecture that here too man is finally conceived of as conversing only with himself. And indeed 'religious symbols are created in the process of religious history' (p. 206). 'One has a right to say that, e.g., Christ and Buddha are symbols in so far as the unconditionally transcendent can be viewed in them' (p. 104). 'God as Object is a representation of what is ultimately intended in the religious act' (p. 103). 'The unconditionally transcendent goes beyond any positing of an essence, even a supreme essence. In so far as such is posited, it is also abrogated again in the religious act. This abrogation, the atheism immanent in the religious act, is the depth of the religious act' (p. 102). 'The truth of a symbol rests upon its inner necessity for the symbol-creating consciousness' (p. 103). 'At the point where – apart from all material connexions – the spiritual expresses itself, it expresses itself religiously' (p. 94).

On this view the ideas of speech, word, proclamation and preaching, which in themselves might all still point to the juxtaposition of God and man, must obviously disappear in the general concept of operation or movement or into the notion of a general dynamic or even meaning which embraces God and man, which is in some way the vehicle of the existence of each and all of us, and which somehow – this is where proclamation is needed – is to be articulated by us. But then Logos in its isolation as word spoken back and forth necessarily becomes one symbol among many others. 'I cannot possibly rate the word so highly,' i.e., as an expression of that dynamic or meaning. The question now becomes in all seriousness: Why do I choose precisely these symbols, talk about God and this form of it, namely, actual exposition of the Bible, along with these two or seven sacraments? Are these really the truest symbols when my spiritual nature should and would express itself? Might there not be truer ones than these?

[...]

And over and above all this the ultimate question may and must arise: Why proclamation at all? Why symbols at all? Why not better be silent? Why not, as the truest word we can utter, renounce all special talk about God, all use of symbols whatsoever?

'Undoubtedly the supreme aim of a theological work would be to discover the point at which reality itself speaks unsymbolically both of itself and also of the unconditioned, to discover the point at which reality itself without a symbol becomes a symbol, at which the antithesis between reality and symbol is removed.' Would it not be the most powerful expression of what is in us if we were to omit all expression in favour of 'immediate talk about things so far as they impinge on us unconditionally, so far as they stand in the transcendent' (P. Tillich, *Rel. Verwirkl.*, p. 208)?

What needs to be said in criticism of this teaching is said clearly enough by the teaching itself. Understanding of the concept of proclamation along these lines can end only with its dissolution. Proclamation as self-exposition must in the long run turn out to be a superfluous and impossible undertaking. To a large degree it has obviously turned out this way already. The distinction between such proclamation and the other functions of the Church cannot be shown to be essential. But if it is not, do not these other functions also become inessential as answers (answers to what?)? What is the Church, what is it meant to be, if it has no centre, if man is not really addressed in it? Can the truth of its being really be that man is alone in and with his world? Is it not plain that there is here a fateful confusion between the man of the present, the man of the kingdom of grace, and the man of eternal glory, who, as we saw at the outset, neither needs nor will need any special talk about God, and consequently any being addressed by God, and consequently any Church? If we are not this man, whence does the Modernist doctrine get its legal ground?

All that Evangelical faith cannot understand about this alien belief on the left may be summed up in the questions of Rom. 10.14: How then shall they call on him in whom they have not believed? and how shall they believe in him of whom they have not heard? and how shall they hear without a preacher? And how shall they preach, except they be sent? ... So then faith cometh by hearing, and hearing by the word of God.

The other no less serious difference that requires treatment here separates us from Roman Catholic dogmatics. In the first place, but only in the first place, it does not concern the main concept of proclamation but the mutual relations of the concepts of preaching and sacrament. The Roman Catholic Church is expressly and consciously the church of the sacrament. Its dogmatics cannot emphasise strongly enough that the Church lives by and in this means of grace.

The sacraments are the channels of grace, the vessels containing the medicine against sin and death, the foundation and linchpin of the Christian life, the river which flows out of Eden according to Gen. 2.10, the seven pillars on which wisdom has built her house according to Prov. 9.1, the bond of peace of Eph. 4.16 (H. Hurter, S.J., *Theol. dogm. compend.*, 12th edn. 1908, Vol. III, p, 214). 'The Church's work in performing them is the truest revelation and the outer confirmation of its mysterious life; they are the essential content of the Church's cultus and therefore the most excellent means of preserving the visible Church in unity and making it recognisable and distinguishable. Reception of them is the most essential mark of the Church's fellowship, their administration the most excellent and sublime activity of its priests ...' They are 'the most concentrated expression and the inmost kernel of the Church's faith and life' (Scheeben-Atzberger, *Handb. d. kath. Dogm.*, Vol. IV, 1903, p. 463). Cf. also Bartmann, *Lehrb. d. Dogm.*, 7th edn., Vol. 2, 1929, p. 207.

But one might ask quite seriously whether the superlatives we have just heard do not always say too little when one realises that in this dogmatics preaching is not only assigned less importance, but virtually no importance at all compared to the sacrament which is received and celebrated so zealously. Nor is it merely that Roman Catholicism overemphasises the sacrament in the same way as Protestantism does oral preaching.

This schematism becomes pure nonsense when Klaus Harms (in his 95 theses of 1817) advances the exaggerated view that the Roman Church inclines to cling to the sacrament and build its life around this, that the Reformed Church does the same with the Word, but that the Lutheran Church 'more splendidly than either' honours both sacrament and Word (briefly reproduced by Max Geiger, *Unsere Taufe*, 1931, p. 4). For one thing, Lutheran Protestantism, if it stays to any degree at all in Luther's footsteps, cannot wish to take middle ground and to break solidarity with Reformed Protestantism in respect of the greater emphasis on preaching and its higher ranking as compared with the sacrament. Again, for all the greater emphasis on preaching and its higher ranking, the importance which is assigned to the sacrament in the practice of the Reformed Church, and the care with which the problem of the sacrament has been and is treated in Reformed dogmatics, cannot possibly be regarded as parallel to what happens to preaching in Roman Catholic dogmatics. One would have to say the same even about Modernist dogmatics. Neither Schleiermacher's nor Troeltsch's estimation of the sacraments – judge them materially as one may – can be compared with what happens to preaching on principle and without exception, so far as I can see, in Roman Catholic dogmatics.

The fate of preaching here is quite simple: most profound silence. Roman Catholic dogmaticians pass on from the treatise on grace or from that on the Church to the treatise on the sacraments. They develop the doctrine of the sacrament of the priestly order. They consistently speak of the teaching office of the Church as though preaching did not even exist as an indispensable means of grace that claims serious attention. The only points of interest in preaching, and naturally these have only passing interest, are legal questions like those about primary and secondary bearers of legitimate Church doctrine, the necessity of a special canonically valid mission for preaching, etc.

[…]

If we are to understand this peculiar situation on the Roman Catholic side and then the meaning and significance of the opposing Evangelical thesis, we have to realise above all else that Roman Catholicism – not unlike Modernism in this respect – sees something quite different from proclamation take place at that centre of the Church's life which we have described as proclamation. Proclamation must mean repetition of the divine promise. On the basis of the Word which God has spoken to His Church attention is drawn in His Church, through men, to the Word which He wishes to speak to His Church. The presence of God is thus the grace of God, i.e., His unfathomably free act at a given time in which He recognises the attention drawn and therewith fulfils the promise in a twofold sense: by making the repetition effected by men a true one, and by corresponding to the proclaimed promise by a real new coming of His Word. The grace of this twofold fulfilment meets man, then, quite simply in his hearing of the promise and his obedience to it. It meets him only in faith. This is how the Reformers understood that event at the heart of the Church's life. They understood it in terms of proclamation, i.e., of the *promissio* repeated by man's act, because they thought they could understand the presence of the holy God among unholy men only as the grace of the strictly personal free Word of God which reaches its goal in the equally personal free hearing of men, the hearing of faith, which for its part, too, can be understood only as grace. This presupposition is missing in Roman Catholic dogmatics. It, too, describes the event at the heart of the Church's life as grace. But it understands by grace not the connexion between the Word and faith, but the connexion between a divine being as cause and a divine-creaturely being as effect. With due reservations one might even say that it understands it as a physical, not a historical, event. It sees the presence of Jesus Christ in His Church, the mystical unity of the Head with the whole body, in the fact that under certain conditions there flows forth from Jesus Christ a steady and unbroken stream of influence of divine-human being on His people.[8]

At this particular point one can scarcely fail to see the inner connexion between the Roman Catholic view and the Modernist view. The assertion of fellowship between God and man in the form of an operation beyond the juxtaposition of the divine and human persons, beyond the act of divine and human decision, is at least common to both even if one has to remember that this synthetic operation is regarded as man's work on the side of Modernism and as God's on that of Roman Catholicism. But of what importance here (and not only here) is the distinction between 'anthropocentric' and 'theocentric' theology? Both agree in the unwillingness to recognise the ultimate necessity of proclamation.

Proclamation obviously cannot be the term for this event. Grace here neither is (and remains) God's free and personal Word nor is (and remains) hearing faith. It neither has to be just Word from God nor faith in man. Man neither needs to listen to a Word of God already spoken nor to wait for a Word of God yet to be spoken. Faith neither has to grasp the promise made as made by God nor to wait for a fulfilment still to come. Blessedness is not seen in this grasping and waiting nor judgment discerned in a situation other than this grasping and waiting. All this can obviously be regarded only as partly inadequate, partly superfluous, and partly distorted if both from the standpoint of the divine Giver and also from that of the human recipient grace is an

This was my problem in the Church as sacrament class!!!

---

8   Barth sees the same fundamental error in Roman Catholic dogmatics: the Word of God is transmuted into an immanent voice. In the Catholic context, however, it is not the 'spirit of all men' (as in Schleiermacher) but the spirit of the church (what he terms a 'steady and unbroken stream of influence of divine-human being on his people'). Barth sees both the 'Modernist' and the 'Roman Catholic' dogmatic traditions inhibiting the extrinsic and alien nature of the Word of God; in his view, this limits their appreciation of God's freedom, the fallibility of dogmatics, and the need for constant reformation by the Word.

operation, an influence, an action and passion which takes place, not essentially and ultimately between person and person, but materially between God as author on the one hand and the ground of being in the human person on the other.

Protestant polemics is urgently recommended not to use the word 'magical' in this connexion.[9] The authentic Roman Catholic view of this material process cannot be brought under any meaningful definition of the term 'magic'. Cf. on this whole subject Damasus Winzen O.S.B. *Die Sakramentenlehre der Kirche in ihrem Verhältnis zur dialektischen Theologie, Catholica,* 1932, p. 19 f.

We are faced with a basic decision at this point. For the man who can interpret an operation or influence of an impersonal kind as the grace of Jesus Christ, the rest follows self-evidently. On this view the sacrament has to become the one and all. As act in distinction from spoken Word it is well adapted, if influence be the thing that takes place between God and man in the Church, to be the medium and channel of this influence.

9   Barth clearly has serious concerns about Roman Catholic theology and its concomitant views of the church's being and power. He thinks this dogmatic tradition too easily identifies the life of the church with the Word of God. Nevertheless, this small-print section shows that he wants to give an honest and fair assessment of Roman Catholic teaching on its own terms and in its best forms. He refuses to use the category of 'magic' to depict its views of nature and grace (for example, the notion of papal infallibility or the teaching authority of the magisterium). This qualification exemplifies his constant forays into historical theology and ecumenical engagement, where Barth models a concern to understand various ecclesiastical voices in their own terms (though, admittedly, he does not always succeed). For an exceptional account of Barth's historical theology (via focused studies on some of his early lecture series), see John Webster, *Barth's Earlier Theology* (London: T & T Clark, 2005). Regarding historical study of Roman Catholic dogmatics specifically, it should be noted that Barth became familiar with this ecclesiastical tradition in the 1920s and remained conversant with it throughout his teaching career, culminating in a visit to Vatican City in 1966 and a book that offered his reflections on the Second Vatican Council (*Ad Limina Apostolorum: Reappraisal of Vatican II* [trans. Keith Crim; Edinburgh: St. Andrew, 1968]).

CHAPTER 5

THE PERFECT GOD

When we ask questions about God's being, we cannot in fact leave the sphere of His action and working as it is revealed to us in His Word. God is who He is in His works. He is the same even in Himself, even before and after and over His works, and without them. They are bound to Him, but He is not bound to them. They are nothing without Him. But He is who He is without them. He is not, therefore, who He is only in His works. Yet in Himself He is not another than He is in His works. In the light of what He is in His works it is no longer an open question what He is in Himself. In Himself He cannot, perhaps, be someone or something quite other, or perhaps nothing at all. But in His works He is Himself revealed as the One He is.[1]

Dogmatics in each and all of its divisions and subdivisions, with every one of its questions and answers, with all its biblical and historical assertions, with the whole range of its formal and material considerations, examinations and condensations, can first and last, as a whole and in part, say nothing else but that God is.[2]

Volume 2 of the Church Dogmatics addresses the doctrine of God – his perfections (part 1) and his electing determination to be God for us in Jesus Christ (part 2). This portion of part 1 addresses Barth's discussion of the knowledge of God (§25–27) and then of the 'reality of God' as 'the One who loves in freedom' (§28–31). The editorial introduction to part one notes two dangers that Barth sought to avoid: 'Here Barth is concerned to correct the scholastic and philosophical separation between the being of God and His actions and attributes, but he is equally careful to avoid the other error which thinks of God's being only in terms of His ways and works as if it were exhausted in them or passed wholly into them' (II/1: viii). Theology (God in Himself) is revealed in the economy (God with us), over against speculative philosophical theology that bases the doctrine of God on logical *a priori* reasoning. Yet theology is not

---

1   *CD* II/1.260.
2   *CD* II/1.258.

exhausted by the economy, over against pragmatic reductionism and Hegelian historicism in modern theology. Therefore, Barth addresses the twin topics, then, of God's freedom (his eternal fullness in and of himself) as well as his love (his turning toward the creature in grace and mercy).

Bibliography

Christopher R. J. Holmes, *Revisiting the Doctrine of the Divine Attributes: In Dialogue with Karl Barth, Eberhard Jüngel, and Wolf Krötke* (Issues in Systematic Theology 15; New York: Peter Lang, 2007), ch. 3.

Rob Price, *Letters of the Divine Word: The Perfections of God in Karl Barth's Church Dogmatics* (T & T Clark Studies in Systematic Theology 9; London: T & T Clark, 2011).

Text (*CD* II/1.322, 341–350)

God's being consists in the fact that He is the One who loves in freedom. In this He is the perfect being: the being which is itself perfection and so the standard of all perfection; the being, that is, which is self-sufficient and thus adequate to meet every real need; the being which suffers no lack in itself and by its very essence fills every real lack.[3] Such a being is God. He is this being because He lives as such. It is as we return to life as the fundamental element in the divine being that we also move forward to God's perfections. The one perfection of God, His loving in freedom, is lived out by Him, and therefore identical with a multitude of various and distinct types of perfection. There is no possibility of knowing the perfect God without knowing His perfections. The converse is also true: knowledge of the divine perfections is possible only in knowledge of the perfect God,

---

3   It is worth noting that Barth's favourite hymn, 'Now Thank We All Our God' (by M. Rinkart) addresses the eternally rich and 'bounteous', that is, self-sufficient and free God displayed in the gospel:

> Now thank we all our God, with heart and hands and voices,
> Who wondrous things has done, in Whom this world rejoices;
> Who from our mothers' arms has blessed us on our way
> With countless gifts of love, and still is ours today.

> O may this bounteous God through all our life be near us,
> With ever joyful hearts and blessed peace to cheer us;
> And keep us in His grace, and guide us when perplexed;
> And free us from all ills, in this world and the next!

> All praise and thanks to God the Father now be given;
> The Son and Him Who reigns with Them in highest heaven;
> The one eternal God, whom earth and Heaven adore;
> For thus it was, is now, and shall be evermore.

of His loving in freedom. But because God lives His perfect being the knowledge of His perfections is also a way — the way which in the presence of the living God we must tread. In other words, even in the knowledge of the one perfect God we are confronted by His richness. The real God is the one God who loves in freedom, and as such is eternally rich. To know Him means to know Him again and again, in ever new ways — to know only Him, but to know Him as the perfect God, in the abundance, distinctness and variety of His perfections.

[...]

A fully restrained and fully alive doctrine of God's attributes will take as its fundamental point of departure the truth that God is for us fully revealed and fully concealed in His self-disclosure.[4] We cannot say partly revealed and partly concealed, but we must actually say wholly revealed and wholly concealed at one and the same time. We must say wholly revealed because by the grace of revelation our human views and concepts are invited and exalted to share in the truth of God and therefore in a marvellous way made instruments of a real knowledge of God (in His being for us and as He is in Himself). We must say wholly concealed because our human views and concepts (the only ones at our disposal for the knowledge of God, and claimed by God Himself as a means to this end) have not in themselves the smallest capacity to apprehend God. A true doctrine of the divine attributes must in all circumstances attest and take into account both factors — God's self-disclosure and His self-concealment.[5] The knowledge of God must not be swallowed up in the ignorance. Nor, again, must the ignorance be swallowed up by the knowledge. Both demands are laid upon us by God Himself in His revelation: the obedience of knowledge and the humility of ignorance. And in laying down both requirements God

---

4   Before we get to the fact that we must know God as both revealed and yet concealed (stated here), we must first consider Barth's claim that the 'fundamental point of departure' for knowledge of God's character is his 'self-revelation'. In other words theological knowledge is always God's gift. Elsewhere Barth puts it this way: 'The eternal correlation between God and us, as shown in God's revelation, is grounded in God alone and not partly in God and partly in us' (II/1.281).

5   Barth here addresses the nature of theological knowledge and language. God reveals himself. Yet God reveals himself in human form. Thus, there is a dialectic relationship of veiling and unveiling, of revelation and mystery, of exposure and concealment. Theologians have often clarified by saying that we can adequately and really know God, though we cannot comprehensively and perfectly know God. The key doctrinal issue is that an infinitely free God cannot be captured by finitely limited minds or words. This is no mere abstract theorem for Barth, however. He sees a Christological clarification. Jesus does interpret God for us (John 1.18), but he does so by becoming the Word of God *incarnate*; therefore, the unveiled God is still veiled in human nature.

is equally the one true God. The one grace of His self-revelation is at the root of both, and, because His self-revelation is His truth, we must add: He Himself, His own most proper reality. And in both ways, through His self-disclosure and His concealment, He is at one and the same time knowable and unknowable to us. In other words, in His self-revelation and concealment He has become for us an object of our human knowledge while remaining completely unknowable to us in both aspects (even in that of revelation). The relation between the two is not such that in His self-unveiling we have grounds for knowing Him, and in His self-concealment for not knowing Him; in the former case for speaking, in the latter for being silent. We have to know Him integrally and therefore in both these aspects. At every point, therefore, we have to be silent, but we have also to speak. The honour which we give Him is in both cases alike problematical. But we are summoned to both alike. We can evade neither. We have thus to recognise Him both in His hiddenness and in His self-disclosure. It will certainly be true that in both cases He remains completely unknowable to us even as we may and must know Him. In all our thinking and speaking about Him we never become His masters. We are always and must always be His servants, and indeed quite unprofitable servants. But it is also true – and this must be stated just as vigorously – that in both cases He becomes completely recognisable by us, not because of our capacity, thinking and speaking, but because of the grace of His revelation, which we cannot refuse to receive, however little we may be able to control it. In order to do justice to this whole state of affairs it is obviously incumbent upon a doctrine of divine attributes to say two things. We cannot confess simultaneously both our knowing and our not knowing. Nor should we try to do so. For it is in such a way that the two things do not exist simultaneously, but only alongside of each other and in succession, that God has revealed Himself in Jesus Christ. Nor does a temporal simultaneity, if we are to trust His revelation, correspond to God's own reality. But, again, we may not and should not wish to confess the one to the exclusion of the other, thus allowing our knowledge to be swallowed up in a presumed absolute and final ignorance, or on the other hand our ignorance to be dissolved in a presumed absolute and final knowledge. For in God's self-revelation and therefore in God's reality there is no such merging of the one in the other. God's reality is of such a character that the one exists with the other, in the other, alongside of and after the other, an eternal simultaneity and successiveness. So, then, we are not compelled to retire within the limitations of our capacity for knowledge, but speak directly in view of the reality of the object itself, when we say that in any doctrine of divine attributes both factors must be particularly emphasised, alongside each other and therefore successively – God's self-disclosure and also His concealment.

This unity and this distinction corresponds to the unity and distinction in God's own being between His love and His freedom.[6] God loves us. And because we can trust His revelation as the revelation of His own being He is in Himself the One who loves. As such He is completely knowable to us. But He loves us in His freedom. And because here too we can trust His revelation as a self-revelation, He is in Himself sovereignly free. He is therefore completely unknowable to us. That He loves us and that He does so in His freedom are both true in the grace of His revelation. If His revelation is His truth, He is truly both in unity and difference: the One who loves in freedom. It is His very being to be both, not in separation but in unity, yet not in the dissolution but in the distinctiveness of this duality. And this duality as the being of the one God necessarily forms the content of the doctrine of His perfection. The doctrine must consequently treat of the perfections of His love and also of the perfections of His freedom. According to all that we have said, this cannot mean that we shall now begin to speak of two different subjects. The unity of self-disclosure and concealment, of the knowability and unknowability of God, constitutes the biblical idea of the revelation of God, just as the unity of love and freedom constitutes the biblical idea of the being of God. In both cases therefore – and in respect of each individual characterisation – we shall have to speak of the one God integrally. Therefore, explicitly or implicitly, when we speak of the love of God we shall have to speak also of His freedom, when we speak of His freedom we shall have to speak also of His love, and when we speak of one individual aspect we shall have to speak also of all the others. But if we do not wish to deviate from Scripture, the unity of God must be understood as this unity of His love and freedom which is dynamic and, to that extent, diverse. What we have here is, then, a complete reciprocity in the characterisation of the one Subject. Always in this reciprocity each of the opposing ideas not only augments

6   Barth offers a dialectical approach to the divine attributes/perfections. His *a posteriori* approach to the divine perfections reveals that they must be thought about together – the one true God is loving and free, gracious and perfectly self-sufficient. To understand God's love rightly, one must know that it is the love of a perfectly free, self-sufficient, fully alive God. In other words, it is not the love of a God with needs or lacks or insufficiencies. It is a love flowing out of excess (what Barth earlier calls 'richness') rather than stemming from lack. As Barth says elsewhere: 'While God is everything for Himself, He wills again not to be everything merely for Himself, but for this other' (II/1.280). Elsewhere (in IV/1) Barth will tease out the way that God's love is displayed in Christ the servant, while God's freedom is displayed in Christ the Lord; Christ *is both simultaneously*.

but absolutely fulfils the other, yet it does not render it superfluous or supplant it. On the contrary, it is only in conjunction with the other – and together with it affirming the same thing – that each can describe the Subject, God.[7]

Apart from Frank, T. Haering is the modern theologian who has shown a particularly felicitous touch in these matters, and he evinces a fine understanding of this reciprocity. He expresses it by speaking of 'the absolute personality' of God on the one hand and His 'holy love' on the other. The emphasis in the former case is on the adjective and in the latter on the substantive. In this way, we are continually reminded of the counterbalancing second concept which is so indispensable for a true understanding: in the one case, that the attributes of the personal God are those of the Self-existent; and in the other, that whichever name we may give we can speak only of one and the same God. But we cannot speak rightly of this one God except in the mutual characterisation and limitation of these two names – of His love by His freedom, and of His freedom by His love.

For us too, then, there arises the necessity of speaking of God's attributes in a twofold series. The unity and distinction of the complete trust and the complete humility in which the Christian knowledge of God is attained (in view of the complete disclosure and the complete concealment of the one God in His revelation), and the unity and difference in which God loves as the One who is free, and is free as the One who loves, make any other way but this impossible to us.[8] Therefore the two fundamental features of the being of God – His love and His freedom in their unity and diversity – necessarily indicate the two directions in which we shall have to think, now that it can no longer be a question of analysing our knowledge of God as such, but of presenting the One already known. In the following sections, then, we

---

7   The two cannot be thought apart from each other, though they must be distinguished from each other. So there is an intended parallelism in his presentation of divine love and freedom. As Barth focuses on the 'perfections of the divine loving' (II/1.351–439), he summarizes the approach in this way: 'The divinity of the love of God consists and confirms itself in the fact that in Himself and in all His works God is gracious, merciful and patient, and at the same time holy, righteous and wise' (II/1.351). As Barth focuses on the 'perfection of the divine freedom' (II/1.440–677), he summarizes the approach in this way: 'The divinity of the freedom of God consists and confirms itself in the fact that in Himself and in all His works God is One, constant and eternal, and therewith also omnipresent, omnipotent and glorious' (II/1.440). Note that both the divine loving and the divine freedom 'consists and confirms itself ... in Himself and in all His works'. Both are eternally true as well as temporally confirmed.

8   Barth sees a link between the character of God and the character of our posture before him. God is loving and free, thus we are to turn to him in 'complete trust' (believing him to be loving) and simultaneously in 'complete humility' (believing him to be free and, thus, not externally required to give us grace).

shall have to treat of the perfections of divine love and the perfections of divine freedom.

But before we adopt this line of approach which we know to be basically and generally that of a whole theological tradition, we must come to an understanding with regard to the question how far we may or may not associate ourselves with this tradition. What has previously been attempted on this generally and basically acceptable path is not so consistent, unambiguous and secure that even in regard to the question as a whole, quite apart from any details, we do not have to avoid certain misunderstandings and make certain corrections. Three decisive points are at stake.

1. It is in the nature of the case that when we speak of God's love we have occasion to think chiefly of God in His fellowship with the other, or, to be more specific, with the world which He has created. And on the other hand, when we speak of God in His freedom, it would appear to be chiefly a question of His transcendence over against all that is not Himself and therefore over against the created world. But this cannot be a true and basic distinction.[9] For it is also a question of God's transcendence over everything that is not Himself even in His fellowship with the world which He has created. And again, this transcendence is itself no other than that which He discloses and exercises in His fellowship with the world. God is not first the One who loves, and then somewhere and somehow, in contradistinction to that, the One who is also free. And when He loves He does not surrender His freedom, but exercises it in a supreme degree. The principle of division which we recognise at this point cannot mean that out of the distinction suggested but also overcome in revelation we have to establish a separation between a God in Himself and a God for us, in which the essential being of God will probably be decisively sought in His sovereign freedom and the perfections proper to it, eternity, omnipotence and so on, while the love of God and its perfections, holiness, justice, mercy and so on, are treated nominalistically or semi-nominalistically as a question of mere economy, as non-essential, as perhaps purely noetic determinations, so that the final and decisive word in our doctrine of God is the affirmation of God as the impersonal absolute.

It is not to be denied (it would be surprising if it were otherwise) that the various bases of distinction suggested by the Lutheran Orthodox

---

9   Barth wants to insist that both love and freedom are true of God eternally and in his engagement
     with creaturely time. As he puts it in the summary of paragraph 28: 'God is who He is in the
     act of His revelation. God seeks and creates fellowship between Himself and us, and therefore he
     loves us. But He is this loving God without us as Father, Son, and Holy Spirit, in the freedom of
     the Lord, who has His life from Himself' (II/1.257).

theologians point more or less plainly in this direction. Therefore, if we do not repudiate the principles as such, we must add by way of elucidation that there are no absolute attributes which are not also relative, no dormant attributes which are not also active, no metaphysical attributes which are not also moral, and on the other hand, no external attributes which are not also internal, no transcendent attributes which are not also immanent, no derivative attributes which are not also primary. Even the distinction favoured by the Reformed between communicable and incommunicable attributes can be admitted only as a distinction, but in no sense as a separation. For which of the attributes of God, in which as Creator, Reconciler and Redeemer He allows His creatures to share, is not, as His own, utterly incommunicable from the creaturely point of view, i.e., communicable only by the miracle of grace? And again, which of these incommunicable attributes has not God nevertheless communicated to the creature in that His Word was made flesh? Is not God's mercy completely unfathomable and inaccessible to us? And has He not implanted His eternity utterly in our hearts? In His Son God has opened up to us and given us all, His own inmost self. How then can His sovereign freedom be understood as a limitation of His love? How can it be sought elsewhere than in this love itself? Again, the very fact that we know Him and possess Him only because He has revealed Himself and given Himself to us in the miracle of His grace means inevitably that He stands over against us in all the austerity of His majesty and difference from us, and that we ill recognise His love if we do not see in it His freedom. The knowledge of the majesty of God must not be misused to set up that idol of the one and absolute which is 'properly' without motion, utterance, or action. Nor must the knowledge of God's condescension be so misused that finally we seek Him only in certain relations in which we must stand and which have to be interpreted as such. But as in the former aspect God must be recognised as eternal love, so in the latter He must be understood as the freedom personally entering our world of time. What He is there in the height for us and for our sakes, here in the depths He is also in Himself. And we are speaking of God only when we know that He is both – and both in this reciprocal relation, and differentiated unity.

We cannot, then, attribute to this whole distinction between God in Himself and God in His relation to the world an essential, but only a heuristic, significance.[10] It does, of course, have this significance. That

---

10   Barth is willing to acknowledge a distinction between the immanent Trinity and the economic Trinity, to be sure, but he specifies its reality: a 'heuristic' and not an 'essential' significance. In other words, it is a distinction in our understanding of God, but not in his very being, for the immanent Trinity is the same God, who wishes to be with us and not apart from us. Barth wants

God is both knowable and unknowable to us, the One who loves and the One who is free, becomes actually clear to us in this distinction. Neither of the two aspects is self-explanatory. Neither can be simply assumed. Both must become clear to us. The truth of both becomes manifest in the event of revelation in which God makes the transition from there to here, from His being in Himself to His being in fellowship with us, thus disclosing the truth of both these aspects, not in the form of a separation but of a distinction, as the same thing in distinguishable forms. By this distinction in God of His being in Himself and for us, as it is brought out in the event of revelation, the distinction between His love and His freedom can and must become clear to us; His love in that God as He is in Himself wills also to be God for us, His freedom in that He will and can be for us no other than as He is in Himself. We recognise the latter distinction through the former, and with it the division of the divine attributes. But we cannot allow it an essential significance if we wish to avoid the well-known traps into which the orthodox doctrine of God has fallen.

2. The division of the divine perfections according to this twofold principle can involve the temptation of attempted epistemological deduction. If, for example, the distinction between God in Himself and God for us is interpreted at this point as primary, it is only a step to the consideration that if the freedom of God is identical with God's being in Himself in its transcendence over all that is distinct from it, its perfections obviously cannot be described by the aid of concepts whose proper objects can be sought only in the realm of realities distinct from God.[11]

---

to affirm God's love (so God just is the God of the gospel, eternally determining to be with us and to make possible that fellowship in Jesus by the Spirit) as well as God's freedom (so God can be thought of apart from us). Much twentieth century Trinitarian thought has focused primarily on the former to the exclusion or detriment of the latter (for a survey, see Stanley J. Grenz, *Rediscovering the Triune God: The Trinity in Contemporary Theology* [Minneapolis: Fortress, 2004]).

11   Barth here begins with the reality of our knowledge of God by his gift. If this is so – if we really have a Word from God – then God must be such that this is not only possible but actual. Barth regularly moves from actuality to possibility (and not the other way, as in so much speculative philosophical thought about a most perfect being and its potentialities). Here Barth infers that God must be capable of being spoken about in terms drawn from 'the realm of realities distinct from God'. Thus, there must be some relationship or analogy made possible by God's drawing near to us, even more basic by God's being the kind of being that draws near to us. Barth calls this the 'analogy of faith', where we trust that God makes analogous use of creaturely media to give graciously a Word. In volume three, Barth will unpack the notion of an 'analogy of relations' that enables us to speak of God in creaturely terminology. He continues to find this opposed to an 'analogy of being' (*analogia entis*) as functions in Roman Catholic dogmatics, because he believes the 'analogy of being' conflates the divine and creaturely by locating them in the same category ('Being'). It ought to be noted that Barth's criticisms of the 'analogy of being' in the 1920s actually led to modifications in some Roman Catholic thinking on the subject, so that his 'analogy of relations' comes to be quite similar to later, modified Roman Catholic thought

This being the case, it is necessary in describing them to transcend these realities. But how is this possible since our ideas are indissolubly bound up with these realities of quite a different order? Obviously there is only one answer – which is thought to be the true one – that we have to employ negative concepts, i.e., those which express the negation of the realities which are properly denoted by human ideas, but which through this negation point beyond these realities and therefore – so it is supposed – to God as the One who in sovereign freedom stands over against this realm of earthly reality. And if, on the other hand, the love of God is identical with His being for us, in His fellowship with the world which He has created, the perfections of this divine love cannot be characterised by concepts which have as their content the being and nature of the created world as such, but we can attempt to render these ideas transcendental by expanding, elevating and enriching them, by using them in the superlative, so that they receive a form in which they can no longer denote the world but – so it is supposed – only the love of God turned to the world and manifested in the world. The two possibilities may then be completed, or rather grounded and comprehended, in a third possibility, according to which God in Himself and God for us is seen to confront the world as its basis, and the world is therefore a negative and positive witness to the perfection of its divine basis. Thus human concepts properly denoting the realities of this world may be employed to denote the being of God and its perfections.

[...]

3. The order in which these two series of divine attributes are formulated is not a matter of indifference. It is, of course, true that in both cases, whether we are speaking of the love or of the freedom of God, we are concerned with the one God, with the glory of the Lord in its fullness, in which there can be no more or less and therefore no before and after. At a first glance, then, it may well appear that we can begin and end at either point without deriving any particular advantage and without incurring any particular danger. But this conclusion is overhasty.

on the matter (see Keith Johnson, *Karl Barth and the Analogia Entis* [T & T Clark Studies in Systematic Theology; London: T & T Clark, 2010]). We might add that earlier Roman Catholic thought on the 'analogy of being' (e.g. in Thomas Aquinas' *Summa Theologiae*) is not very far from what Barth means by his 'analogy of relations', in as much as both Barth and Thomas mean to acknowledge the reality of our knowing God through creaturely means made actual by God and yet that God transcends those very means and is the perfect God (see Fergus Kerr, *After Aquinas: Versions of Thomism* [Oxford: Blackwell, 2002], ch. 12; and Peter S. Oh, *Karl Barth's Trinitarian Theology: A Study in Karl Barth's Analogical Use of the Trinitarian Relation* [London: T & T Clark, 2006], especially part 1, which makes available some astute reflections by German Barth scholar Eberhard Jüngel).

The logical rigour of the dialectic which occupies us must not conceal from us the fact that we are not concerned with any sort of dialectic but with the very special dialectic of the revelation and being of God, in the apprehension of which we are not left to chance or caprice but must adjust ourselves to the order intrinsic to the theme, or realised in it. It is important not to miss this order if we are not to miss the thing itself. But it is undeniable that this order, and to a great extent also the thing itself, has been fairly generally missed in the tradition to which in essentials we have adhered. For instance, theologians have nearly always treated first of the absolute, dormant, incommunicable attributes, etc., i.e., of the perfections of the divine majesty, or, as we would term it, the divine freedom, and only then have they been willing to discuss the relative, operable, communicative attributes, etc., i.e., the perfections of the divine love. The fundamental error of the whole earlier doctrine of God is reflected in this arrangement: first God's being in general, then His triune nature – with all the ambiguities and sources of error which must result from this sequence.[12] Its nominalism or semi-nominalism is also reflected in it, for the order undoubtedly implies that it is a question first of what the being of God is properly in itself, and only then of what it is improperly in its relationship to that outside of himself. And finally there is reflected what is actually the most doubtful feature of its conception of God: that God is first and properly the impersonal absolute, and only secondarily, inessentially and in His relationship to that outside of himself the personal God of love with

---

12 Barth here begins to offer a genealogical account of a modern theological error. He suspects that the medieval, Reformation, and especially post-Reformation dogmatic tradition considered the notion of theism prior to the names of the Trinity, in other words, the idea of divinity prior to the identity of the God of the gospel. Barth sees such an approach in the liberal Protestant tradition of his youth and in the atheistic criticisms of religion's cultured despisers. It ought to be noted, however, that the modern approach to a scientific and objective study of God, focusing on universally available knowledge (a bland theism) rather than on the revealed nature of the Trinity (a specifically Christian doctrine of God), is not continuous with the classical Christian tradition of the medieval, Reformation, and early post-Reformation eras. In fact, the order of teaching in that classical Christian tradition was based not on scientific method (moving from universals to particulars, e.g., in Schleiermacher's *The Christian Faith*, which only discusses the Trinity at the very end) but on canonical revelation (moving from the revelation of the one God of Israel to the fuller revelation of that God's triunity in the life of Jesus Christ). Here Barth seems limited by the historical resources available at his time, and, thus, he wrongly conflates the classical and the contemporary dogmatic traditions. See, e.g., the survey of the formative influence of the 'divine names' on thinking about the divine nature in post-Reformation Reformed dogmatics in Richard A. Muller, *Post-Reformation Reformed Dogmatics: The Rise and Development of Reformed Orthodoxy, ca. 1520 to ca. 1725*, volume three: *The Divine Essence and Attributes* (Grand Rapids: Baker Academic, 2003), 244–70 (especially the analysis of Wolfgang Musculus' *Loci Communes* and Peter Martyr Vermigli's *Loci Communes* on 246–7 and 253, respectively).

the attributes of wisdom, justice, mercy, etc.[13] But this sequence corre-sponds neither to the order of revelation nor to the nature of the being of God as known in His revelation. In God's revelation the disclosure of God is in fact the first and the last, the origin and the end, of the ways of God. God's revelation is first and last a Gospel, glad tidings, the word and deed of divine grace. Not without concealment, for in His revelation God shews Himself to be the secret of all secrets; not without the revelation of His omnipotence and eternity, of His hidden majesty; not without the Gospel becoming for us Law and judgment; not without exposing our sin and helplessness, our distance from God and therefore the transcendence of God over all that He Himself is not. Nor is all this involved only provisionally or apparently or incidentally, in such a way that this aspect of the divine speaking and action can be ignored. It is involved in such a way that this second aspect is seen as complementary to the first, as included in it, and manifesting itself truly only in the light of it. Only now that the mystery of God is disclosed is it seen to be a mystery: for what do we know of the mystery of God without revelation? Only as God reveals Himself does He also conceal Himself. Only as God speaks and acts do His omnipotence and eternity become real to us. Only as He gives Himself to us as the One who loves does He withdraw from us also in His holy freedom. Only through the power of the Gospel does there arise for us a divinely binding and authoritative Law, and a knowledge of our sin, and therefore of our creatureliness, our distance from God, and therefore the recognition of God's transcendence in Himself and over against all that He is not. It is not that God in His revelation is the second of these aspects to a lesser degree than He is the first. The truth is that He is it differently. He is it Himself in this relationship of the second with the first. He is it in this sequence. And a knowledge of His being and attributes which is to be faithful to the intrinsic character of His revelation must adhere to this sequence. The same point results from a consideration of the being of God as knowable in His revelation. We have seen that the essence of the divine being is to be the One who loves us and who loves in Himself, the One who is active in founding and maintaining fellowship. But He is this as the One who is free, in His freedom, and therefore as the self-existent One, unconditioned by anything else, Himself conditioning everything else. He is it, therefore, in His majesty, omnipotence and eternity. He is it in His aseity. Nor again is He all this

---

13   This is Barth's clearest description of the bland theism that he finds so troubling. To avoid this approach – which privileges transcendence and thus relegates immanence to a secondary appendage – Barth began the *Church Dogmatics* with the doctrine of the Word of God by way of Trinitarian analysis (I/1).

provisionally, apparently or incidentally, in such a way that this aspect of His being can be ignored. Even in His freedom He is the One who loves. Therefore His Godhead, in so far as it is to be understood as His freedom, is the Godhead of His love. It is as the personal triune God that He is self-existent. And although the converse is certainly true, it is only because we must first say that it is as the personal triune God that He is self-existent; as the One who loves that He is the One who is free. If there is full reciprocity, as we have seen, this order obtains even in the full reciprocity, not signifying a difference of value between the two aspects of divinity, but the movement of life in which God is God, corresponding exactly to His revelation of Himself as God. And in our apprehension and exposition of the perfections of God we must adhere to this order and sequence.

It is clear that the older scholastic doctrine, to whose basic thoughts we formally adhere, will be given a greatly changed appearance by these three modifications and especially by the third – the reversal in the order of the two categories. But it is surely the appearance corresponding to the compulsion of the subject.

CHAPTER 6

THE ELECTION OF JESUS CHRIST

The doctrine of election is the sum of the Gospel because of all words that can be said or heard it is the best: that God elects man; that God is for man too the One who loves in freedom. It is grounded in the knowledge of Jesus Christ because He is both the electing God and elected man in One. It is part of the doctrine of God because originally God's election of man is a predestination not merely of man but of Himself. Its function is to bear basic testimony to eternal, free and unchanging grace as the beginning of all the ways and works of God.[1]

Of all his many contributions to theology, Karl Barth is undoubtedly most widely known for his revisions to the doctrine of election. Inspired by a 1936 lecture given by Pierre Maury on 'Election and Faith', where Maury proclaimed that 'outside of Christ, we know neither of the electing God, nor of His elect, nor of the act of election'.[2] Barth was henceforth set on a course of rethinking the centrality of Christ for all theology, especially as it relates to election in Christ: 'in these years I had to learn that Christian doctrine, if it is to merit its name and if it is to build up the Christian Church in the world as she must needs be built up, has to be exclusively and conclusively the doctrine of Jesus Christ – of Jesus Christ as the living Word of God spoken to us men and women … I should like to call it a Christological concentration'.[3] Barth's doctrine of election proves pivotal in marking this 'Christological concentration', namely, that the only God, and thus the only gospel, of which we may speak involves the Triune determination to have fellowship with us. Barth does teach a double predestination – Jesus Christ is elect and reprobate, exalted and humiliated – that shows God's singular purpose in reconciling all things in Christ. Barth teases out this approach by offering lengthy exegetical excurses that show the Christological shape of Old Testament passages of election (e.g. Saul and David).

---

1   *CD* II/2.3.
2   Pierre Maury, *Erwählung und Glaube* (Theologische Studien 8; Zurich: EVZ, 1940), p. 7.
3   Karl Barth, *How I Changed My Mind* (Edinburgh: The Saint Andrew Press, 1969), p. 43.

Eventually Barth does address many of the same issues so often covered under the doctrine of election in Reformed divinity: the relationship of divine and human action, the link between divine sovereignty and human freedom, etc. In III/3 his doctrine of providence makes plain that God freely and lovingly governs all human history – he gives new yet faithful expression to a classical Augustinian and Reformed approach to the doctrine of providence. But that is not the word of election for Barth: election is a word about God's self-determination to be with us and not without us in Jesus Christ (II/1.275). As he says earlier (II/2.13–14): 'The election of grace is the whole of the Gospel, the Gospel *in nuce*. It is the very essence of good news … God is God in His being as the One who loves in freedom. This is revealed as a benefit conferred upon us in the fact which corresponds to the truth of God's being, the fact that God elects in His grace, that He moves towards humanity in His dealings within this covenant with the one man Jesus and the people represented by Him. All the joy and benefit of His whole work as Creator, Reconciler, and Redeemer … all these are grounded and determined in the fact that that God is the God of the eternal election of His grace. In the light of this election the whole of the Gospel is light'. God really does love us – this is no façade and no illusion. God really does have skin in the game – in Jesus, we see that 'it was the will of the LORD to bruise him' (Isa. 53.10). This one, humiliated for our transgressions, exalted for our glory, forever receives our praise and provides our rest. He does this, because he is that kind of being: he is *Immanuel*.

Bibliography

Karl Barth, 'The Humanity of God', in *The Humanity of God* (trans. John Newton Thomas; Louisville: Westminster John Knox, 1960), pp. 37–68.

G. C. Berkouwer, 'The Triumph of Election', in *The Triumph of Grace in the Theology of Karl Barth* (Grand Rapids: Eerdmans, 1956), pp. 89–122.

David Gibson, *Reading the Decree: Exegesis, Election, and Christology in Calvin and Barth* (T & T Clark Studies in Systematic Theology 4; London: T & T Clark, 2009).

George Hunsinger, 'Election and the Trinity: Twenty-Five Theses on the Theology of Karl Barth', *Modern Theology* 24, no. 2 (2008): 179–98.

Bruce L. McCormack, 'Grace and Being: The Role of God's Gracious Election in Karl Barth's Theological Ontology', in *The Cambridge Companion to Karl Barth* (ed. John Webster; Cambridge: Cambridge University Press, 2000), pp. 92–110.

Text (*CD* II/2: 101–106, 115–118)

The choice or election of God is basically and properly God's decision
that as described in Jn. 1.1–2 the Word which is 'the same,' and is called
Jesus, should really be in the beginning, with Himself, like Himself, one
with Himself in His deity. And for this reason it is in itself an election
of grace. This is not, of course, self-evidently the case. God would not
be God, He would not be free, if this had to be so. 'What is man, that
thou art mindful of him? and the son of man, that thou visitest him?'
(Ps. 8.5). The eternal God was not under an obligation to man to be
in Himself the God whose nature and property it is to bear this name.
That He is, in fact, such a God is grace, something which is not merited
by man but can only be given to him. And that God is gracious, that in
assuming this name He gives Himself to the man who has not merited
it, is His election, His free decree. It is the divine election of grace. In
a free act of determination God has ordained concerning Himself; He
has determined Himself. Without any obligation, God has put Himself
under an obligation to man, willing that that should be so which
according to Jn. 1.1–2 actually is so. It is grace that it is so, and it is
grace that God willed it to be so.

In the beginning, before time and space as we know them, before
creation, before there was any reality distinct from God which could be
the object of the love of God or the setting for His acts of freedom, God
anticipated and determined within Himself (in the power of His love
and freedom, of His knowing and willing) that the goal and meaning of
all His dealings with the as yet non-existent universe should be the fact
that in His Son He would be gracious towards man, uniting Himself
with him. In the beginning it was the choice of the Father Himself to
establish this covenant with man by giving up His Son for him, that
He Himself might become man in the fulfilment of His grace. In the
beginning it was the choice of the Son to be obedient to grace, and
therefore to offer up Himself and to become man in order that this
covenant might be made a reality. In the beginning it was the resolve
of the Holy Spirit that the unity of God, of Father and Son should
not be disturbed or rent by this covenant with man, but that it should
be made the more glorious, the deity of God, the divinity of His love
and freedom, being confirmed and demonstrated by this offering of
the Father and this self-offering of the Son. This choice was in the
beginning. As the subject and object of this choice, Jesus Christ was
at the beginning. He was not at the beginning of God, for God has
indeed no beginning. But He was at the beginning of all things, at
the beginning of God's dealings with the reality which is distinct from
Himself. Jesus Christ was the choice or election of God in respect of

this reality. He was the election of God's grace as directed towards man. He was the election of God's covenant with man.

We are following an important insight of J. Coccejus (*S. Theol.*, 1662, c. 37, 2) when we trace back the concept of predestination to the biblical concept of the covenant or testament, the self-committal first revealed to Noah (Gen. 9.14) as God's covenant with 'every living creature of all flesh that is upon the earth,' then (Gen. 17.7f.) as His covenant with Abraham and his posterity, and later (Is. 55.3, Jer. 32.40, Ezek. 16.60, 37.26 and cf. Jer. 50.5) as His covenant with Israel. By its definition as eternal covenant (*bᵉrith'olam*) this self-committal is characterised (no matter what time-concepts may be presupposed) as a relationship which is not haphazard and transitory, but which derives its necessity from God Himself.[4] It is more steadfast than the hills (Is. 54.10). God has sworn it by Himself (Gen. 22.16, Ex. 32.13, Is. 45.23, 54.9, 62.8, Ps. 110.4, Heb. 6.13). In Mic. 5.2 (cf., too Is. 9.7, Dan. 7.13f.) it can be said of the Messiah that 'his goings forth have been from of old, from everlasting.' As the Jews are aware in Jn. 12.34, He 'abideth' for ever. According to Heb. 7.16f. (cf. Ps. 110.4), He 'is a priest for ever' 'after the power of an endless life.' 'Through the eternal Spirit he offered himself without spot to God' (Heb. 9.14). 'Before Abraham was,' He was, and 'Abraham rejoiced to see his day' (Jn. 8.56f.). We also find references to this divine past in the 'I am pleased' of Mt. 3.17, the 'he was pleased' of Col. 1.19, the 'he assigned' of Lk. 22.29, and the 'he purposed' of Eph. 1.9. Now it is quite impossible to distinguish all these from the reality which is treated of in the New Testament passages which speak of the election in express connexion with the name and person of Jesus. In Eph. 1.3–5 the one follows directly on the other: there is a general mention of the blessings with which we have been blessed 'in heavenly places' in Christ; he has blessed us in Christ, and then there is the particular statement: 'he chose us in Him before the foundation of the world, having predestined us for adoption through Jesus Christ, and for him, according to the good pleasure of his will.' Again, in Eph. 1.9–11 there is the general: 'he purposed his will … to bring all things together in Christ,' and the particular 'in him, in whom we were appointed, having been predestined according to the purpose of the one who works all things according to the counsel of his will.' From these passages, and

---

4   Covenant is a biblical term, employed with great frequency in the tradition of Reformed dogmatics (including the work of Johannes Coccejus), to describe a structured relationship between two persons. Barth emphasizes that such formal relationships (with promises and responsibilities, blessings and curses, ceremonies and constitutions) are not happenstance but eternally determined by God's gracious decision in Christ. God and humanity are not two ships that happen to pass in the night; rather, God brings light out of the darkness to make possible face to face fellowship with humanity.

from Eph. 3:4, we gather that the concrete form of the divine blessing, and of the will of the eternal purpose is in fact that predestination which will be made known by the existence of the Church (Eph. 3.10), so assuredly did God 'purpose his eternal purpose in Jesus Christ our Lord.' And conversely, what we now experience as our deliverance and calling takes place only because it is gifted to us as God's own purpose and grace: 'in Christ before all ages' (2 Tim. 1.19); because Christ as the Lamb without blemish and without spot was 'foreknown before the foundation of the world' (1 Pet. 1.20, cf. Rev. 13.8); because 'from the foundation of the world' His high-priestly suffering was necessary (ἔδει) (Heb. 9.26). 'Him, being delivered by the determinate counsel and foreknowledge (πρόγνωσις) of God, ye have taken, and by wicked hands have crucified and slain' (Ac. 2.23). 'For to do whatsoever thy hand and thy counsel determined before to come to pass,' both Herod and Pilate, with the Gentiles and the peoples of Israel, were gathered together against thy holy servant Jesus (Ac. 4.27f.). Again, the glory with which Jesus prayed that He might be glorified (in Jn. 17.5) is none other than that glory which He had with the Father before the world was. In these texts it is not of any importance whether the mention of God's will and purpose preceding the history, or more specifically the expressions 'before all ages' and 'before' or 'from the foundation of the world,' are meant to refer to the eternity of God in itself, or 'only' to the beginning of the creation, and therefore of the universe and time. What is certain is that in all the passages the reference is to the beginning of all God's ways and works outside of Himself. And it is also certain that all these passages describe this beginning under the name of Jesus Christ, whose person is that of the executor within the universe and time of the primal decision of divine grace, the person itself being obviously the content of this decision.

In its simplest and most comprehensive form the dogma of predestination consists, then, in the assertion that the divine predestination is the election of Jesus Christ. But the concept of election has a double reference – to the elector and to the elected. And so, too, the name of Jesus Christ has within itself the double reference: the One called by this name is both very God and very man. Thus the simplest form of the dogma may be divided at once into the two assertions that Jesus Christ is the electing God, and that He is also elected man.[5]

In so far as He is the electing God, we must obviously – and above all – ascribe to Him the active determination of electing. It is not that He does not also elect as man, i.e., elect God in faith. But this election can

---

5   Jesus is Lord and Servant simultaneously. Barth will tease out the Christological metaphysics involved here in volume IV/1–3.

only follow His prior election, and that means that it follows the divine electing which is the basic and proper determination of His existence.

In so far as He is man, the passive determination of election is also and necessarily proper to Him. It is true, of course, that even as God He is elected; the Elected of His Father. But because as the Son of the Father He has no need of any special election, we must add at once that He is the Son of God elected in His oneness with man, and in fulfilment of God's covenant with man. Primarily, then, electing is the divine determination of the existence of Jesus Christ, and election (being elected) the human.

Jesus Christ is the electing God. We must begin with this assertion because by its content it has the character and dignity of a basic principle, and because the other assertion, that Jesus Christ is elected man, can be understood only in the light of it.

We may notice at once the critical significance of this first assertion in its relation to the traditional understanding of the doctrine. In particular, it crowds out and replaces the idea of an absolute decree. That idea does, of course, give us an answer to the question about the electing God. It speaks of a good-pleasure of God which in basis and direction is unknown to man and to all beings outside God Himself. This good-pleasure is omnipotent and incontrovertible in its decisions. If we are asked concerning its nature, then ultimately no more can be said than that it is divine, and therefore absolutely supreme and authoritative. But now in the place of this blank, this unknown quantity, we are to put the name of Jesus Christ. According to the witness of the Bible, when we are called upon to define and name the first and decisive decision which transcends and includes all others, it is definitely not in order to answer with a mysterious shrug of the shoulders. How can the doctrine of predestination be anything but 'dark' and obscure if in its very first tenet, the tenet which determines all the rest, it can speak only of an absolute decree? In trying to understand Jesus Christ as the electing God we abandon this tradition, but we hold fast by Jn. 1.1–2.[6]

Jesus Christ was in the beginning with God. He was so not merely in the sense that in view of God's eternal knowing and willing all things may be said to have been in the beginning with God, in His plan and decree. For these are two separate things: the Son of God in His

---

6   Barth believes the traditional Augustinian approach to election focuses on an 'absolute decree' (*decretum absolutum*) that suggests that God's love, grace, and gospel are secondary and accidental, rather than tethered to the very being and character of the electing God. Barth worries that such an approach posits a chasm in between the revelation of Jesus and the real nature of the eternal God; over against this, he suggests that John 1 teaches that Jesus really is and really reveals God's nature: 'No one has ever seen God; the only God, who is at the Father's side, he has made him known' (Jn. 1.18).

oneness with the Son of Man, as foreordained from all eternity; and the universe which was created, and universal history which was willed for the sake of this oneness, in their communion with God, as foreordained from all eternity. On the one hand, there is the Word of God by which all things were made, and, on the other, the things fashioned by that Word.[7] On the one hand, there is God's eternal election of grace, and, on the other, God's creation, reconciliation and redemption grounded in that election and ordained with reference to it. On the one hand, there is the eternal election which as it concerns man God made within Himself in His pre-temporal eternity, and, on the other, the covenant of grace between God and man whose establishment and fulfilment in time were determined by that election. We can and must say that Jesus Christ was in the beginning with God in the sense that all creation and its history was in God's plan and decree with God. But He was so not merely in that way. He was also in the beginning with God as 'the first-born of every creature' (Col. 1.15), Himself the plan and decree of God, Himself the divine decision with respect to all creation and its history whose content is already determined. All that is embraced and signified in God's election of grace as His movement towards man, all that results from that election and all that is presupposed in such results – all these are determined and conditioned by the fact that that election is the divine decision whose content is already determined, that Jesus Christ is the divine election of grace.

Thus Jesus Christ is not merely one object of the divine good-pleasure side by side with others. On the contrary, He is the sole object of this good-pleasure, for in the first instance He Himself is this good-pleasure, the will of God in action. He is not merely the standard or instrument of the divine freedom. He is Himself primarily and properly the divine freedom itself in its operation outside of Himself. He is not merely the revelation of the mystery of God. He is the thing concealed within this mystery, and the revelation of it is the revelation of Himself and not of something else. He is not merely the Reconciler between God and man. First, He is Himself the reconciliation between them.[8] And so He is not only the Elected. He is also Himself the Elector, and

---

7   Two subjects are defined by election. First, God is manifest as the electing God, who wishes to be with us and not without us. Second, humanity is made by, through, and for the electing God. Barth believes the Augustinian/Reformed tradition honours the latter, though not the former assertion. Note, however, that Barth's historical analysis of the tradition has been criticized as misguided: see, for example, Richard A. Muller, *Christ and the Decree: Christology and Predestination in Reformed Theology from Calvin to Perkins* (2nd ed.; Grand Rapids: Baker Academic, 2008).

8   If election involves the determination of a relationship between God and humanity, Barth wishes to clarify here that Jesus is a person on both sides (fully God and fully human). He is not just reconciler – he is reconciliation itself, because his person mediates the relationship.

in the first instance His election must be understood as active. It is true
that as the Son of God given by the Father to be one with man, and to
take to Himself the form of man, He is elected. It is also true that He
does not elect alone, but in company with the electing of the Father and
the Holy Spirit. But He does elect. The obedience which He renders
as the Son of God is, as genuine obedience, His own decision and
electing, a decision and electing no less divinely free than the electing
and decision of the Father and the Holy Spirit.[9] Even the fact that He
is elected corresponds as closely as possible to His own electing. In the
harmony of the triune God He is no less the original Subject of this
electing than He is its original object. And only in this harmony can He
really be its object, i.e., completely fulfil not His own will but the will of
the Father, and thus confirm and to some extent repeat as elected man
the election of God. This all rests on the fact that from the very first He
participates in the divine election; that that election is also His election;
that it is He Himself who posits this beginning of all things; that it is
He Himself who executes the decision which issues in the establishment
of the covenant between God and man; that He too, with the Father
and the Holy Spirit, is the electing God. If this is not the case, then in
respect of the election, in respect of this primal and basic decision of
God, we shall have to pass by Jesus Christ, asking of God the Father,
or perhaps of the Holy Spirit, how there can be any disclosure of this
decision at all. For where can it ever be disclosed to us except where
it is executed? The result will be, of course, that we shall be driven to
speculating about an absolute decree instead of grasping and affirming
in God's electing the manifest grace of God. And that means that we
shall not know into whose hands we are committing ourselves when
we believe in the divine predestination. So much depends upon our
acknowledgment of the Son, of the Son of God, as the Subject of this
predestination, because it is only in the Son that it is revealed to us as the
predestination of God, and therefore of the Father and the Holy Spirit,
because it is only as we believe in the Son that we can also believe in
the Father and the Holy Spirit, and therefore in the one divine election.
If Jesus Christ is only elected, and not also and primarily the Elector,
what shall we really know at all of a divine electing and our election?
But of Jesus Christ we know nothing more surely and definitely than
this – that in free obedience to His Father He elected to be man, and as
man, to do the will of God. If God elects us too, then it is in and with
this election of Jesus Christ, in and with this free act of obedience on

---

9   Augustine anticipated Barth's concern in showing that the Son is not merely object of election,
     but also subject just as much as the rest of the Trinity: 'The invisible Father and the invisible Son
     sent the Son to become visible' (*De Trinitate*, II.5.9).

the part of His Son. It is He who is manifestly the concrete and manifest form of the divine decision – the decision of Father, Son and Holy Spirit – in favour of the covenant to be established between Him and us. It is in Him that the eternal election becomes immediately and directly the promise of our own election as it is enacted in time, our calling, our summoning to faith, our assent to the divine intervention on our behalf, the revelation of ourselves as the sons of God and of God as our Father, the communication of the Holy Spirit who is none other than the Spirit of this act of obedience, the Spirit of obedience itself, and for us the Spirit of adoption. When we ask concerning the reality of the divine election, what can we do but look at the One who performs this act of obedience, who is Himself this act of obedience, who is Himself in the first instance the Subject of this election.[10]

The passages in Jn. 13.18 and 15.16, 19, in which Jesus points to Himself as the One who elects His disciples, are not to be understood loosely but in their strictest and most proper sense. It is clear that at this point John knows nothing of a rivalry which can and should be dissolved by subordination.[11] If Jesus does nothing 'of himself' (ἐφ’

---

10 Notice the personal application of the election of the Son – all others are elect 'in Him' – that speaks volumes about the doctrine of assurance (see below). Elsewhere in this volume, Barth addresses the so-called 'practical syllogism' (II/2.335–340), whereby the Puritan tradition grounded assurance not only in the objective work of Christ but also in the subjective fruits of that union with Christ (namely, in sanctifying evidences of justification in Christ). Barth believes assurance is entirely in Christ, and that the practical syllogism denies that Jesus is obedient for us, just as He is accursed for us. He fills both sides of the covenantal relationship (for Barth's covenant theology and the place of Christ's human faithfulness within it, see R. Michael Allen, *The Christ's Faith: A Dogmatic Account* [T & T Clark Studies in Systematic Theology; London: T & T Clark, 2009], ch. 5).

11 Barth does affirm a subordination of the Son, though it is a personal and not an essential subordination. In this regard, he follows the Western theological tradition, which speaks of a necessary doubled way of talking about each Trinitarian person (first, pertaining to their divinity or essence; second, pertaining to their unique personal character). On this point, see especially Gilles Emery, 'Essentialism or Personalism in the Treatise on God in St. Thomas Aquinas?' in *Trinity in Aquinas* (trans. Matthew Levering; Naples FL: Sapientia Press, 2003), pp. 165–208. The Son is God 'in Himself', but He is Son 'from the Father'; pertaining to divinity or essence, he is fully God, but pertaining to personal character, he is subordinated to the Father as the obedient Son, who goes into the far country (see IV/1.164). Barth describes it this way, with reference to the dual teaching of John's Gospel on the Son's divinity and his subordination: 'it should again be emphasized that the same Gospel of John which leaves no possible doubt about the deity of Christ in His unity with the Father no less plainly – and with particular reference to His way of suffering and death – represents Him as the One who is sent, who has a commission and who has to execute it as such, as the Son who lives to do His Father's will, to speak His words, to accomplish His work and to seek His glory' (IV/1.194). Barth does not see human subordination as competitive with divine lordship in the person and work of Jesus, precisely because Barth does not see divine and human action as competitive in general (see Kathryn Tanner, 'Creation and Providence', in *Cambridge Companion to Karl Barth* [ed. John B. Webster; Cambridge: Cambridge University Press, 2000], pp. 123–6 [111–26]).

ἑαυτον, Jn. 5.19, 30), there is the closely corresponding verse: 'Without me ye can do nothing' (Jn. 15.5). The statement 'All mine are thine,' is balanced by the further statement: 'Thine are mine' (Jn. 17:10). Jesus was 'sent,' but He also 'came.' As He is in the Father, the Father is also in Him (Jn. 14.10). 'As the Father hath life in himself, so hath he given to the Son to have life in himself' (Jn. 5.26). The Father glorifies Him, but He, too, glorifies the Father (Jn. 17.1–5). It is Jesus' 'meat to do the will of him that sent him' (Jn. 4.34), but the Father abiding in Him doeth His works (Jn. 14.10). The Father is greater than He (Jn. 14.28), but 'he hath given all things into his hand' (Jn. 3.35), and 'hath given him power over all flesh' (Jn. 17.2). In the same breath He says: 'Believe in God, and believe also in me' (Jn. 14.1). No man can come unto Jesus except it be given unto him of the Father (Jn. 6.65). He who comes must have 'heard and learned of the Father' (Jn. 6.45). He must have been 'drawn' by the Father (Jn. 6:44). He must have been given Jesus by the Father (Jn. 6.37, 17.6, 9, 24). But again, He, Jesus, is the way, the truth and the life, and no one cometh unto the Father but by Him (Jn. 14.6). The Father is the husbandman, but He, Jesus, is the true vine (Jn. 15.1f.). And for this reason He prays(!): 'Father, I will that they also, whom thou hast given me, be with me where I am; that they may behold my glory, which thou hast given me' (Jn. 17.24). In the light of these passages the electing of the disciples ascribed to Jesus must be understood not merely as a function undertaken by Him in an instrumental and representative capacity, but rather as an act of divine sovereignty, in which there is seen in a particular way the primal and basic decision of God which is also that of Jesus Christ. And so, too, behind that summons to 'discipleship' which is so frequent in the Synoptics, there stands the statement of Mt. 11.27: 'Neither knoweth any man the Father, save … he to whomsoever the Son will reveal him.' And that other statement in Mt. 16.17, that the Son may be known only by revelation of the Father, does not in any way restrict this truth, but rather expounds it according to its true sense. Even in those places where it is said of Christ that He 'emptied' Himself and 'humbled' Himself (Phil. 2.7f.), or that He 'gave' Himself (Gal. 1.4, 1 Tim. 2.6), or that He 'offered' Himself (Gal. 2.20, Eph. 5.2), or that He 'sacrificed' Himself (Heb. 7.27, 9.14); even in those passages which treat of His obedience (Phil. 2.8, Heb. 5.8), we cannot but see the reflection of the divine spontaneity and activity in which His own existence is grounded, and together with it the covenant between God and man.[12]

12   Barth interprets the 'emptying' (*kenosis*) of Philippians 2.7 by way of addition; 'God gives Himself, but He does not give Himself away' (IV/1.185; cf. 180–183, 188–192 on exegesis of Phil. 2), and He gives Himself by assuming and fulfilling the calling of sinful flesh.

[…]

The election of Jesus Christ is the eternal choice and decision of God.[13]
And our first assertion tells us that Jesus Christ is the electing God.
We must not ask concerning any other but Him. In no depth of the
Godhead shall we encounter any other but Him. There is no such thing
as Godhead in itself. Godhead is always the Godhead of the Father, the
Son and the Holy Spirit. But the Father is the Father of Jesus Christ and
the Holy Spirit is the Spirit of the Father and the Spirit of Jesus Christ.
There is no such thing as an absolute decree. There is no such thing as
a will of God apart from the will of Jesus Christ. Thus Jesus Christ is
not only the manifestation and mirror of our predestination. And He is
this not simply in the sense that our election can be known to us and
contemplated by us only through His election, as an election which,
like His and with His, is made (or not made) by a secret and hidden
will of God. On the contrary, Jesus Christ reveals to us our election as
an election which is made by Him, by His will which is also the will of
God. He tells us that He Himself is the One who elects us. In the very
foreground of our existence in history we can and should cleave wholly
and with full assurance to Him because in the eternal background of
history, in the beginning with God, the only decree which was passed,
the only Word which was spoken and which prevails, was the decision
which was executed by Him. As we believe in Him and hear His Word
and hold fast by His decision, we can know with a certainty which
nothing can ever shake that we are the elect of God.

Jesus Christ is elected man. In making this second assertion we
are again at one with the traditional teaching. But the christological
assertion of tradition tells us no more than that in His humanity Jesus
Christ was one of the elect. It was in virtue of His divinity that He
was ordained and appointed Lord and Head of all others, the organ
and instrument of the whole election of God and the revelation and
reflection of the election of those who were elected with Him.

Now without our first assertion we cannot maintain such a position.
For where can Jesus Christ derive the authority and power to be Lord
and Head of all others, and how can these others be elected 'in Him,'
and how can they see their election in Him the first of the elect, and
how can they find in His election the assurance of their own, if He is

---

13   Barth summarizes the meaning of Christ's election in this way: 'The election of grace is the
     eternal beginning of all the ways and works of God in Jesus Christ. In Jesus Christ God in His
     free grace determines Himself for sinful man and sinful man for Himself. He therefore takes upon
     Himself the rejection of man with all its consequences, and elects man to participation in His own
     glory' (II/2.94).

only the object of election and not Himself its Subject, if He is only an
elect creature and not primarily and supremely the electing Creator?
Obviously in a strict and serious sense we can never say of any creature
that other creatures are elect 'in it,' that it is their Lord and Head, and
that in its election they can and should have assurance of their own.
How can a mere creature ever come to the point of standing in this
way before God, above and on behalf of others? If the testimony of
Holy Scripture concerning the man Jesus Christ is true, that this man
does stand before God above and on behalf of others, then this man is
no mere creature but He is also the Creator, and His own electing as
Creator must have preceded His election as creature. In one and the
same person He must be both elected man and the electing God. Thus
the second assertion rests on the first, and for the sake of the second the
first ought never to be denied or passed over.

Because of this interconnexion we must now formulate the second
statement with rather more precision. It tells us that before all created
reality, before all being and becoming in time, before time itself, in the
pre-temporal eternity of God, the eternal divine decision as such has as
its object and content the existence of this one created being, the man
Jesus of Nazareth, and the work of this man in His life and death, His
humiliation and exaltation, His obedience and merit. It tells us further
that in and with the existence of this man the eternal divine decision
has as its object and content the execution of the divine covenant with
man, the salvation of all men. In this function this man is the object of
the eternal divine decision and foreordination. Jesus Christ, then, is not
merely one of the elect but *the* elect of God. From the very beginning
(from eternity itself), as elected man He does not stand alongside the
rest of the elect, but before and above them as the One who is originally and properly the Elect. From the very beginning (from eternity
itself), there are no other elect together with or apart from Him, but,
as Eph. 1.4 tells us, only 'in' Him.[14] 'In Him' does not simply mean
with Him, together with Him, in His company. Nor does it mean only
through Him, by means of that which He as elected man can be and do
for them. 'In Him' means in His person, in His will, in His own divine
choice, in the basic decision of God which He fulfils over against every
man. What singles Him out from the rest of the elect, and yet also,
and for the first time, unites Him with them, is the fact that as elected
man He is also the electing God, electing them in His own humanity.

---

14   It is not inaccurate to say that Barth's revision of the doctrine of election stems from his merging
      of Eph. 1.4 with John 1. He believes that humans are elect in the eternal Word, who became
      flesh in Jesus. Criticism of Barth's revision has arisen largely with respect to the biblical breadth
      of his position: does it do justice to the full teaching of the Bible in this regard?

In that He (as God) wills Himself (as man), He also wills them. And so they are elect 'in Him,' in and with His own election. And so, too, His election must be distinguished from theirs. It must not be distinguished from theirs merely as the example and type, the revelation and reflection of their election. All this can, of course, be said quite truly of the election of Jesus Christ. But it must be said further that His election is the original and all-inclusive election; the election which is absolutely unique, but which in this very uniqueness is universally meaningful and efficacious, because it is the election of Him who Himself elects. Of none other of the elect can it be said that his election carries in it and with it the election of the rest. But that is what we must say of Jesus Christ when we think of Him in relation to the rest. And for this reason, as elected man, He is the Lord and Head of all the elect, the revelation and reflection of their election, and the organ and instrument of all divine electing. For this reason His election is indeed the type of all election. For this reason we must now learn really to recognise in Him not only the electing God but also elected man.

The basic passage in Jn. 1.1–2 speaks of the man Jesus. In so doing, it contains self-evidently this second assertion, that Jesus Christ is elected man. All the Johannine passages which speak of His mission, of His doing the will and works of His Father, of His submission, and of the submission of His people to the rule of the Father, really point to this aspect of the matter. Indeed, all the New Testament passages so far quoted find in Jesus Christ this elected man and therefore in a creature distinct from God the divine decree in the very beginning. To that extent do they not all testify to a second and passive meaning of the election of Jesus Christ? More specific testimony is given in the words of Jn. 17.24: 'Thou lovedst me before the foundation of the world'; and quite expressly in Lk. 9.35 and 23.35. It is common to the verses from Luke 'that Jesus is identified as the Christ in the immediate context of His sufferings. He was declared 'my chosen son' at the transfiguration, just before His entry on the way of suffering. His declaration as 'the Christ of God, the chosen one' came when He had already taken the form of the crucified. He is elected man not only in His passion and in spite of His passion, but for His passion' (G. Schrenk in *Theol. W.B. zum N.T.* IV 194, 11 f.). There is little room for doubt that in Jn. 17.24, too, there is a specific reference to the story of the passion. If we compare with it Ac. 2.23, 4.27f., 1 Pet. 1.20, Heb. 9.14 and Rev. 13.8, we can hardly make too much of this aspect of it. Deutero-Isaiah speaks of the Servant whom Yahweh upholds; of the Elect in whom His soul delighteth and upon whom He has set His Spirit, that he may bring forth judgment to the Gentiles (Is. 42.1); of the One who was given as a covenant for the people, for a light of the Gentiles (Is. 42.6, 49.8). And it is of this One that he tells us, at the very climax of his presentation, that 'they made his grave with the wicked, and with the rich in his death; although he had done no violence, neither was any deceit in his mouth. Yet it pleased the Lord to bruise him; he hath put him to grief: when thou shalt make his soul an offering for sin, he shall see his seed, he shall prolong his days, and the pleasure of the Lord shall prosper in his hand' (Is. 53:9f.). And it is in the light of this climax – election for suffering – that the relevant passage in Heb. 2.11f. must certainly be understood: 'For both he that sanctifieth and they that are sanctified are all of one: for which cause he is not ashamed to call them brethren, saying, I will declare thy name unto my brethren, in the midst of the church will I sing praise unto thee. And again, I will put my trust in him. And again, Behold I and the children which God hath given me. Forasmuch then as the children are partakers in flesh and blood, he also himself likewise took part of the same; that through death he might destroy him that had the power of death, that is, the devil.' Behold, the man (Jn. 19.5).

In relation to this passive election of Jesus Christ the great exponents of the traditional doctrine of predestination developed an insight which we too must take as our starting-point, because, rightly understood, it contains within itself everything else that must be noted and said in this connexion. The insight is this: that in the predestination of the man Jesus we see what predestination is always and everywhere – the acceptance and reception of man only by the free grace of God.[15] Even in the man Jesus there is indeed no merit, no prior and self-sufficient goodness, which can precede His election to divine sonship. Neither prayer nor the life of faith can command or compel His election. It is by the work of the Word of God, by the Holy Spirit, that He is conceived and born without sin, that He is what He is, the Son of God; by grace alone. And as He became Christ, so we become Christians. As He became our Head, so we become His body and members. As He became the object of our faith, so we become believers in Him. What we have to consider in the elected man Jesus is, then, the destiny of human nature, its exaltation to fellowship with God, and the manner of its participation in this exaltation by the free grace of God. But more, it is in this man that the exaltation itself is revealed and proclaimed.[16] For with His decree concerning this man, God decreed too that this man should be the cause and the instrument of our exaltation.

---

15   Barth argues that the eternal determination for God to become incarnate in the person of the Son demonstrates its gratuity and freedom: it clearly can neither be compelled nor be contingent upon human achievement. Rather, 'it was the will of the Lord to bruise him' (Isa. 53.9, which Barth quotes on this page); the very existence of the man Jesus owes itself only to God's gracious will and character, not to any absolute but arbitrary decree and not to any human compulsion.

16   Barth reinterprets the history of Israel in light of the election of Jesus in II/2; for analysis of one example (Barth's re-reading of the story of Saul and David), see Michael Allen, 'Theological Politics and the Davidic Monarchy: Three Examples of Theological Exegesis', *Horizons in Biblical Theology* 30, no. 2 (2008), pp. 138–43 (pp. 137–62).

CHAPTER 7

THEOLOGICAL ETHICS

True man and his good action can be viewed only from the standpoint of the true and active God and His goodness. It is this connexion with dogmatics which guards ethics against arbitrary assertions, arguments or conclusions, and allows it to follow a secure path to fruitful judgments.[1]

Barth makes a decision at the inception of the *Church Dogmatics* regarding the place of ethics. Ethics will be subsumed within the dogmatic task (*contra* modern liberal Christianity, where Barth thinks ethics is either separate from or entirely supplants the dogmatic task). He later says:

> dogmatics asks concerning the covenant between the true God and true man established in Him from all eternity and fulfilled in Him in time. But true man is characterized by action, by good action, as the true God is also characterized action, by good action. As dogmatics inquires concerning the action of God and its goodness, it must necessarily make thorough inquiry concerning active man and the goodness of his action. It has the problem of ethics in view from the very first, and it cannot legitimately lose sight of it (III/4.3).

So Barth's dogmatics will be an 'ethical dogmatics' through and through.

Furthermore, ethics will be organized in a layered approach co-ordinated with theological reality. In the preface to the first volume he writes: 'What is called ethics I regard as the doctrine of the command of God. Hence I do not think it right to treat it otherwise than as an integral part of dogmatics, or to produce a dogmatics which does not include it. In this dogmatics the concept of the command of God in general will be treated at the close of the doctrine of God. The command of God from the standpoint of order will then be discussed at the close of the doctrine of creation, from the standpoint of law at the close of the doctrine of reconciliation, and from the standpoint of promise at the close of the doctrine of redemption' (I/1.xvii).

---

1   *CD* III/4.3.

Note that a metaphysical observation grounds a rhetorical and pedagogical practice. Barth believes human ethics flows from God's command. Thus human agency is primarily discussed by means of divine gift, namely, the command given by God to creatures. Human ethical reflection is not autonomous, rather it must be tethered to the moral order commanded by God himself. Thus *CD* II/2 concludes his doctrine of God himself by looking to God's command. Only then, in the wake of that ethics with respect to God, does Barth proceed to reflect on ethics in relation to God's external works of creation, reconciliation, and redemption. Human ethics is rooted in the divine command, and it is reiterated in the divine works. Barth believes the Reformed confessions and dogmatics give superior expression to the evangelical (and ultimately theological) roots of ethics in grace, over against the Lutheran tradition (see his comments to this effect in his lectures on *The Theology of the Reformed Confessions*).

This portion of text selected is as close to programmematic as can be found in the *CD*. Its concluding paragraph explains the metaphysical and pedagogical approach to Barth's ethics (as mentioned above).

Bibliography

Karl Barth, 'The Gift of Freedom: Foundation of Evangelical Ethics', in *The Humanity of God* (trans. Thomas Wieser; Louisville: Westminster John Knox, 1960), pp. 69–96.

Paul Nimmo, *Being in Action: The Theological Shape of Barth's Ethical Vision* (London: T & T Clark, 2007).

Matthew Rose, *Ethics with Barth: God, Metaphysics, and Morals* (Barth Studies; Surrey: Ashgate, 2011), part 2.

John Webster, *Barth's Ethics of Reconciliation* (Cambridge: Cambridge University Press, 1995).

John Webster, *Barth's Moral Theology: Human Action in Barth's Thought* (Edinburgh/Grand Rapids: T & T Clark/Eerdmans, 1998).

Text (*CD* II/2.543, 546–551)

The way of theological ethics

It is the Christian doctrine of God, or, more exactly, the knowledge of the electing grace of God in Jesus Christ, which decides the nature and aim of theological ethics, of ethics as an element of Church dogmatics. It has its basis, therefore, in the doctrine of God Himself.[2]

---

2   Barth summarizes §36 in this way: 'As the doctrine of God's command, ethics interprets the Law as the form of the Gospel, i.e., as the sanctification which comes to man through the electing God. Because Jesus Christ is the holy God and sanctified man in One, it has its basis

For the God who claims man makes Himself originally responsible for man. The fact that He gives man His command, that He subjects man to His command, means that He makes Himself responsible not only for its authority but also for its fulfilment. Therefore we do not speak completely about God Himself if we do not go on at once to speak also about His command. But it is the Christian doctrine of God, or, more exactly, the knowledge of the electing grace of God in Jesus Christ, which also decides the special way of theological ethics, the special form of its enquiry and reply, the attainment of its fundamental principles. Here, as everywhere, the rightness of these is decided by the matter to which they must be related – the matter which is to be presented by them. Now the matter of theological ethics is the responsibility which God has assumed for us in the fact that He has made us accountable through His command. Its matter is the Word and work of God in Jesus Christ, in which the right action of man has already been performed and therefore waits only to be confirmed by our action.

In view of this matter, we must first refuse to follow all those attempts at theological ethics which start from the assumption that it is to be built on, or to proceed from, a general human ethics, a 'philosophical' ethics. In the relationship between the command of God and the ethical problem, as we have defined it in its main features, there is not a universal moral element autonomously confronting the Christian. It is, therefore, quite out of the question methodically to subordinate the latter to the former, to build it on, or to derive it from, it.

[...]

If we ask first concerning the basis of ethics, the first task which obviously confronts us is to understand and present the Word of God as the subject which claims us. It is to understand and present the Word of God in its character as the command which sanctifies man. This basis will be our particular concern in this final chapter of the doctrine of God.

in the knowledge of Jesus Christ. Because the God who claims man for Himself makes Himself originally responsible for him, it forms part of the doctrine of God. Its function is to bear primary witness to the grace of God in so far as this is the saving engagement and commitment of man' (II/2.509). Barth frequently employs the term 'command' as something approaching a definition of ethics (as here, where ethics simply is 'the doctrine of God's command'). But the command of God is articulated as not only the elaboration of God's will but also the economy of God's redemption. In other words, the address of God situates the hearer as an ethical subject with real responsibility and freedom: it creates moral space for action in light of the Gospel.

The goodness of human action consists in the goodness with which God acts toward man. But God deals with man through His Word. His Word is the sum and plenitude of all good, because God Himself is good. Therefore man does good in so far as he hears the Word of God and acts as a hearer of this Word. In this action as a hearer he is obedient. Why is obedience good? Because it derives from hearing, because it is the action of a hearer, namely, of the hearer of the Word of God. It is good because the divine address is good, because God Himself is good.[3]

We can also put it in this way. Man does good in so far as he acts as one who is called by God to responsibility. To act in and from responsibility to God means to act in commitment. Our action is free in so far as it is our own answer, the answer which we ourselves give to what is said to us by God. But as an answer, it is bound. It is a good action when it takes place in this commitment. Therefore its good consists always in its responsibility. Responsible action is good because the divine address is good, because God Himself is good.

We can also put it in this way. Man does good in so far as his action is Christian. A Christian is one who knows that God has accepted him in Jesus Christ, that a decision has been made concerning him in Jesus Christ as the eternal Word of God, and that he has been called into covenant with Him by Jesus Christ as the Word of God spoken in time. When he knows this, when he is 'judged' by God through confrontation and fellowship with Jesus Christ, his action, too, becomes a 'judged' action. It is in the fact that it is 'judged' that its goodness consists. Therefore its goodness derives from this confrontation and fellowship. His action is good because the divine address which is

3   Barth insists that human obedience is fundamentally listening to God's Word. He does not encourage inactivity, but he encourages a particular sort of activity. He believes that dependent, faithful obedience is always referring back to its lifeblood: 'the Word of God'. The law is always and only meant to be a frame or shape for life in the Gospel; thus, it is necessary at every point to point away from oneself and point toward one's life in Christ. Eventually, Barth will pair 'hearing' (the Word of God) with 'invoking' (in prayer) as another way of emphasizing the ec-centric (dependent) obedience of Christians (see, e.g., Barth, *The Christian Life* [Edinburgh: T & T Clark, 1981], p. 43).

This shapes how he describes the ethical discipline:

[T]he action of man must be one which always and in all directions is open, eager to learn, capable of modification, perpetually ready, in obedience to the exclusively sovereign command of God, to allow itself to be orientated afresh and in very different ways from those which might have seemed possible and necessary on the basis of man's own ideas of his ability and capacity (III/4.629; cf. II/2.180, 646–647).

John Webster has surveyed this emphasis in Barth's evangelical ethics and termed it the 'ecstatic character' of his ethics (*Barth's Ethics of Reconciliation* [Cambridge: Cambridge University Press, 1995], p. 225).

an eternal and temporal event in Jesus Christ is good, because God Himself is good.

In its simplest and most basic expression this is the theological answer to the ethical question. This is the sum and substance of theological ethics. The characteristic feature of the theological answer to the ethical problem is that – although it also answers the question of the goodness of human action – it understands man from the very outset as addressed by God, so that in regard to the goodness of his action it can only point away from man to what God says, to God Himself. 'From the very outset' means from the eternal grace of God as it has eventuated in time, from the lordship of His grace as it is resolved and established by God and cannot now be overthrown by any contradiction or any denial. When we understand man from this point of view, we have a positive answer to give in regard to the goodness of his action, but we have to do it by pointing away from man to what God says, to God Himself. To put it concretely, we have to do it by pointing to God's commanding, to God as Commander. The good of human action consists in the fact that it is determined by the divine command. We shall have to consider more closely what is involved in this command and this determination. But we can never seek the good except in this determination of human action and therefore in the divine command which creates this deter-mination, in God the Commander Himself. We cannot in any sense seek it in human action in itself. 'There is none good but one, that is God' (Mk. 10.18). We must remember, of course, that this is a truth of the Gospel. It is not, then, the affirmation of an abstract transcendence of the good.[4] To receive this truth is not to reject and abandon the question of the goodness of human action. It is only with this truth that we take it up. This truth is its positive answer. For this God who alone is good is the God who is gracious to man. He is not a transcendent being, not even a transcendent being of the good. From all eternity He has determined to turn to man, to make Himself responsible for man. He has dealt with man on the basis of this self-determination, and He does so still. And it is in this self-determination and action – not excluding, but including man – that God alone is good. He is this in the eternal-temporal act of His compassion for man. He is this in Jesus Christ. It is not to any god that we point, but to this God, the God of the Gospel, when, in the question of the goodness of human action,

---

4   Barth insists that we begin with God's being and his perfection to then define 'the good', rather than beginning with an ideal or principle of 'the good' (see, e.g., II/1.276; II/2.709; as well as Karl Barth, *Ethics* [Edinburgh: T & T Clark, 1981], p. 74). Barth believes the epistemic path, then, to know 'the good' is to consider what he calls 'the name of Jesus'. He refers neither merely to the identity, title, or role of Jesus, nor to the ethical teaching of Jesus; rather he points to the enacted history of Jesus as the fulfilment of both sides of the covenant (II/2.568, 576).

we point to the divine command, to God Himself. There is no more positive answer to this question than that which is given when we refer to this God, just because it means that we refer away from man.

The first thing that theological ethics has to show, and to develop as a basic and all-comprehensive truth, is the fact and extent that this command of God is an event.[5] This is the specific ethico-dogmatic task as it now confronts us within the framework of the doctrine of God. We cannot emphasise too strongly the fact that by the ruling principle of theological ethics, by the sanctifying command of God – corresponding to the fact that we do not know God Himself otherwise than as acting God – we have to understand a divine action, and therefore an event – not a reality which is, but a reality which occurs. Not to see it in this way is not to see it at all. It is not seen when we try to see it from the safe shelter of a general theory. It is not seen when we think we see a being and then ask whether and to what extent we can derive from this being this or that obligation. The proposition: 'There is a command of God,' is quite inadequate as a description of what concerns us. For we should naturally have to weigh against it the denial: No, 'there is' no command of God. What 'there is' is not as such the command of God. But the core of the matter is that God gives His command, that he gives Himself to be our Commander. God's command, God Himself, gives Himself to be known. And as He does so, He is heard. Man is made responsible. He is brought into that confrontation and fellowship with Jesus Christ. And his action acquires that determination. The command of God is the decision about the goodness of human action. As the divine action it precedes human action. It is only on the basis of this reality, which is not in any sense static but active, not in any sense general but supremely particular, that theological ethics has to make answer to the ethical question. Its theory is simply the theory of this practice. It is because this practice occurs, because theological ethics cannot escape noticing this practice, in the contemplation of this practice, that theological ethics fashions its

5   Barth sees actualism as important for ethics as for the doctrine of God; see, e.g., Paul T. Nimmo, *Being in Action: The Theological Shape of Barth's Ethical Vision* (London: T & T Clark, 2007). He emphasizes the character of the ethical 'command' as 'event' not because of philosophical commitment to an actualistic principle, but because he believes the daily grace of the Gospel is the ongoing context for the calling of the Christian to spiritual activity (II/2.511, 602). 'Scripture itself is a really living, acting and speaking subject' (I/2.672), only because God employs the Scripture and makes it holy for his commanding purposes. Because Scripture is alive, Barth believes we cannot rest content with past readings – we always read with hope of fresh hearing and with a trust that the Word is faithful and free (see, e.g., I/2.684; II/2.706). Nimmo concludes: 'Barth's actualistic ontology therefore preserves the open possibility of a material identity of the command of God today with Scripture, but does not render it necessary' (*Being in Action*, p. 37).

concepts. The same practice of the Word of God forms the basis of the Christian Church. It is in view of it that there is faith and obedience in the Church. It is in view of it that all theology has its legitimacy and its necessity. It is as God gives man His command, as He gives Himself to man to be his Commander, that God claims him for Himself, that He makes His decision concerning him and executes His judgment upon him. It is as He does this that He sanctifies him, and the good (which is God Himself) enters into the realm of human existence. To understand the command of God as this claim and decision and judgment will therefore be the first task to which we must address ourselves in the present context.

Once this foundation has been laid, in later sections of the *Church Dogmatics* we shall have to show in detail to what extent this divine command is actually directed to man.[6] Even as His command, the Word of God is the Word of His truth and reality in the act of creation, in the act of reconciliation and in the act of redemption. Or we might put it in this way, that it reveals the kingdom of the Lord Jesus Christ as the kingdom of nature, the kingdom of grace and the kingdom of glory. Or we might say that it manifests the pre-temporal, cotemporal and post-temporal eternity of God. Or, alternatively, it speaks to us about our determination for God, our relationship to Him and the goal of our perfection in Him. As the command of God, too, His Word has this threefold meaning and content. The concept of the command of God includes the concepts: the command of God the Creator, the command of God the Reconciler and the command of God the Redeemer. The three concepts are identical with the fundamental concepts of dogmatics which it is the task of theological ethics to explain and recapitulate in their ethical content. They characterise in the shortest possible form the act of the God who in grace has elected man for the covenant with Himself, and in so doing they also characterise the command by which He has sanctified him for Himself. Of course, there can be no question of three parts or even stages of the one Christian truth and knowledge. The position is as in the doctrine of the Trinity. Three times in these three concepts we have to say the one whole, in which Jesus Christ is the presupposition and the epitome of creation and redemption from the dominating centre of reconciliation as it has taken place in Him. As there is only one God, so also there is only one command of God. But as the one God is in Himself rich and multiple, so also His one

6   Barth intended to address the ethical address of God at the end of each subsequent volume of the *CD*, extrapolating the ethical material in his consideration of the economy of redemption (creation, reconciliation, and redemption). 'Dogmatics has no option: it has to be ethics as well' (I/2.793).

command is in itself diverse, and yet there is only one way to achieve the knowledge of it. It is of this inner diversity of God's command and the way to achieve a knowledge of it that we are thinking when we stress these three concepts. We are asking who and what is man in the Word of God and according to the Word of God, that is, the man elected, received and accepted by God in Jesus Christ, and therefore, as such, the recipient of the divine command.[7] We find this man in the person of Jesus Christ Himself. He is the Son of David and of Adam who is determined and created to be the image of God. He is the One who is laden with human sin, and condemned because of it, but loved and preserved as the Son of God even in this judgment. And finally, in His resurrection, sitting at the right hand of God, He is the realisation and revelation of the divine image, received into God's eternal glory. In this threefold determination of the humanity of Jesus Christ we recognise the roots of these three concepts. And if we understand man in general from the humanity of Jesus Christ, it automatically follows that we have to understand him as God's creature, as the sinner pardoned by God, and as the heir-expectant of the coming kingdom of God. In these relations we recognise ourselves, not as in the mirror of an idea of man, but as in the mirror of the Word of God which is source of all truth.[8] And it is obviously not in the framework of unguaranteed concepts borrowed from psychology or sociology, but in that of the concepts arising from these relations, that our sanctification, and the significance of the claim and decision and judgment of the divine command, can and must be understood. In these three relations we know that we are placed under the command of God. We are, therefore, taking as our basis, not a general, abstract concept of man, but the concrete Christian concept when we say that this is the sanctified man who is not the subject, but is certainly the predicate of the statements of theological ethics. Man is the creature of God. He is the sinner to whom grace has been shown. He is the heir of the kingdom of God. It is as all these things that he is addressed in God's command. In all these relations the divine command is the principle of the goodness of his actions. The one whole command of God has this threefold relation. As he lives in the Word of God and according to the Word of God, the one whole man stands in this threefold relation. In accordance with the context, the autonomy, but also the totality of the chief concepts of dogmatics,

---

7   Barth locates human being within that of Jesus Christ: 'The only ultimate and really serious
     determination for the believer is that which proceeds from Jesus Christ. Ultimately and in the
     true sense he is no longer the subject. In and with his subjectivity he has become a predicate to
     the subject Jesus Christ, by whom he is both justified and sanctified, from whom he receives both
     comfort and direction' (I/2.313–314).
8   'Jesus Christ ... is the image to which we have to conform ourselves' (II/2.737).

we shall not, in ethics, isolate any one of these relations from the other two. We shall not be guilty either of preference on the one hand or prejudice on the other in our systematic treatment of the three. On the contrary, we shall have to understand each one separately, not only in its connexion with the others, but also in its autonomy and totality.

The history of Christian ethics tells of numerous conflicts between the different schools of thought which derive from creation, reconciliation and redemption, or from nature, grace and eternal glory, with the one-sided orientation corresponding to this derivation. The movement which lies at the basis of these conflicts is necessary; but the conflicts, the actions and reactions in favour of one or the other of the different relations of sanctification are not necessary. Indeed, although they may often have been important historically, they are fundamentally dangerous. We shall have to understand them as historically meaningful. We shall have to note and consider and estimate their aims and interests. But for our own part we must be careful not to become involved in them. We must avoid the rigidity and the enthusiasm with which one or the other of the equally necessary and possible points of view is constantly seized and more or less absolutised. In this way we must learn from history to do justice to history.

There can be no question even of a systematic combination of the three points of view. The reason for this is that we never at any point know the divine command in itself and as such, but only in its relations. The multiplicity of God Himself obviously resolves itself as little into His unity as His unity can be lost in His multiplicity. God is not dead in a rigid unity. He lives in the multiplicity of His triune essence, of His inner perfections and therefore of His Word and work. This being the case, we have to pursue the knowledge of His command in such a way that we try to understand and bring out its relations as stations on a road which we have to tread, and the unity of which we shall know only as we tread it. Therefore the later task of a specific theological ethics will not be to contemplate a system – either from this point of view or that, or even from a fourth position superior to it – but to traverse this road of knowledge which corresponds to the inner life of God Himself, to execute this movement of knowledge. In it we shall have to realise the fact and extent that the divine command is actually directed to man, and the divine decision concerning man is made in it. It will be an exact repetition of the same movement which dogmatics itself executes on the road indicated by its basic concepts. There is only one difference – and it is not one of matter or method, but merely of fact and practice. It is simply that in it special attention is given to the question of the character of the Word of God as the command of God, and therefore of the claiming of man. The best place to discuss it is, therefore, in a concluding chapter to each of the different parts of dogmatics. In the present instance, this means that 'general' ethics forms the last chapter of the doctrine of God.

CHAPTER 8

CREATION AND COVENANT

He wills and posits the creature neither out of caprice nor necessity, but because He has loved it from eternity, because He wills to demonstrate His love for it, and because He wills, not to limit His glory by its existence and being, but to reveal and manifest it in His own co-existence with it. As the Creator He wills really to exist for His creature. That is why He gives it its own existence and being. That is also why there cannot follow from the creature's own existence and being an immanent determination of its goal or purpose, or a claim to any right, meaning or dignity of its existence and nature accruing to it except as a gift. That is why even the very existence and nature of the creature are the work of the grace of God.[1]

Barth turns in volume three to the first of God's external works: creation. Following the path charted by his doctrine of the Word of God, he looks to revelation for knowledge of the cosmos. Thus, the first paragraph in this volume addresses the need for 'faith in God the Creator' (§40) – noting that creation is neither obvious, nor proven, but it must be believed (III/1.6). Faithful to his doctrine of election, he considers creation within the bounds of his 'Christological concentration'. The next paragraph (§41) considers the link between creation and covenant, noting that they are intertwined with 'creation as the external basis of the covenant' and 'covenant as the internal basis for creation'. Whereas Roman Catholic theology speaks of nature and grace, Barth will speak of creation (the widest circle of God's external works) and covenant (the inner circle of God's external works) – see more comments regarding this comparative analysis in footnote 9.

Barth's doctrine of creation begins with lengthy exegetical and dogmatic analysis of the primeval history found in the first two chapters of the book of Genesis. Per his interpretative practice, Barth employs the insights of historical critics (in this case, the documentary hypothesis and interpretation of the differences between the two creation accounts in Genesis 1–2), but he presses forward to offer theological commentary that builds upon such archaeological

---

1 *CD* III/1.95.

reflections. Barth is attuned to canonical reflections on the link between Genesis 1–11 and the rest of the Pentateuch – as Kathryn Tanner observes, 'Talk of God's creation and providence is a way of showing how what happens to Israel is written into the nature of things more generally' (cf. CD III/1, pp. 268–9).[2] In Barth's terms, we could say that talk of creation signals that what happens in the covenant of grace is woven into the fabric of the whole cosmos.

Bibliography

Karl Barth, 'No! An Answer to Emil Brunner', in Natural Theology: Comprising 'Nature and Grace' by Professor Dr. Emil Brunner and the reply 'No!' by Dr. Karl Barth (trans. Peter Fraenkel; Eugene, OR: Wipf & Stock, 2002), pp. 65–128.

Matthew Rose, Ethics with Barth: God, Metaphysics, and Morals (Barth Studies; Surrey: Ashgate, 2011), part 1.

Robert Sherman, The Shift to Modernity: Christ and the Doctrine of Creation in the Theologies of Schleiermacher and Barth (London: T & T Clark, 2005).

Kathryn Tanner, 'Creation and Providence', in The Cambridge Companion to Karl Barth (ed. John Webster; Cambridge: Cambridge University Press, 2000), pp. 111–26.

John Webster, 'Creation and Reconciliation', in Barth's Ethics of Reconciliation (Cambridge: Cambridge University Press, 1995), pp. 59–98.

Text (*CD* III/1.229–239)

The creature does not exist casually. It does not merely exist, but exists meaningfully. In its existence it realises a purpose and plan and order.[3]

---

2   Kathryn Tanner, 'Creation and Providence', in *The Cambridge Companion to Karl Barth* (ed. John Webster; Cambridge: Cambridge University Press, 2000), p. 113.

3   Earlier Barth introduced §41 (Creation and Covenant) by saying: 'Creation comes first in the series of works of the triune God, and is thus the beginning of all the things distinct from God Himself. Since it contains in itself the beginning of time, its historical reality eludes all historical observation and account, and can be expressed in the biblical creation narratives only in the form of a pure saga. But according to this witness the purpose and therefore the meaning of creation is to make possible the history of God's covenant with man which has its beginning, its centre, and its culmination in Jesus Christ. The history of this covenant is as much the goal of creation as creation itself is the beginning of this history' (III/1.42). Creation is identified as 'first in the series of works of the triune God ... the purpose and therefore the meaning of creation is to make possible the history of God's covenant with man'. So there is a 'purpose and plan, and order' as Barth says here. This purpose and order renders a Christian account – in faith – different from any scientific or philosophical account of creation's origin and telos. As Barth will say later: 'a decision has been made concerning the being and nature of every man by the mere fact that with him and among all other men He too has become a man. No matter who or what or where he may

It has not come into being by chance but by necessity, and therefore
not as an accident but as a sign and witness of this necessity. This is
already implied in the fact that it is a creature and therefore the work of
the Creator, of God. As God Himself does not exist casually but in the
power of His own divine meaning and His own divine necessity, so also
the creature exists by Him and is a revelation of His glory. The act of
creation as such is the revelation of the glory of God by which He gives
to the creature meaning and necessity. The creature could not assume
these, nor could it have, possess or retain them, nor, having lost them,
could it have regained them. But it does not need to do so. Creating
it, God gives it meaning and necessity. Giving it being and existence,
He makes it the exponent of His intention, plan and order. It could
not exist if it were not, in virtue of its being, this exponent; if it were
not, by reason of God's gift, the sign and witness of the divine meaning
and the divine necessity. In and with this creation God makes it this
exponent. This is the revelation of God's glory in the act of creation.
The divine meaning and necessity which the creature reveals, which as
such it denotes and attests, is God's free love, i.e., the love of God in
which He wills and posits another by Himself and is Himself for it – the
free love in which He accomplishes this willing and this positing in His
own power and by His own independent resolve. It is in the same free
love that He Himself is God, i.e., the Father in the Son and the Son in
the Father by the Holy Spirit. Again, it is in the same free love that He
has resolved in Himself from all eternity on His fellowship with man
in the person of His own Son. As this free love is revealed, i.e., made
visible outside His own being, His hidden glory is revealed. And this is
creation to the extent that it makes the creature the exponent, sign and
witness of the divine meaning and necessity. It is from here, from the
free love of God, that the creature receives its meaning and necessity,
and it is given to it to be the bearer of God's intention, plan and order.[4]
From this standpoint it may be said that it was not created other than
to be the recipient of this gift, and that it does not exist otherwise than
as the recipient of this gift. From this standpoint it may be said that,
as it exists, it can only be grateful, and that it necessarily forgets and
denies its existence if it is not prepared to be grateful. Its creation as

---

be, he cannot alter the fact that this One is also man. And because this One is also man, every
man in his place and time is changed' (III/2.133). Ethics relates to ontology; Barth believes that
Nietzschean will-to-power or so-called 'social Darwinism' flow from a loss of the 'purpose and
plan and order' of creation as revealed in Jesus (III/2.231–242, 79–84).

4   Barth connects the doctrine of God (as 'the one who loves in freedom' and 'who elects to be with
us and not apart from us') to the doctrine of creation here by emphasizing that creation flows
from love (and, thus, is not self-caused or self-sufficient) and, in particular, from a free love (and,
thus, is really gratuitous and unconditional).

such is its creation as a grateful being and for a grateful existence. It is and exists solely by reason and in accomplishment of the revelation of the glory of God's free love: the love which God has shown towards it without being under any obligation to do so; the love of the Father and the Son in the Holy Spirit; the love which already in the eternal decree of the giving of His Son for the sake of man did not will to be without a concrete extra-divine object. It was when this love began to be deed and event and therefore to be revealed that creation took place and the creature received its being and existence. The creature owes both the fact that it is, and what it is, to the revelation which has this content.

This is the other aspect of the matter. We have already considered the first aspect, to wit, that creation is the formal presupposition of the covenant in which God fulfils the will of His free love. God loves His creature and therefore a being which originally belongs to Him as the One who loves, to which nothing that happens from the side of God, the Lord of this covenant, can be foreign, and which in this respect cannot assert or maintain any divergent claims of its own. Creation is one long preparation, and therefore the being and existence of the creature one long readiness, for what God will intend and do with it in the history of the covenant. Its nature is simply its equipment for grace. Its creatureliness is pure promise, expectation and prophecy of that which in His grace, in the execution of the will of His eternal love, and finally and supremely in the consummation of the giving of His Son, God plans for man and will not delay to accomplish for his benefit. In this way creation is the road to the covenant, its external power and external basis, because for its fulfilment the latter depends wholly on the fact that the creature is in no position to act alone as the partner of God, that it is thrown back wholly and utterly on the care and intercession of God Himself, but that it does actually enjoy this divine care and intercession. What we now see is that the covenant is the internal basis of creation.[5] It is certainly not its external basis.[6] Its external basis

---

5   Barth works with these paired statements: 'creation as the external basis of the covenant' and 'covenant as the internal basis of creation'. Eberhard Busch offers apt analysis: 'The two statements belong together. The first one says that creation has autonomous special life of its own. The second tells us that the grace of the covenant God has no special sphere of its own. The first one guards against the idea of a worldless God; the second against the idea of a godless world' (*The Great Passion*, p. 183).

6   There is an order here: the external basis determines creation; the goal of this determination is its internal basis, the fellowship of God with creatures in Jesus Christ. The external basis is the triune God. Creation exists of God's loving freedom: 'For from him and through him and to him are all things' (Rom. 11.36). The internal basis is that fellowship between the triune God and creatures in Jesus Christ. Creation exists for this fellowship in Jesus: 'all things were created through him and for him' (Col. 1.16).

is the wisdom and omnipotence of God, who is sure of Himself as Creator because He is God, who at the creation of the world and man, at the laying of the presupposition of the covenant, at the preparation of the creature for His grace, is never at a loss for the right ways and means, but whose Word is sufficient to give being and existence to the creature as the object of His love and as the partner of His covenant. But creation also has − and this is what we have now to consider − its internal basis. This consists in the fact that the wisdom and omnipotence of God the Creator was not just any wisdom and omnipotence but that of His free love. Hence what God has created was not just any reality − however perfect or wonderful − but that which is intrinsically determined as the exponent of His glory and for the corresponding service. What God created when He created the world and man was not just any place, but that which was foreordained for the establishment and the history of the covenant, nor just any subject, but that which was to become God's partner in this history, i.e., the nature which God in His grace willed to address and accept and the man predestined for His service. The fact that the covenant is the goal of creation is not something which is added later to the reality of the creature, as though the history of creation might equally have been succeeded by any other history. It already characterises creation itself and as such, and therefore the being and existence of the creature. The covenant whose history had still to commence was the covenant which, as the goal appointed for creation and the creature, made creation necessary and possible, and determined and limited the creature.[7] If creation was the external basis of the covenant, the latter was the internal basis of the former. If creation was the formal presupposition of the covenant, the latter was the material presupposition of the former. If creation takes precedence historically, the covenant does so in substance. If the proclamation and foundation of the covenant is the beginning of the history which commences after creation, the history of creation already contains, as the history of the being of all creatures, all the elements which will subsequently meet and be unified in this event and the whole series of

---

7   Here we see Barth's leanings toward a revised supralapsarian position (over against infralapsarian positions). Supralapsarians believe that God's decree of election precedes his knowledge of the fall to come (the *lapsum*), whereas infralapsarians believe that God's election is premised upon his knowledge of the fall to come. So supralapsarians believe that God always planned to redeem in Jesus, while infralapsarians characterize redemption as a plan contingent on not only creation but also the fall. Barth does not leave traditional supralapsarianism untouched, but he clearly prefers it to the infralapsarian position (see II/2.133–145). For a similar approach from a Reformed contemporary, see Herman Bavinck, *Reformed Dogmatics*, volume two: *God and Creation* (ed. John Bolt; trans. John Vriend; Grand Rapids: Baker Academic, 2004), pp. 383–92.

events which follow; in the history of Israel, and finally and supremely in the history of the incarnation of the Son of God.[8]

From this outline of the new problem and theme it may be seen that the object in question is really the same. It may be seen that there are no factual contradictions; that nothing can be added to what has been said, or subtracted from it. The only change is in respect of the direction and dimension in which it is considered; of the concern and emphasis. The main interest now is not how creation promises, proclaims and prophesies the covenant, but how it prefigures and to that extent antici-pates it without being identical with it; not how creation prepares the covenant, but how in so doing it is itself already a unique sign of the covenant and a true sacrament; not Jesus Christ as the goal, but Jesus Christ as the beginning (the beginning just because He is the goal) of creation.[9] This is what we have now to maintain and appreciate. It must

---

8   For more on how the history of Israel reveals what is true of the world at large, see III/1.268–269, 275. Barth has been criticized for being supersessionistic, that is, for failing to honour the enduring specificity of Israel in God's economy. While he did stand up valiantly against the Nazis, his protest, which was formalized in the Theological Declaration of Barmen, did not address the problem of anti-Semitism. Barth's student Friedrich Marquardt fears that 'at times, Barth is tempted to reduce the Jews to a cipher, to a mirror that reflects life but lives none of its own' (Friedrich-Wilhelm Marquardt, Die Entdeckung des Judentums für die christliche Theologie: Israel im Denken Karl Barths [Munich: Christian Kaiser, 1967], p. 317; cited in Katherine Sonderegger, 'That Jesus Christ Was Born a Jew': Karl Barth's Doctrine of Israel [University Park, PA: Pennsylvania State University Press, 1992], p. 146). Sonderegger argues that matters are much more subtle (see especially pp. 170–1).

9   Creation and covenant function for Barth like nature and grace function in many other dogmatics (see especially Roman Catholic dogmatics). Barth argues here that creation 'prefigures' and 'anticipates' the covenant, 'without being identical with it'; he argues that there is an analogy between the fulfilment of creation in covenant and creation's own intrinsic capacities. Grace works within (III/1.331) and yet also far outstrips and expands the bounds of creation (cf. II/1.80, 569–572, 579; III/1.431). In the work of a number of ressourcement theologians in the Roman Catholic world (oftentimes called the nouvelle théologie – Yves Congar, Hans Urs von Balthasar, and especially Henri de Lubac – this movement is especially important in that it shaped the Second Vatican Council as well as the papacies of John Paul II and now Benedict XVI), nature is inclined toward grace, but must have grace added to it; furthermore, nature has an intrinsic desire for grace, so that there is a deep continuity between the two. To be sure, Barth worries about this continuity, thinking that it downplays the radical nature of sin and the freshness of God's Word given in Christ Jesus. However, a number of interpreters have begun to argue that Barth's proposal is closer to that of the nouvelle théologie than most observers have concluded (indeed, more so than Barth concluded!). See the essays in Thomas Joseph White (ed.), The Analogy of Being: Invention of the Anti-Christ or the Wisdom of God? (Grand Rapids: Eerdmans, 2010), as well as Kenneth Oakes, 'The Question of Nature and Grace in Karl Barth: Humanity as Creature and as Covenant Partner', Modern Theology 23, no. 4 (Oct 2007), pp. 595–616; the classic argument in this direction (toward a rapprochement between Roman Catholic views of nature and grace and the Christocentric approach to creation and covenant in Barth, see Hans Urs von Balthasar, The Theology of Karl Barth: Exposition and Interpretation (trans. Edward T. Oakes; San Francisco: Communio, 1992), especially pp. 381–9. George Hunsinger offers a helpful analysis of Barth's thinking about grace and nature (or, in terms of this volume, of creation and covenant): 'Grace

be conceded at once that without the existence of the second creation narrative we could hardly have the temerity to do this. But since the Bible offers us this second account we must and may attempt it.

In Gen. 2:4b–25 we are dealing in some sense with a history of creation from inside.[10] We have left the sphere of the Priestly witness with his architectonics and lucidity. It is no longer a question of building in a great nexus which will later reveal at a definite point the meaning and purpose of the whole. More than one expositor has at least raised the question whether the theme is really creation in any true sense. It is only on the periphery, as it were, that we discover that the second witness too is thinking of the foundation of 'the heavens and earth, and all the host of them.' His explicit statements concern only a tiny selection of the great cosmic happenings recorded in the first account. There can be no doubt that we are again in the sphere of the beginning and becoming of all things; it is again a question of historically explaining their being, and therefore the history of the covenant, by what has taken place prior to this history as the divine foundation of the creature. But in this case the explanation is limited to the narrowest possible sphere. And this sphere is as near as possible to that of the history which follows. What takes place is depicted wholly in the manner and with the colours of this later history. Only the fact that it has to do with a divine activity, and indeed a basic divine activity, shows us unmistakeably that here too we are in fact dealing with creation history. But the smallness of the sphere, the narrowness of the selection made,

that is not disruptive is not grace – a point that Flannery O'Connor well grasped alongside Karl Barth. Grace, strictly speaking, does not mean continuity but radical discontinuity, not reform but revolution, not violence but nonviolence, not the perfecting of virtues but the forgiveness of sins, not improvement but resurrection from the dead. It means repentance, judgment, and death as the portal to life. It means negation and the negation of the negation. The grace of God really comes to lost sinners, but in coming it disrupts them to the core. It slays to make alive and sets the captive free. Grace may of course work silently and secretly like a germinating seed as well as like a bolt from the blue. It is always wholly as incalculable as it is reliable, unmerited, and full of blessing. Yet it is necessarily as unsettling as it is comforting. It does not finally teach of its own sufficiency without appointing a thorn in the flesh. Grace is disruptive because God does not compromise with sin, nor ignore it, nor call it good. On the contrary, God removes it by submitting to the cross to show that love is stronger than death. Those whom God loves may be drawn to God through their suffering and be privileged to share in his sufferings in the world, because grace in its radical disruption surpasses all that we imagine or think' (*Disruptive Grace: Studies in the Theology of Karl Barth* [Grand Rapids: Eerdmans, 2000], pp. 16–17). However, see the comparative analysis of Roman Catholicism and Karl Barth on nature and grace in Matthew Rose, *Ethics with Barth: God, Metaphysics, and Morals* (Barth Studies; Surrey: Ashgate, 2011), p. 58 fn. 78.

10 Barth agrees with the common historical-critical exegesis that sees 1.1–2:4a coming from a Priestly hand and 2.4b–25 coming from a different hand. Here he suggests that the second creation account focuses on the 'internal basis' of creation: God's covenant fellowship with creatures, manifest in the Edenic life of Adam and Eve with God.

the consequent limitation of horizon, and the immediate proximity of the later history – all these features of the second narrative involve an essential foreshortening of the teleology of the first. There is no trace of the expectant and straining march from sphere to sphere up to the decisive centre. Without having first to look ahead, or to fill out what has gone before by what follows, we find ourselves from the very first in the middle of things. It is only in the great final act of the creation of woman, and here in contrast to the meagreness of the first account, that there is a striking teleological tension. Even here, however, the solution – 'And the Lord God said, It is not good that the man should be alone; I will make him an help meet for him' – is formally antici-pated in the opening words. And we certainly cannot say that this final item is itself the goal of creation as we have it in the accounts of the sixth and seventh days in the first record. The creation of woman as the helpmeet of man is a strongly emphasised aspect of the goal of the totality, but the creation of man in the concreteness here ascribed to him, the planting of the Garden of Eden, and the planting of the two special trees, are in their own way aspects of the same goal of creation. From the very outset we are already at the goal, and this not merely in the form of a forward prospect and reference, but in such a way that the end is already present and visible in the beginning itself and as such.

It does not seem to fit in with the normal characterisation of the two sources which must here be presupposed, but it is worth considering whether it would not help to characterise them more profoundly if it were agreed that in Gen. 1 we have a prophetical view of creation, whereas the view contained in Gen. 2 might usefully be described as sacramental.

It would be quite out of place, therefore, to apply the method used in relation to Gen. 1, selecting a certain point in the passage and using it as a criterion in our understanding of the rest. If we ask what the story is really leading up to, a general answer is given by its direct connexion with the ensuing account of the fall. It is palpable that it aims immediately at the commencement of the history of the covenant between God and man which takes place when the man created by God becomes disobedient and has to bear the consequences of this disobedience, but God for His part does not really cease but continues to be his God and faithful to him in this modification of the relationship between the Creator and the creature, as the One who controls the conflict which has broken out. The history of creation in Gen. 2 is the immediate presupposition of this event. It describes the coming into being of the world, and supremely of man as that of the being in whose nature and mode of existence there is prefigured the history which follows, and particularly this first event in this history, for all that it is so new and incomprehensible in relation to creation. It describes in the form of history the situation which forms the background to this event; the wall which gives rise to both the light and shadow of this event; the sphere within which this event will take place. It describes creation as the sign and witness of the event which will follow. To this extent it presupposes and prefigures it. Of course it does not say that man will sin against God, or that even if he does God will have to be faithful to him. It does not question the freedom which there will be on both sides in the history which follows. But it describes the relationship, willed and ordered by God as the Creator of all that is, within which there will be these dealings on both sides. As a description of this relationship, and therefore in connexion with the aim of the whole, all the elements of the passage are equally important, and none of them can be picked out and used as a dominant exegetical motif for the understanding of the rest. On the contrary, we have to see that for all their historical succession they all stand together in the foreshortened and therefore impressive teleological connexion of the whole with what follows.

The first obvious sequence is to be found in Gen. 2.4b–7. And the first point to call for consideration – and it is decisive for all that follows – is that we now have to do with a new name for God. The God whose creative work is to be described is from the very outset called Yahweh Elohim: the God who reveals His name to Israel; who under this name has chosen and called Israel and has dealt with it as its Lord. So close are we here to the history of the covenant which commences after the completion of creation that even in the history of creation God must bear this name.[11] So much is the story of creation to be considered as the presupposition of the history of the covenant, indeed as the visible prefiguration of its beginning! The Israelite who hears or reads about the Creator is to think at once of the One to whom he and his nation owe everything, against whom he and his people have sinned a thousand times, but who incomprehensibly has never failed to be faithful to him and his people. This God is the God of creation.

And this God made 'the earth and the heavens.' This striking inversion of the order is the second point to be noted. The fact that God is also the Creator of the heavens is true and familiar. But it is mentioned only once and incidentally and dependently and secondarily in the first

---

11   Barth addresses a thorny question for source critics and theological exegetes alike: though God first gives the divine name (YHWH) to Moses and through him to Israel in Exodus 3, the name appears frequently in Genesis! Barth argues that the name was used by later authors/editors to demonstrate that the same God of Israel created the whole world (for a similar argument about how Genesis forms the backdrop to the covenant life of Israel, see R. W. L. Moberly, *The Old Testament of the Old Testament: Patriarchal Narratives and Mosaic Yahwism* [Overtures to Biblical Theology; Minneapolis: Fortress, 1992]).

sentence. The heavens are not overlooked or denied, but in this saga attention is focused on the earth. What interests the man who speaks here is the fact that God has made this lower earthly sphere visible and attainable to man, and that in it and from its elements He has made man himself. He praises the Creator because He is the Creator of the earth. This is natural enough in view of the fact that God has appointed the earth to be the sphere of man, and that He will accept the man who lives on earth and is himself taken from it, and that even in his creation He has already allied Himself so wonderfully with him. But from what follows it is the earth itself which is important to him. Even man – this saga is not as anthropocentric as it is often made out to be – is first introduced only as the being who had to be created for the sake of the earth and to serve it. For we are told that the earth was originally barren because God had not yet sent rain and man was not there to till it. This twofold condition of a fruitful earth bearing trees and plants had still to be fulfilled in the onward course of creation: first, by a mist which went up from the earth and watered the whole face of the ground; and then – as part of the same perfecting of the earth – by the creation of man. That man has the concrete duty to cultivate and tend the things which God has planted will be emphasised later in the story of the Garden of Eden. After the fall – although in very different circumstances – man is immediately sent to work on the land. Here, too, creation is really the creation of the heavens and the earth (with an emphasis on the terrestrial sphere), and not just that of man; indeed, it is the creation of the man who must work and serve under the heavens and on earth, i.e., in relation to his fellow-creatures. It is to be noted how different this is from the first account, which is far more anthropocentric at this point, suggesting that the world of vegetation was ordained and created only to be the food of men and animals. For in this account it is a kind of end in itself. The perfect earth is not a dry, barren or dead earth, but one which bears shrubs and vegetation and is inhabited. God will plant it. But to make that which has been planted thrive, God needs the farmer or gardener. This will be the role of man. He thus appears as the being which must be able and ready to serve in order to give meaning and purpose to the planting of the earth. He has a gap to fill at this point. He is just as necessary as the watering without which the earth cannot be brought to completion. In view of his complete integration into the totality of the created world, there can be no question of a superiority of man supported by appeals to his special dignity, or of forgetfullness not merely of a general but of the very definite control of Yahweh Elohim over man. In spite of all the particular things that God may plan and do with him, in the first instance man can only serve the earth and will continually have to do so.

What is said at the end of these verses – more concretely than in the first saga – about the process of the special creation of man points in the same direction of the indispensable humility of man's existence. In the first place, we are told that God had formed him of 'the dust of the ground.' The verbal connexion in the Hebrew is unmistakeable: man is a formation consisting of detached and individual portions of the earth which is arid, barren and dead in itself. Of course he is more than this. But he is this too. He is not a new element planted by God like shrubs and vegetation. Seen even from this standpoint, he has no independent position in the totality of creation. His nature is that of the earth on which he lives and moves. He owes his existence wholly and utterly to the fact that from a particular handful of the dust of the earth God willed to make him. That God made him and that He made him of the earth are both things which he has in common with the beast. The only difference between him and the beast is that he is dust formed into a human body. But the human frame no less than the animal has a natural tendency to return to the earth from which it was taken. Primarily, then, the distinctive election of man is merely that he is formed from this dust as opposed to all other dust and given this form which is distinct from that of the beasts. On the other hand, what robs him of all claim is that while his nature is differentiated from the earth and the beast it is still related to them, retaining its earthly and animal character. He is not even distinguished from the beast – although from the earth – by the fact that he became a 'living soul,' that he is a being which not only possesses a body but also a soul, and finally that it is the breath of God which makes him such a being. And if this is an exaltation and distinction which man as such a being shares with the beast, he also shares with it the problematical and threatened and transitory nature of his existence. God does not owe him the breath which, apart from his bodily existence, makes him a living soul, nor does it become his own in virtue of the fact that God made him for this purpose. If man is not renewed, the fact that he was once quickened will not prevent him from sharing the fate of the beast and becoming again what he was: arid, barren, dead, dust of dust, earth of earth; a soul without form or dwelling, assigned with the body to the depths of the earth, condemned without the Spirit of God to an impotent hopelessness. Thus from the beginning he stands under the law of humility and the fear of God. In what sense, then, does his election really distinguish him from the earth and the beast? According to the second creation narrative – and we have here a material parallel to what the first account called his divine likeness – only in one respect. The divine quickening is general, so that the animal kingdom too exists in virtue of it. But man becomes a living soul as God breathes the breath of life into his nostrils; in this most

direct and personal and most special act.[12] To no beast does God turn
in this way, nor does any of the things which He has formed become
a living soul in this way. It is to man, and to man alone, that God gives
breath in this manner. It is man, and man alone, who becomes a living
soul in this way. And this, and this alone, is the distinguishing feature of
man – his humanity – according to this passage. And it is to be noted
that this rests on the wholly free and special election and compassion
of God, and that it stands or falls with it. As long as it stands, God,
who can repeat this in-breathing even when man's frame of dust has
returned to dust, is always the confidence of the one whom He has
elected and addressed in this way. If it falls, man's only future and
prospect is to return to dust. The fact that he is not just earth moulded
into a body, and not just a soul, but a soul quickened and established
and sustained by God in a direct and personal and special encounter of
His breath with this frame of dust, is the differentiating exaltation and
distinction of man. In spite of his earthly and animal nature, indeed in
this earthly and animal nature, God in his creation gave him cause to
put his confidence in Him directly, personally and specifically, to hold
to the One who already in his creation has covenanted with him. His
nature is still problematical, threatened and transitory. He is set under
the law of humility and the fear of God. But in all this, God is his
refuge and hope. He is this because He willed to accept him of all His
creatures. It was not by reason of any immediacy to God proper to
himself, but only by reason of God's free immediacy in His attitude to
him, that he triumphed over the aridity, barrenness and deadness of the
dust to which he is still subjected. When we say this we must not lose
sight here of the beginning of the passage. On the contrary, we have to
understand the passage as a self-enclosed circle. It is just because man,
with God as his refuge and hope, can triumph over the earthiness of
earth from which he comes and to which he must return, that he is
destined, within the totality of the creaturely world, to serve the earth
as a husbandman and a gardener. The hope of the arid, barren and
dead earth is that it will bear the vegetation planted by God. According
to the second account of creation, we must add that this is the hope
of the whole creaturely world. It proceeds from death to life. But the
realisation of this hope waits for man as the being which, earthy by
nature, will triumph over the aridity, barrenness and deadness of the
earth because God is his refuge and hope, because God has constituted
Himself as such. His existence will be the sign which will contradict
the whole earthiness of earth. His act will be an act of release for the

---

12   Human dignity, then, is based on divine fellowship; more specifically, human dignity is based on
the Christological *telos* of humanity.

earth too, and for the whole creaturely world. And what he will take with him when he returns to earth will be the promise of life for everything terrestrial.[13] Thus the existence of man within the whole is indeed the existence of one who is commissioned to serve and work. He must give himself to till and keep the earth in order that it may have meaning when God will bring it to perfection. In this function man is responsible to both God and the creature. And in this function he fulfils the meaning of his own existence. Yet it must not be forgotten that it is not he but God who will plant the earth and therefore fulfil its hope and bring about its perfection. And it is not he but God who will create the other condition for the fulfilment of this hope, who will provide a mist for the earth and therefore rain and the humidity without which the service and work of man would be in vain. Nor has man assumed this function which is the meaning of his existence; he has received it from God.[14] Thus it is not he but God who is the ground which gives courage and confidence to all creation. But he is the sign of this courage and confidence – a sign which he is permitted to erect in his existence and work and service, and even in his necessary return to dust. The law of humility and the fear of God still remain even under this aspect. But the matter is also characterised by the fact that it is man whom God has chosen and created as a sign of the future which He has destined for all creation as such. We see, then, that properly understood, and taking into account all its aspects, it is full of prefigurative significance. From the very outset we are indeed in the middle of things. And it is not for nothing – even the first verses force us to say this – that this form of the creation saga gives to the Creator of the world the covenant name of Yahweh Elohim.

Self-evidently what we have here is in the first instance a childlike description of human existence, of the contradiction and unity of its visible corporality and invisible quickening or animation; and at

13 Barth distinguishes but does not separate heaven and earth: 'Heaven is not earth and earth is not heaven. Yet they do not stand in a relationship of equilibrium and symmetry. Heaven undoubtedly has a definite superiority over earth … Earth for its part is not without God. But it is also not without heaven. It is under it, and in this way it participates in its distinction. But it has its own dignity, which in relationship to God is not less, but which is determined and ordered by God through its inner creaturely relationship with heaven' (III/1.18). John Webster has noted that the most underdeveloped section of Barth's doctrine of creation is his account of nature, no doubt left thin due to his worry about natural theology, his fear that scientific rationality will serve as judge of revelation, and his Christocentric focus (see Webster, *Barth*, pp. 111–12). It is worth noting that Barth clearly wants to affirm the dignity of the earth (III/1.18), though he sees it 'determined and ordered by … its inner creaturely relationship with heaven'.

14 Earlier Barth describes 'the proposition that God created heaven and earth and man' as containing 'within itself a negative and a positive': 'The negative is that the world is not alone … And the positive is that God is before the world' (III/1.7).

the same time a description of the basis of the twofold reality of man in the direct will and activity of God. And again self-evidently we also have in the first instance and the same childlike form a magnifying of the state of the husbandman, his divine election and call.

It is inherently improbable, however, that these themes explain the origination or even the adoption of this account in the Old Testament sphere. Behind these prefigurative pictures, which have their own meaning as such, there stands the whole of Old Testament anthropology. Like the beast, man is formed of dust, animated by God and destined to return to dust and non-existence. But in contrast to the beast, he is animated by God directly and personally. Of all creatures he is chosen and called by Him immediately. And he stands or falls by reason of the fact that God does not abrogate this relationship to him but maintains and continues it. And this man is set in the service of the ground from which he was taken, of which he has need and to which he will return. He is set in this service because, in that which it will bear and produce in the power and goodness of God, the ground also has a hope for the fulfilment of which man must be prepared with his existence and ability to work.

But it must not be overlooked that behind this anthropology as such there stands directly − conditioned and predestined by the will and act of Yahweh Elohim − the election and calling of Israel, its existence and position within the world of nations to which it belongs, its selection and special training from among these nations, its antithesis to them, but also its role as a mediator on their behalf, its being (subject to destruction) as light in their darkness, the responsibility of its mission, the exaltation and humility of its status as God's servant to them, and the insoluble connexion of its hope with the hope of the whole cosmos. In all the dialectic here ascribed to man, there did not first arise and live, as the Old Testament sees it, either individual man or man in general, but the people of Israel. And it is because the people of Israel lived out this dialectic that this account of creation had to ascribe it to man.

It is difficult, however, for exposition merely to affirm that the riddle of Israel is the final subjective content of this passage, since throughout the Old Testament this riddle of Israel and therefore of man is a hard but also a hopeful eschatological riddle − a riddle which points beyond itself. And it is impossible for exposition to stop at this point if the hopeful riddle which might have confronted the writer as something final has not objectively pointed beyond itself in vain but found its fulfilment in Jesus as the Messiah of Israel. If we do not deny but believe this, we shall have to press forward to a final and deepest meaning of the content of the passage.[15] He, Jesus Christ, is the man whose existence was necessary for the perfecting of the earth; for the redemption of its aridity, barrenness and death; for the meaningful fulfilment of its God-given hope; and especially for the realisation of the hope of Israel. He is the man who, taken from all creation, all humanity and all Israel, and yet belonging to them and a victim of their curse, was in that direct, personal and special immediacy of God to Him a creature, man, the seed of Abraham and the Son of David. He is the man whose confidence and hope was God alone but really God; who is what He is for all, for all Israel, all humanity, and even the whole world; who in the deepest humility and the fear of God gave up Himself wholly to the fate of the creature, man and Israel, and in this way was decisively exalted and reigns over all creatures, the King of Israel and Saviour of the world, triumphing over all their weakness. He is the man who did not return emptyhanded, but with the spoils of hope, to the earth from which He was taken but for which He was also given. The man of whom the saga spoke, objectively if not subjectively, is – in respect of the solution of the riddle of Israel and the fulfilment of its hope – this man Jesus.[16] So near are we in this second creation history to the threshold of the history of the covenant and salvation that, even though we continue to give due attention to the other strata of its content, we cannot interpret it finally, and therefore decisively, in any other way than this.

---

15 Old Testament scholars have noted frequently that the creation accounts of Genesis were composed to give necessary background to the religion of Israel (e.g., Gerhard von Rad). Barth agrees (III/1.63–65). But Barth thinks they fail to move forward far enough: not only the Song of Songs and the Prophets, but also the New Testament expresses the goal of this creation (see III/1.320–321, 239–249).

16 This Christological reading of Genesis 1–2 explains why Barth begins his account of the doctrine of creation with the following statement: 'The insight that man owes his existence and form, together with all the reality distinct from God, to God's creation, is achieved only in the reception and answer of the divine self-witness, that is, only in faith in Jesus Christ, i.e., in the knowledge of the unity of Creator and creature actualized in Him, and in the life in the present mediated by Him, under the right and in the experience of the goodness of the Creator towards His creature' (III/1.3).

CHAPTER 9

PROVIDENCE

If God is who God is in Jesus, God should be at work everywhere in much the same way: directing, in an irresistible but non-coercive fashion, a history between God and creatures whereby the two are one in act yet remain completely themselves. In short: no synergism (as if God and creatures were agents on the same plane); no monism (as if God were the only actor); no determinism (as if God pulled creatures away from their own best inclinations).[1]

Karl Barth moves forward in his doctrine of creation to focus upon anthropology (III/2). He then addresses the doctrine of providence (III/3). Like creation before it, this doctrine is a tenet of faith revealed in Jesus Christ, not reasoned out in empirical fashion (§48). In §49 Barth addresses three aspects of the God of the gospel's providential work: 'God fulfills His fatherly lordship over His creature by preserving, accompanying, and ruling the whole course of its earthly existence. He does this as His mercy is revealed and active in the creaturely sphere in Jesus Christ, and the lordship of His Son is thus manifested to it' (III/3: 58). In due course, then, he turns to related doctrines: sin as nothingness (§50), and then 'the kingdom of God, the ambassadors of God and their opponents' (§51).

Barth's attention to providence is attuned to ethical concerns, namely, to sketching out the shape of human agency. While he is criticized by many as christomonist – as giving insufficient space to creaturely agency – his dogmatic approach is not meant to supplant, but to situate human agency. In his ethical reflections, he will address the crucial concept of freedom, following the early Reformed tradition in affirming real human freedom while defining it as freedom 'within the limits which correspond to its creaturely existence' (III/3.61). Barth affirms what seems contradictory to those who believe human and divine agency exist in a competitive fashion: 'That the creature may continue to be by virtue of the divine preserving means

1   Kathryn Tanner, 'Creation and Providence', in *The Cambridge Companion to Karl Barth* (ed. John Webster; Cambridge Companions to Religion; Cambridge: Cambridge University Press, 2000), pp. 124–5.

that it may itself be actual within its limits: actual, and therefore not a mere appearance engendered by some heavenly or hellish power; itself actual, and therefore not an emanation from the being of God ... God preserves the creatures in the reality which is distinct from His own. It is relative to and dependent upon His reality, but in its relativity and dependence autonomous towards it, existing because it owes its existence to Him, as a subject with which He can have dealings and which can have dealings with Him' (III/3.86). Barth argues that divine providence in no way rules out creaturely agency, though it does locate such human freedom within the economy of grace. Barth will even speak of human autonomy, though he will always maintain that it is an autonomy given by God – a counter-intuitive sort of autonomy if ever there were one.

Bibliography

Karl Barth, 'The Gift of Freedom: Foundations of Evangelical Ethics', in *The Humanity of God* (trans. Thomas Wieser; Louisville: Westminster John Knox, 1960), pp. 69–96.

George Hunsinger, 'Double Agency as a Test Case', in *How to Read Karl Barth: The Shape of His Theology* (New York: Oxford University Press, 1991), pp. 185–224.

Kathryn Tanner, *God and Creation in Christian Theology: Tyranny or Empowerment?* (Minneapolis: Fortress, 2005).

John Webster, 'Freedom in Limitation: Human Freedom and False Necessity in Barth', in *Barth's Moral Theology: Human Action in Barth's Thought* (Edinburgh/Grand Rapids: T & T Clark/Eerdmans, 1998), pp. 99–123.

Text (*CD* III/3.41–43, 47–57)

But our primary emphasis must now be upon the fact that this accompaniment of the history of the covenant of grace by that of creaturely being, this co-ordination, integration and co-operation of the latter, is the work of God. It is this no less than creation, and the establishment of the covenant in and with creation, and the history of the covenant. If in its continued existence the creature may serve the will of God in His covenant, grace and salvation, it does this in the individuality and particularity given it with its creation by God, in the freedom and activity corresponding to its particular nature. The creatures of the earth thus live their own lives. Man, too, lives his own life in accordance with the particular spirit which is the basis of human nature. All creation is made to exist in this relationship according to its own manner and freedom. But the fact that it actually does this is first and last the direct work of God.[2] For neither generally nor in detail has God created a machine which works at once in harmony with His will and therefore with the history of the covenant of grace. To the relative freedom and autonomy in which the creature has begun and continues to exist in face of Him, there corresponds the perfect sovereignty in which God is present in its whole history and in which He Himself co-ordinates and brings it into a positive relationship with the history of the covenant of grace. As He is free in His dealings with the patriarchs and Moses, with judges, kings and prophets, and finally in His incarnate Son, and as He is gracious and omnipotent in His freedom, so He is in the dealings with and to and through and in creation with which He accompanies this history at every step. The perfection of creation is not the power with which the latter sets and maintains itself in motion in this sense. The power in which it does this is the perfection of God, and concretely the perfection of His free and omnipotent grace, and even more concretely the perfection of the kingdom of Jesus Christ. Creation has its own perfection. We are told that God considered what He had made, 'and behold, it was very good.' But the goodness and even perfection of creation consists in the fact that God has made it serviceable for the rule of His free and omnipotent grace, for the exercise of the lordship of Jesus Christ. But this serviceability would be futile and concealed if there were no such rule and lordship, if it were not the living good-pleasure of God actually to use it. In other hands than His it cannot render the service for which it was ordained. There is needed the Master who has fashioned this instrument if its goodness and perfection are to be effective and revealed. This meets all the complaints of the creature against its supposed imperfection, which can be raised only by those who cannot control or see it in its perfection because it is not for them to use it. It also takes from creation all boasting or self-glory, because its glory can consist only in the fact that God has made and found it useful for Himself, and especially in the fact that He will and does use it in the service of the 'kingdom of his dear Son' (Col. 1:13). It is not glorious in itself; it can become so only in the right hand of the living God. That He uses it in the service of this kingdom; that He co-ordinates and integrates it with His

---

2   Barth does intend to speak of creaturely freedom and agency, but he wants to clarify that this is a reality as a gift from God: 'The doctrine of providence deals with the history of created being as such, in the sense that in every respect and in its whole span this proceeds under the fatherly care of God the Creator, whose will is done and is to be seen in His election of grace, and therefore in the history of the covenant between Himself and man, and therefore in Jesus Christ' (III/1.3). As seen here, he affirms the reality of 'history of created being', indeed 'in every respect and in its whole span'. But it proceeds not autonomously, materialistically, or randomly, but 'under the fatherly care of God the Creator', the same God who came to dwell amongst us in Jesus Christ.

work in this kingdom; that He causes it to co-operate in the history of this kingdom, this is the rule of His providence. In so doing God acts with a sovereignty which has its self-evident limit in His own being, in the unity and steadfastness of His will, in His own glory and mercy, in the immutability of His purpose.[3] Accordingly it has its limit also in the nature of creation, in the goodness and perfection given it, in its serviceability to Him. But in what this consists is known only by God Himself as its Creator and Lord. We can perceive it, and therefore the limit of the sovereignty of God which it sets, only when we perceive the use which God wills to make and does make of it. The extent of this use is the extent of its nature, goodness and perfection, and the extent of His sovereignty over it. Since we do not know the totality of His rule, it is not for us to fix the limit of His sovereignty.[4] It certainly cannot have its limit in what we know of it, or of creation.

[...]

There is one indispensable presupposition of the covenant of grace and the kingdom of Christ and its history even outside the free and gracious will of God. It consists in the fact that God is not alone but with the creature, so that the latter has existence and continued existence alongside and outside Him. In order that God may work for and to and in it, it must be there in its distinct reality. But to its being, and therefore to God's dealings with it, there also belongs the fact that it has time, space and opportunity both to exist and to do so for God's glory.

---

3   What does sovereignty and providence actually look like? '[W]hatever may take place in the history of the creature, and however this may appear from the standpoint of its own law and freedom, it never can nor will escape the lordship of its Creator. Whatever occurs, whatever it does and whatever happens to it, will take place not only in the sphere and on the ground of the lordship of God, and not only generally in His direct presence, but concretely, in virtue of His directly effective will to preserve, under His direct and superior co-operation and according to His immediate direction ... The Lord is never absent, passive, nonresponsive or impotent, but always present, active, responsible and omnipotent. He is never dead, but always living; never sleeping, but always awake; never uninterested, but always concerned; never merely waiting in any respect, but even where He seems to wait, even where He permits, always holding the initiative. In this consists His co-existence with the creature' (III/1.13).

4   Barth reminds us that providence is God's governance of created being and its history for the sake of his election in Jesus Christ. In other words, God does not possess bare power directed to arbitrary ends; rather, God possesses absolute power directed specifically to ends flowing from his will and, thus, befitting his character. Barth expresses worry that earlier theologians – ranging from the medieval to the Protestant orthodox eras – gave insufficient attention to the link between God's election in Jesus and God's providence, with the result that providence was not tied specifically to God's plans revealed in his Word (see III/1.30–33; 60–62, 75). To combat such drift, Barth will say that biblical history is the 'inner basis' for viewing all of world history (III/1.183–184, 196–204).

The psycho-physical life of man, and therefore the God who addresses Himself to this man in His grace, needs this. It must all be co-ordinated and integrated with the work of His grace and co-operate in it. It cannot in any degree help to effect this work. It cannot be its subject. It is genuinely an external and not an internal basis of this work, whether as primary cause or secondary cause. But it is indeed the external basis of this work. It is its necessary condition. This work of God, which is not a work inside God like the inner acts of the trinitarian God but most definitely a work outside of God, needs outside (outside of God) a theatre on which it can be enacted and unfolded. The created cosmos including man, or man within the created cosmos, is this theatre of the great acts of God in grace and salvation. With a view to this he is God's servant, instrument and material. But the theatre obviously cannot be the subject of the work enacted on it. It can only make it externally possible. This is done by the history of the creature as such. As it fulfils this purpose, it is indispensable. And the fact that it really serves this purpose is the meaning and problem of the doctrine of providence. This tells us that provision has been and is continually made for this theatre of the history of the covenant of grace, for time, space and opportunity for the divine work of grace and salvation. It tells us that this provision is made by God Himself. It speaks of the specific and as it were supplementary divine work of this provision. There will be time, space and opportunity for the history of the covenant of grace, for faith, knowledge, repentance, love and hope, until this history reaches its divinely appointed end. In great and little things alike all this will be continually furnished by the sustaining and overruling sway of God as the Lord of heaven and earth.[5] This is the divine co-ordination and integration of cosmic history with the history of salvation. It is seen by the Christian faith in providence as follows. Even as God's creatures, and within the world of other creatures, caught up in the great drama of being, we are not in an empty or alien place. It is not God's fault if we

---

5   Barth insists that human history is real – even at a 'psycho-physical' level (see above) – and, thus, creaturely agency is real. But the primary character in this cosmos is God, who creates, governs, and brings it to its end in Jesus. The electing God determines to be with us in Jesus; thus, we will exist and have significance, but we do so only as those shaped ec-centrically by God's determination and God's grace in Christ. Barth is advocating a form of *concursus* or compatibilism – the belief that divine sovereignty and real human responsibility concur or are compatible and, thus, are noncompetitive – as he expresses throughout the volume (III/1.132–133). He will also take up the traditional language of primary and secondary causality to make this point (see III/1.148, 160). For a wonderful analysis of Barth's noncompetitive view of divine and human agency, see Kathryn Tanner, *God and Creation in Christian Theology: Tyranny or Empowerment?* (Minneapolis: Fortress, 2005); George Hunsinger, 'Double Agency as a Test Case', in *How to Read Karl Barth: The Shape of His Theology* (New York: Oxford University Press, 1991), pp. 185–224. A classic example of the *concursus* doctrine is Thomas Aquinas, *Summa Theologiae*, 1a.22.

do not feel at home in our creatureliness and in this creaturely world.[6] This is a notion which can obtrude only if we suspend as it were our faith in God's providence and do not take seriously our membership of the kingdom of Christ. If we take this seriously, our eyes are open to the fact that the created world including our own existence fulfils that purpose and constitutes that theatre of God's glory. It and we are present in order that God may have time, space and opportunity to pursue in the history of the covenant of grace the work which is the goal of His creative will and to hasten towards which He has made it His own most proper cause with the interposition of Himself in Jesus Christ. We are in the house of our Father, in a world ordered according to His fatherly purpose, as we are in the created cosmos, under heaven and on earth, and ourselves cosmic creatures. It cannot help us, or deliver us, or reconcile us with God, that we are at home in this sense. Our salvation and future glory do not have their source here. Yet it is not a matter of indifference, nor can we perceive it without joy and gratitude. The fact that we are given by God Himself the necessary condition, the time, space and opportunity without which we could not have a share in the kingdom of Christ, is co-ordinated and integrated with the divine work of grace and salvation. We certainly cannot and must not say that even the picture of the theatre and home is wholly adequate. It lacks the things which are plainly brought out concerning God's working through the creature by the pictures of the servant and instrument, and concerning the creature as the object of God's working by that of the material. But in the sense indicated it does at least indicate the way in which the teleology of the divine work is to be described.

But the question as to the concrete meaning of that co-ordination, integration and co-operation can be carried a step further, and may finally be put as follows. What recognisable character is proper to creaturely occurrence in relation to what it has to accompany under God's providence? What does it mean for an understanding of creaturely occurrence that it takes place in this co-ordination under the divine rule? We venture to answer, as we may well do in the light of 1 Corinthians

---

6   To help us 'feel at home in our creatureliness', Barth considers common metaphors for God's providential care over creatures: first, the metaphor of Lord/servant; second, the metaphor of an instrument used by a master/doctor (see III/1.46–47). The first fails to note the true distinction between Creator and creature (for, really, servants are not of a different sort than lords), while the second fails to honour the activity of the creature (by employing the entirely passive metaphor of an instrument). Barth then acknowledges that concerning attempts to explain our 'co-operation in this history, we cannot give any true definition, but only some inadequate comparisons' (III/1.47). Barth immediately draws out the positive aspects of the servant/lord metaphor, and he will later return to the metaphor of an instrument (III/1.170–175), in both cases he critically appropriated the concept to serve theological ends.

13.12, that creaturely occurrence acquires in this co-ordination the character of a mirror. The distinction and inter-connexion of the two historical sequences are both brought out in this comparison. The original, God's primary working, is the divinely ruled history of the covenant. The mirror has nothing to add to this. In it the history of the creature as such cannot play any role. The mirror can confront it only as a reflector. It cannot repeat it, or imitate its occurrence. It can only reflect it. And as it does so it reverses it, the right being shown as the left and *vice versa*. Yet the fact remains that it gives us a correspondence and likeness. The creature does not exist for nothing in this co-ordination. It does not have for nothing the same Lord in both cases. Its history under His lordship as Creator is indeed a different one from that of the covenant instituted and fulfilled by the same Lord. But its twofold history is comparable as creature is comparable with creature (for even the history of the covenant takes place in the creaturely sphere). Jesus Christ as very God and very man, the basis and fulfilment of the history of the covenant, is certainly not to be found again in general creaturely occurrence. This cannot then be more than a mirror and likeness. And everything thus takes place differently for all the similarities. Yet there are similarities. The contrast and connexion of heaven and earth, of the inconceivable and conceivable world, is not the same as that of God and man in Jesus Christ; but it is similar. The confrontation and fellowship of man and woman in marriage is not the same as that of Christ and His community; but it is similar. The antitheses of above and below, of light and dark, of beautiful and ugly, of becoming and perishing, of joy and sadness, which are obviously to be found in creaturely occurrence, are certainly not the same as the true antithesis of grace and sin, deliverance and destruction, life and death, in the history of the covenant; but they are at least similar. In the same way there is something of good and bad, right and wrong, spirit and the opposite, if not in cosmic history as a whole, at least in the history of man. How strange it is that there is still a people Israel, and that this people is so brightly spotlighted in our own day! Nor is there lacking the phenomenon of gods and their worship, of sacrifices, prayers and the like, of religious history. We must be careful not to identify the reflection with the original, the history of the creature with the true history of salvation. For reasons which have nothing to do with its creatureliness, the former is one long history of the very opposite of salvation, as emerges even more clearly in religious history, and in what is known as 'Israel' in world history. But we cannot overlook or deny the fact that creaturely history is still similar in every respect to the history of salvation, as a reflection resembles the original. Creaturely history is not for nothing the theatre of the great acts of God, the Father's house. In virtue of its origin and in its whole structure its occurrence is calculated to reflect and illustrate and echo these acts of God. And this is what actually happens.

'The heavens declare the glory of God; and the firmament sheweth his handywork. Day unto day uttereth speech, and night unto night sheweth knowledge. There is no speech nor language; their voice is not heard. Yet their line is gone out through all the earth, and their words to the end of the world' (Ps. 19.1f.). What can be known of God is manifest (φανερόν) among men because God 'hath shewed it unto them' (ἐφανέρωσεν). His invisible being, namely, His eternal power and Godhead from the creation of the world, may well be understood as seen in His works (νοούμενα καθορᾶται, Rom. 1.19f.). But is this image really seen, this reflection recognised, this likeness under-stood? Are there the necessary seeing eyes to see it? The original must obviously be known to make this possible. But to know the original we need faith in God's Word and revelation to have a part in the history of the covenant, and then genuinely in creaturely history.[7] If we are children of the Father, we certainly recognise His house in more and more likenesses. But we shall certainly not be guilty of the confusion of thinking that the house of the Father, what can be only a similitude, is the matter itself. We shall always see the likenesses as such. We shall always hear the echo as such. We shall therefore be at home even in creaturely occurrence. Is it not the case that the biblical view of cosmic occurrence, of natural and universal history, is one which, as opposed to every kind of dualism, is open and relaxed, and in the best sense attentive and grateful? It can and must be this, for its presupposition is that creaturely occurrence has its meaning and substance and centre solely but genuinely in the history of the covenant. The Bible regards creaturely occurrence as the circumference of this centre. It sees it set in the light in view of this centre. This light is not extinguished by the

---

7   Barth follows the teaching of Calvin that the world is God's theatre. Barth elsewhere expresses great concern that sinful humans could perceive naturally what God is doing in the world; for example, he spoke out against Nazi propaganda that identified the Third Reich with the kingdom of God. Earlier in his career Barth stringently criticized Emil Brunner, another well-known Protesant theologian identified with the 'dialectical theology' movement in the 1920s. Barth thought Brunner minimized the effects of sin upon human knowledge of God – his hyperbolic rhetoric makes itself evident in the title of his reply to Brunner: *Nein!* (a very stark 'No'!). For a brief sketch of the lengthy and at times vociferous debate, see John Hart, 'The Barth-Brunner Correspondence', in *For the Sake of the World: Karl Barth and the Future of Ecclesial Theology* (ed. George Hunsinger; Grand Rapids: Eerdmans, 2004), pp. 35–40. But Barth never denies that God's revelation occurs throughout history; he consistently distinguishes between its presence and our perception, finding the difficulty to reside in the latter (III/1.223; cf. I/1.55). For a helpful analysis of Barth on nature, natural theology, and providence, see George Hunsinger, 'Epilogue: Secular Parables of the Truth', in *How to Read Karl Barth: The Shape of His Theology* (New York: Oxford University Press, 1991), pp. 234–80.

fact that what takes place outside the history of salvation is a history of the very opposite. This light is still light even when it becomes so deceptive in the perverted eyes of men, even when it causes so much of that confusion, even when it usually summons them to so much natural theology (in complete misunderstanding of the truth which is to be joyfully but soberly recognised at this point).

In great and little things alike world-occurrence is a reflection and likeness. We can and must say, of course, that this description, too, is not without its faults. It has something static about it. It gives rise to the impression that creaturely occurrence is an object which can simply be speculatively contemplated, whereas it, no less than the history of the covenant, is really an occurrence which comes upon man as such, and claims him totally, and leaves him no place for mere contemplation or idle experience. A mirror is indeed a futile implement which can be dispensed with if necessary. And when creaturely occurrence is called a mirror it may easily be forgotten that in it there take place service, work and action. Speculative thinkers are warned that they can find no entrance here; that this is only one aspect of the problem; that this aspect cannot be absolutised as such but can have significance only in respect of the character of creaturely occurrence in its relation to the divine activity of grace and salvation. And those who perhaps fear the rightly suspect 'analogy of being' are reminded of the earlier descriptions in which it is quite clear that there can self-evidently be no question of anything but the 'analogy of faith' or relation even in this description of creaturely occurrence as a mirror and likeness.[8]

As we sum up, we must try to be more precise. For not only this final venture but the whole discussion of the concrete meaning of the divine co-ordination and integration of creaturely history with that of the covenant of grace, or of the divinely occasioned co-operation of the creature in this matter, stands in need of more precise statement. We have spoken of the function of creaturely occurrence, and described it as that of a servant or instrument. We have spoken of its *telos*, and described it by calling the created world a theatre. We have spoken of its character, and finally described it as a mirror and likeness. These

---

8   As seen in the last chapter, Barth expressed worries about the Roman Catholic approach to nature and grace (the so-called 'analogy of being': *analogia entis*), which he thought conflated Creator and creature; in its place, he proposed the existence of an 'analogy of faith': *analogia fidei*. This approach highlights the fact that our understanding of fellowship between God and humans is the reasoning of faith, rather than an observation of direct links or points of contact between the two (in this case: Barth's worry that providential governance might be assumed to be discerned via some intrinsic purpose to human history; cf. III/1.102). As seen in the last chapter, though, Barth may have overstated the differences between (at least some versions of) the two approaches.

statements constitute a legitimate answer to the question of the meaning and purpose of this occurrence, and a permissible description of it as the external basis of the history of the covenant, so long as they are all taken together, the fragmentary nature of each of them being perceived and therefore none of them understood or asserted as though it were absolute. Each is merely an imperfect indication of what is here to be described, namely, the divine rule operative in creaturely occurrence. We are not to think, therefore, that what is to be described is really indicated or introduced in any one of these descriptions.

This condition, on which alone all that we have said here is valid, must finally be given an even stricter formulation. What we have said is legitimate only if we realise that it cannot be said of creaturely occurrence in itself and as such, but only of creaturely occurrence as it takes place under the sway of God's sovereign and actual providence. It cannot be said of qualities and determinations inherent to it, but only of qualities and determinations ascribed and imparted to it by God's action in the power of His omnipotent mercy. Creation in itself and as such never has the power, capacity or competence on the basis of the election of grace to be the servant and instrument of the God who acts in the covenant of grace and kingdom of Jesus Christ, to be the theatre of His action and therefore to afford it time, space and opportunity, to be for His children their Father's house and as such a mirror and likeness of His fatherly action. It has no power for this. How could it have? It was not with God when His counsel of grace took shape concerning it. It can know and fulfil the will of God only to the extent that in this counsel decision is made concerning its existence as such. But as creation it has no knowledge of the ways which God will take with it as it exists, and no control of the part which He will allot it. It can neither take, give nor keep the function, purpose and character in which God will and does use it in His dealings with it. We cannot say, therefore, that in itself and as such it possesses and has these qualities and determinations. It possesses and has them only as it receives them, as they are given it by God.[9] We thus say too much if in the sense of an ontological definition we try to say that creation *is* God's servant and instrument, the theatre, mirror and likeness of His gracious and saving action. At this point any 'is' can strictly relate only to moments in God's universal rule in which creation may become a servant and instrument, a theatre, mirror and likeness, by God's sovereign and actual will. It is all this as

9   Not only covenant, but also providence comes as a second topic to be considered after creation (see III/1.8–9). Contrary to modern notions of progress and evolutionary optimism, Barth believes there is no intrinsic purpose to history apart from the Gospel, which is the inbreaking of an ec-centric purpose (III/1.36, 170–175, 184).

He takes it into His omnipotent and merciful hand in the execution
of His plan, giving it these qualities and determinations. It is it in the
event of the divinely accomplished co-ordination and integration, in
the event of the co-operation for good, to which it is called, authorised
and capacitated by Him. That it is created good and even very good by
Him means only that it is prepared by Him to be grasped in this way.
He has not prepared the creature in vain or for anything else. But as
He speaks and commands, it is so (Ps. 33.9). And it is so in the manner
and form, in the function, with the *telos* and character, which it is to
have ineluctably and with supreme objectivity, and therefore not merely
in the sense of a human opinion, but with God's own truth. We must
not abstract from this divine Speaker and Commander if we are to give
a legitimate answer to this question of the concrete sense of creaturely
occurrence. We must think always of God's living hand which continually lends creaturely occurrence this concrete sense. As the creature
cannot anticipate its creation, or give itself existence and essence, so it
cannot anticipate God's providence or its use in God's living hand, as
though it already were what it must be in this use, or already had what it
must have in it. It can only be ready for God, or more exactly for God's
action in the covenant of grace and kingdom of Christ. It can only wait
for His omnipotent mercy, acquiring its function, *telos* and character,
and becoming God's servant and action, the theatre of His action and
mirror and likeness of His glory, in the event of His rule and dominion.
We must see clearly that this rule of God's providence over and in
creation does not give up or break off, and has and leaves no gaps.
It is not the case, then, that sometimes the creature does not acquire
these qualities and determinations. The hand of God never rests. And
it will never withdraw. Everything is always involved in its power and
therefore in that receiving and becoming. For the faithfullness of God
never ceases in the kingdom of His grace. There is no moment, place
or situation in which His creature escapes Him or becomes indifferent,
in which He has no further use for His creature or some part of it, or
in which He forgets it. But we must be clear that it is God's faithfullness
alone if creation in its totality is in fact always involved in this receiving
and becoming, and may thus have this function, *telos* and character, and
be this servant and instrument, this theatre, mirror and likeness. God
does not owe it His love. He is under no obligation to co-ordinate and
integrate it with His work in this way, and enable it to co-operate in
His action. It has no glory of its own in this. It can only participate in
His glory and glorify Him. What help would it be to have existence
and essence by God's creation, and therefore to be made ready for His
use, if He did not continually take it to Himself, and lend it this dignity
and significance, and cause it to participate in His work, and give it the

appropriate glory? What would it be without this active good-pleasure of its Creator? It can only receive, and receive grace for grace, and receive of His fullness (Jn. 1.16).

This is the insight without which there could be no legitimate answer to the question of the concrete sense of creaturely occurrence under God's providence, and of its participation in the doing of God's gracious and saving will. We shall conclude by mentioning some of the important deductions to be drawn from this insight.

1. We began this final discussion with the assertion that there can be no question of an independent co-operation of creation in the establishment, direction and fulfilment of the history of the covenant of grace, of a participation of creation in the procuring, attainment and mediation of the love of God which comes to it in this covenant.[10] We made this assertion without giving any reason for it in this particular context. We can now give this specific reason. It takes the form of a conclusion from the lesser to the greater. There is no question of an independence of creation in its co-ordination and integration with the divine work of grace, or in respect of its determination as a servant and instrument, a theatre, mirror and likeness of the kingdom of grace. The free love of God alone can give it this function, *telos* and character, and not its own goodness. But if this is so in this sphere, how much more is it the case when it is a matter of the preservation, reconciliation and redemption of the creature fallen into sin and hopelessly threatened in consequence! Since it has no glory, merit or claim of its own on the one side, since God has no obligations towards it, since it is referred exclusively to the active good-pleasure of its Creator in this whole sphere, how could it possibly add anything to God's work on the other with its own capacity and action? How could it possibly be a creature who is co-redeemer?

2. Creaturely occurrence is the external basis of the history of the covenant. How far this is the case we have tried to show in our consideration of its concrete meaning. But after our last and more precise statement, we cannot overemphasise the fact that it is this external basis, and has therefore constitutive significance even for the occurrence of the history of the covenant, to the extent that it is enacted under God's providence, and this significance is not withdrawn from it, but continually given it by God.[11] It thus has it, but only as it may receive it. Not

---

10   Barth's first inference is that creaturely history is dependent on a distinct history: God's own perfect life (see III/1.160–164, 430).

11   Barth's second inference is that creaturely history has real integrity and is no façade or delusion (see III/1.430). Again, there is a noncompetitive relationship between God's sovereign lordship and real human agency. As Kathryn Tanner has said: 'A non-competitive relation between creatures and God means that the creature does not decrease so that God may increase. The

even momentarily, therefore, can we think away God's free faithfullness towards it if we are to see this significance, and see it in its capacity as the external basis of the history of the covenant. God Himself and God alone continually sees to this external basis of the history of the covenant. He Himself and He alone makes creaturely occurrence His servant and instrument, the theatre, mirror and likeness of His action. It thus follows that we can recognise it as such only in faith in God and His free faithfullness. Hence there follows the simple but pregnant fact that in this respect we walk by faith and not by sight. We can never have this recognition if we look past the internal basis of the history of the covenant, namely, the divine election of grace revealed in Jesus Christ. This recognition can thus take place only in the act of hearing the Word of God, in the act of adoring His inconceivable goodness, in the act of gratitude and the corresponding willingness and readiness to do the will of God. It can be achieved only in the light and power of the Holy Ghost and by the man whom the Father draws to the Son and the Son to the Father. In relation to this recognition we do not find ourselves in a forecourt but in the very centre of the sanctuary. As the kingdom of Jesus Christ is revealed to men in Jesus Christ, so too is the sway of divine providence, the determination of creaturely occurrence, its function, *telos* and character. It is always a matter of recognition from within outwards, from the cross and resurrection of Jesus Christ to all other occurrence, from God's grace to the world of its addressees and recipients. The freedom of the divine providence by which all things are upheld and sustained and meaningful and right can be known only in the freedom of faith which has its origin where God Himself does the work for the sake of which He has created all things, and where He is revealed in this work.

3. This way can be traversed only in this direction. Not even subsequently can this sequence be reversed.[12] We are confronted by the necessary impotence of all systems which radically or practically, primarily or subsequently, abstract from God's work of grace and the kingdom of Jesus Christ. In making this abstraction, they forfeit their inward and outward vision. They lack that which alone could justify their vaunting claims. Even without the freedom of faith, as those who are closed to the revelation of God, we could investigate in all

---

glorification of God does not come at the expense of creatures. The more full the creature is with gifts the more the creature should look in gratitude to the fullness of the gift-giver. The fuller the giver the greater the bounty to others' (*Jesus, Humanity, and the Trinity: A Brief Systematic Theology* [Minneapolis: Fortress, 2001], pp. 2–3).

12 Barth's third inference is that God's agency must be considered before the creature's reality: first God, then the creature (III/1.52, 108–109, 134, 430). The material order of the gospel – the living God gives life to others – must shape the epistemological or pedagogical order.

kinds of ways the meaning of creaturely occurrence. But on what principle of exposition could we give an answer? If we do not know of a Creator, we do not know that in world-occurrence we have to do with a creaturely and therefore relative occurrence taking place in a definite connexion and definitely ruled in this connexion. We shall therefore posit absolutely one of its aspects, even perhaps that of its insolubility. But how then can we avoid ascribing to it an autonomous significance supposedly found in this aspect? How can we escape the unending debate whether this significance of the external world is to be found more in its historical aspects or more in its natural, more in its law-abiding or more in its contingent, more in its spiritual or more in its material, or in what combination of all of them? How can we justify ourselves in ascribing this particular significance to world-occurrence? World-occurrence as such does not speak unequivocally. If we hear it say this or that, how can we justify ourselves except on the basis of a significance with which we ourselves have already encountered it? From world-occurrence as such there are obviously only arbitrary and highly debatable ways to a world principle whose superiority, power and credibility can even remotely be compared with the world rule of God. And in that centre from which man in the freedom of faith and under the constraint of the Word of God can continually see afresh the ever new and living work of His hand, he stands quite alone, renouncing his own cleverness and responsibility, his own decision for this or that possibility, his own opinion. What is a world-view if it does not consist in the contemplation of a world rule, and therefore of a reality which is superior to the world and all its contemplation and interpretation, and can effectively order and co-ordinate world-occurrence? But how can there be the contemplation of a world rule if there can be no question of that of a world Ruler?

4. We have said that this sequence, and this way of considering it, cannot subsequently be reversed but must always be from within outwards. But this means that there can be a contemplation of the divine world-rule, and therefore of world-occurrence under this rule, and therefore a Christian view of things, only in the movement of faith itself from within outwards, and in the concrete realisation of its perception.[13] We have said that this perception or recognition is possible only in the light and power of the Holy Ghost, in the freedom of faith in which the freedom of the divine providence is manifested. But on both sides this means that there cannot be a closed and static Christian

---

13   Barth's fourth inference is that the ec-centric nature of providence (that human life is governed by someone outside the sphere of human existence: a Creator) means that this governance is perceived only by faith.

system. What might be given this name can only be the insight of many or few individuals grounded in a concrete perception of God's work of grace and then expressed as such in an equally concrete perception of God's action in the creaturely sphere. This insight can never take the more solid form of a more permanent view, of theoretical notions of what constitutes God's work in the creaturely sphere, of definitive assertions concerning the extent to which creaturely occurrence is God's servant, instrument, theatre, mirror and likeness. For the freedom of faith in which alone this insight is possible must always be given to man afresh as the gracious gift of the Holy Spirit. And when it is given afresh, it must always be a new freedom. The establishment of a fixed Christian view, of a lasting picture of the relationship between Creator and creature, would necessarily mean that in taking to-day the insight given him to-day man hardens himself against receiving a new and better one to-morrow. Having thought and spoken as a believer to-day, he would no longer do so to-morrow, but place himself on the same level as the unhappy inventors and champions of non-Christian systems. For what distinguishes him from them but the freedom of faith? What will distinguish him from them if he renounces the freedom of faith to-morrow? The knowledge received in enlightening and empowering by the Holy Ghost will never be closed but always open. Yet it is the objective side which is really decisive. As we have seen, we do not have to perceive immanent qualities and determinations of creaturely occurrence, but divine actions by which it is continually given afresh its function, *telos* and character. In the freedom of faith man follows the way and movement of the divine providence which is free in a very different sense. What God has done to-day, and revealed to man as His action, He will do again to-morrow, but He will perhaps do it quite differently, and reveal it to man in a very different form. That to-morrow as to-day He will give creaturely occurrence its function, *telos* and character is the faithfullness of God on which we can and should count, the constant element for which the believer will look even in respect of to-morrow. But what he cannot say is how God will do it. His world-view as his understanding of creaturely occurrence and the divine providence reigning in and over it will always be that which corresponds to the present measure of his faith and knowledge, to the insight given him by God to-day. It will certainly be a modest insight. Probably it will not usually concern itself with larger or total issues. It will be content to be a clear perception of individual points and questions making possible practical decisions for the next stretches of the way. It will probably consist less in the maintaining of principles and leading tendencies than in the discovery of a small series of promising standpoints. It will probably display many reservations and gaps. In this form it is less likely to acquire a form which will compel the believer sooner or later to become entangled in blatant self-contradictions. It will not become so easily the basis of a programmeme or party, or an object of debate. It will be an instrument to promote understanding with as many others as possible. But within these limits it will always be sure of itself and fruitful. If the matter is understood within these limits, we may well say that as the believer has faith in God's providence in world-occurrence he may live with a partial world-view which is provisional and modest but also binding. He will not, of course, believe in this partial world-view.[14] But as he believes only in God the Lord, he will have enough light to make some such partial view of world-occurrence – the part which meets his own requirements – indispensable. And he will be the more glad of it the more he is prepared to be continually led from this point.[15] Man has always many new things to see even when he ostensibly made a serious beginning long ago, and has thus acquired no little genuine skill, in having open eyes for the ways of God in creaturely occurrence.

14 Faith is directed to the providential God, not to one's perception of that providential work.
15 Here and elsewhere Barth addresses the practical import of the doctrine of providence (III/1: 14, 149, 154), following the tradition of the Heidelberg Catechism: 'Q. 28. What advantage comes from acknowledging God's creation and providence? A. We learn that we are to be patient in adversity, grateful in the midst of blessing, and to trust our faithful God and Father for the future, assured that no creature shall separate us from his love, since all creatures are so completely in his hand that without his will they cannot even move'.

CHAPTER 10

NOTHINGNESS: SIN AS THE IMPOSSIBLE POSSIBILITY

There are few heresies so pernicious as that of a God who faces nothingness more or less unaffected and unconcerned, and the parallel doctrine of man as one who must engage in independent conflict against it. We know well enough what it means to be alien and adverse to grace and therefore without it. A graceless God would be a null and evil God, and a self-sufficient, self-reliant creaturely subject a null and evil creature. If a doctrine of nothingness is not unyielding on this point, nothingness itself will triumph.[1]

Barth's doctrine of sin appears in volume three, following his teaching on creation, anthropology, and providence. It is followed by his angelology and demonology. The paragraph on sin (§50) addresses four matters by focusing on sin as nothingness (*Das Nichtige*): 'the problem of nothingness', 'the misconception of nothingness', 'the knowledge of nothingness', and 'the reality of nothingness'.

Barth will go on in volume four to address the concrete forms of sin: as pride (§60), as sloth (§65), and as falsehood (§70). Sin arises in his discussion of salvation, because 'the verdict of God pronounced in the resurrection of Jesus Christ crucified for us discloses who it was that was set aside in His death' (IV/1: 358). By attending to the revelation of the saving solution of the gospel, the believer can understand something of the nature of their problem. John Webster has observed what Barth is and is not doing in presenting sin in relation to the work of Christ: 'Barth's Christological determination of sin is not so much an attempt to dislocate "theological" from "empirical" reality, as an argument born of a sense that human persons are characteristically self-deceived'.[2] In other words, to speak of sin is not the same as saying something is 'bad', though sin is surely 'bad'; sin is a term spoken by faith and affirmed only in light of the gospel's defeat of it, precisely because humans are so inclined to fantasy and delusion.

---

1   *CD* III/3.360.
2   John Webster, '"The Firmest Grasp of the Real": Barth on Original Sin', in *Barth's Moral Theology: Human Action in Barth's Thought* (Edinburgh/Grand Rapids: T & T Clark/Eerdmans, 1998), p. 69.

Barth consistently employs the terms 'impossible possibility' and 'ontological impossibility' to refer to sin. Since God has elected humans for fellowship in Jesus Christ, sin has no ground or basis in God – indeed it has no foundation whatsoever (III/3.353). Though it is 'under the control of God' (III/3.289), sin is against his will.[3] Sin is absurd and parasitic: a negation and a nothingness. 'Nothingness is that which God does not will. It lives only by the fact that it is that which God does not will. But it does live by this fact' (III/3.352). It may be nothing and unwilled by God, but it lives and cannot be denied. Furthermore, he will even say that sin is 'real nothingness' (III/3.349), a seemingly oxymoronic thing to say. Barth addresses the seeming oddity of saying that nothingness can be real in this excerpt from III/3.

Bibliography

Karl Barth, *Christ and Adam: Man and Humanity in Romans 5* (Edinburgh: Oliver & Boyd, 1956).

Wolf Krötke, *Sin and Nothingness in the Theology of Karl Barth* (Studies in Reformed Theology and History NS10; trans. Philip Ziegler; Princeton: Princeton Theological Seminary, 2005).

John Webster, ' "The Firmest Grasp of the Real": Barth on Original Sin', in *Barth's Moral Theology: Human Action in Barth's Thought* (Edinburgh/Grand Rapids: T & T Clark/Eerdmans, 1998), pp. 65–76.

Text (*CD* III/3.349–356)

What is real nothingness?[4]

1. In this question objection may well be taken to the word 'is.' Only God and His creature really and properly are. But nothingness is

---

3   Traditional dogmatics has employed a distinction between God's revealed/moral will (spoken of here, namely, what God teaches as befitting his character) and God's hidden/decretive will (not referenced here, but referring to God's providential rule over all things, mentioned here tangentially with reference to sin being 'under the control of God' in the paragraph summary on III/3.289). See Herman Bavinck, *Reformed Dogmatics*, volume 4: *God and Creation* (ed. John Bolt; trans. John Vriend; Grand Rapids: Baker Academic, 2004), pp. 242–9. While Barth expresses great concern at any notion of a hidden will (what he so often calls a *decretum absolutum* in II/2), he nonetheless operates with something like this distinction throughout the discussion of providence here in III/3 (see, e.g., III/3.196ff.) and the material on human freedom to following in III/4.

4   Barth introduces 'nothingness' in §50, summarized as follows: 'Under the control of God world-occurrence is threatened and actually corrupted by the nothingness which is inimical to the will of the Creator and therefore to the nature of His good creature. God has judged nothingness by His mercy as revealed and effective in Jesus Christ. Pending the final revelation that it is already refuted and abolished, God determines the sphere, the manner, the measure and the subordinate relationship to His Word and work in which it may still operate' (III/3.289).

neither God nor His creature. Thus it can have nothing in common with God and His creatures. But it would be foolhardy to rush to the conclusion that it is therefore nothing, i.e., that it does not exist. God takes it into account. He is concerned with it. He strives against it, resists and overcomes it. If God's reality and revelation are known in His presence and action in Jesus Christ, He is also known as the God who is confronted by nothingness, for whom it constitutes a problem, who takes it seriously, who does not deal with it incidentally but in the fullness of the glory of His deity, who is not engaged indirectly or mediately but with His whole being, involving Himself to the utmost. If we accept this, we cannot argue that because it has nothing in common with God and His creature nothingness is nothing, i.e., it does not exist. That which confronts God in this way, and is seriously treated by Him, is surely not nothing or non-existent. In the light of God's relationship to it we must accept the fact that in a third way of its own nothingness 'is.' All conceptions or doctrine which would deny or diminish or minimise this 'is' are untenable from the Christian stand-point. Nothingness is not nothing.[5] Quite apart from the inadmissibility of its content, this proposition would be self-contradictory. But it 'is' nothingness. Its nature and being are those which can be assigned to it within this definition. But because it stands before God as such they must be assigned to it. They cannot be controverted without misap-prehending God Himself.

2. Again, nothingness is not simply to be equated with what is *not*, i.e., not God and not the creature. God is God and not the creature, but this does not mean that there is nothingness in God. On the contrary, this 'not' belongs to His perfection. Again, the creature is creature and not God, yet this does not mean that as such it is null or nothingness. If in the relationship between God and creature a 'not' is involved, the 'not' belongs to the perfection of the relationship, and even the second 'not' which characterises the creature belongs to its perfection. Hence it would be blasphemy against God and His work if nothingness were to be sought in this 'not,' in the non-divinity of the creature. The diversities and frontiers of the creaturely world contain many 'nots.' No single creature is all-inclusive. None is or resembles another. To each belongs its own place and time, and in these its own manner, nature and existence. What we have called the 'shadow side' of creation is consti-tuted by the 'not' which in this twofold respect, as its distinction from God and its individual distinctiveness, pertains to creaturely nature. On

---

5   Here the Christian tradition has spoken often of sin as parasitic or of sin as absence and lack (technically 'privation'). Of course, an absence or a lack is not itself something; rather, it is the parasitic removal of something.

this shadow side the creature is contiguous to nothingness, for this 'not' is at once the expression and frontier of the positive will, election and activity of God. When the creature crosses the frontier from the one side, and it is invaded from the other, nothingness achieves actuality in the creaturely world. But in itself and as such this frontier is not nothingness, nor has the shadow side of creation any connexion with it. Therefore all conceptions and doctrines which view nothingness as an essential and necessary determination of being and existence and therefore of the creature, or as an essential determination of the original and creative being of God Himself, are untenable from the Christian standpoint. They are untenable on two grounds, first, because they misrepresent the creature and even the Creator Himself, and second, because they confound the legitimate 'not' with nothingness, and are thus guilty of a drastic minimisation of the latter.

3. Since real nothingness is real in this third fashion peculiar to itself, not resembling either God or the creature but taken seriously by God Himself, and since it is not identical either with the distinction and frontier between God and creation or with those within the creaturely world, its revelation and knowledge cannot be a matter of the insight which is accessible to the creature itself and is therefore set under its own choice and control. Standing before God in its own characteristic way which is very different from that of the creature, the object of His concern and action, His problem and adversary and the negative goal of His victory, nothingness does not possess a nature which can be assessed nor an existence which can be discovered by the creature. There is no accessible relationship between the creature and nothingness. Hence nothingness cannot be an object of the creature's natural knowledge. It is certainly an objective reality for the creature. The latter exists objectively in encounter with it. But it is disclosed to the creature only as God is revealed to the latter in His critical relationship. The creature knows it only as it knows God in His being and attitude against it. It is an element in the history of the relationship between God and the creature in which God precedes the creature in His acts, thus revealing His will to the creature and informing it about Himself. As this occurs and the creature attains to the truth – the truth about God's purpose and attitude and therefore about itself – through the Word of God, the encounter of the creature with true nothingness is also realised and recognised. Of itself, the creature cannot recognise this encounter and what it encounters.[6] It experiences and endures it. But it also misin-

---

6   Barth insists that the creature is totally depraved, that is, sinful in every aspect of their being. Therefore, their spiritual perception is thwarted and distorted and incapable of identifying sin within them. The sinner is 'crooked even in his knowledge of his crookedness' (IV/1.361).

terprets it, as has always happened. Calumniating God and His work, it misrepresents it as a necessity of being or nature, as a given factor, as a peculiarity of existence which is perhaps deplorable, perhaps also justifiable, perhaps to be explained in terms of perfection or simply to be dismissed as non-existent, as something which can be regarded as supremely positive in relation to God, or even as a determination of God Himself. All these conceptions and doctrines, whatever their content, are untenable from a Christian standpoint if only because they are contingent upon an arbitrary and impotent appraisal of what can only make itself known in the judgment of God, and is thus knowable only as God pronounces His sentence, while its malignity and corruption find supreme expression in the assumption of the creature that of itself and at its own discretion it is able to discover its nature and existence.

4. The ontic context in which nothingness is real is that of God's activity as grounded in His election, of His activity as the Creator, as the Lord of His creatures, as the King of the covenant between Himself and man which is the goal and purpose of His creation. Grounded always in election, the activity of God is invariably one of jealousy, wrath and judgment. God is also holy, and this means that His being and activity take place in a definite opposition, in a real negation, both defensive and aggressive. Nothingness is that from which God separates Himself and in face of which He asserts Himself and exerts His positive will. If the biblical conception of the God whose activity is grounded in election and is therefore holy fades or disappears, there will also fade and disappear the knowledge of nothingness, for it will necessarily become pointless. Nothingness has no existence and cannot be known except as the object of God's activity as always a holy activity. The biblical conception, as we now recall it, is as follows. God elects, and therefore rejects what He does not elect. God wills, and therefore opposes what He does not will. He says Yes, and therefore says No to that to which He has not said Yes. He works according to His purpose, and in so doing rejects and dismisses all that gainsays it. Both of these activities, grounded in His

Friedrich Nietzsche expresses the sinful denial of this truth in an aphorism: '"I did this," says my memory. "I cannot have done this," says my pride, remaining inexorable. Eventually, my memory yields' (Aphorism 68). Flannery O'Connor expresses the Christian discovery of this truth in a dialogue: '"For myself", she continued, "... I believe that what's right today is wrong tomorrow and that the time to enjoy yourself is now, so long as you let others do the same. I'm as good, Mr. Motes," she said, "not believing in Jesus as a many a one that does." "You're better," he said, leaning forward suddenly. "If you believed in Jesus, you wouldn't be so good."' (*Wise Blood* [New York: Farrar, Strauss, and Giroux, 2007], p. 221). Barth castigates Protestant as well as Roman Catholic theology that identifies knowledge of sin with a gospel-less 'natural law' given to all people (III/3.308; IV/1.365, 388–389, 403). It is worth noting that Barth's characterization of 'natural law' approaches does not fit every such programme, for many approaches do accent the gracious nature of even such 'natural' knowledge.

election and decision, are necessary elements in His sovereign action. He
is Lord both on the right hand and on the left. It is only on this basis that
nothingness 'is,' but on this basis it really 'is.' As God is Lord on the left
hand as well, He is the basis and Lord of nothingness too. Consequently
it is not adventitious. It is not a second God, nor self-created. It has no
power save that which it is allowed by God. It, too, belongs to God.
It 'is' problematically because it is only on the left hand of God, under
His No, the object of His jealousy, wrath and judgment. It 'is,' not as
God and His creation are, but only in its own improper way, as inherent
contradiction, as impossible possibility. Yet because it is on the left hand
of God, it really 'is' in this paradoxical manner. Even on His left hand the
activity of God is not in vain. He does not act for nothing. His rejection,
opposition, negation and dismissal are powerful and effective like all His
works because they, too, are grounded in Himself, in the freedom and
wisdom of His election. That which God renounces and abandons in
virtue of His decision is not merely nothing. It is nothingness, and has
as such its own being, albeit malignant and perverse. A real dimension
is disclosed, and existence and form are given to a reality in its own
category, in the fact that God is wholly and utterly not the Creator in
this respect. Nothingness is that which God does not will. It lives only
by the fact that it is that which God does not will. But it does live by this
fact. For not only what God wills, but what He does not will, is potent,
and must have a real correspondence. What really corresponds to that
which God does not will is nothingness.

The first and most impressive mention of nothingness in the Bible is
to be found at the very beginning in Gen. 1.2 (cf. *CD.*, III, 1, p. 101 f.),
in which there is a reference to the chaos which the Creator has already
rejected, negated, passed over and abandoned even before He utters His
first creative Word, which He has already consigned to the past and to
oblivion even before the beginning of time at His command. Chaos
is the unwilled and uncreated reality which constitutes as it were the
periphery of His creation and creature. It is that which, later depicted in
very suitable mythological terms and conceptions, is antithetical both to
God Himself and to the world of heaven and earth which He selected,
willed and created. It is a mere travesty of the universe. It is the horrible
perversion which opposes God and tempts and threatens His creature. It
is that which, though it is succeeded and overcome by light, can never
itself be light but must always remain darkness. Note that the first creative
work (Gen. 1.3f.) is simply separation – the separation of light from
darkness, of the waters on the earth from the threatening waters above
the firmament, of the dry land from the seas. Note also that with this
separation there arises even within the good creation of God a side which
is as it were the neighbour and frontier of chaos. But chaos is not night,

or the waters above the firmament, or the earthly sea. It still remains not merely distinct from the works of God, but excluded by the operation of God, a fleeting shadow and a receding frontier. Only in this way can we say that it 'is.' But in this way it undoubtedly 'is,' and is thus subject to the divine sovereignty. In this way it is present from the very outset with God and His creature. In this way it is involved from the very outset in the history of the relationship between God and His creature, and therefore from the very outset the biblical witness to this history takes its existence into account. The sin of man as depicted in Gen. 3 confirms the accuracy of our definition. It is purely and simply what God did not, does not and cannot will. It has the essence only of non-essence, and only as such can it exist. Yet the sin of man also confirms the real existence of nothingness. Nothingness is a factor so real that the creature of God, and among His creatures man especially in whom the purpose of creation is revealed, is not only confronted by it and becomes its victim, but makes himself its agent. And all the subsequent history of the relationship between God and His creature is marked by the fact that man is the sinner who has submitted and fallen a victim to chaos. The issue in this whole history is the repulse and final removal of the threat thus actualised. And God Himself is always the One who first takes this threat seriously, who faces and throws Himself against it, who strives with chaos, who persists in His attitude, who continues and completes the action which He has already undertaken as Creator in this respect, negating and rejecting it. As He affirms and elects and works His proper work, the work of His grace, God is always active in His strange work as well. And He is always holy. Therefore He always wills that His creature should be holy. He wills to take part in its conflict. Since it is really His own cause, He wills to place Himself alongside it in this conflict.

Nothingness 'is,' therefore, in its connexion with the activity of God. It 'is' because and as and so long as God is against it. It 'is' only in virtue of the fact that God is against it in jealousy, wrath and judgment. It 'is' only within the limits thus ordained. But within these limits it 'is.' From the Christian standpoint, therefore, any conception must be regarded as untenable if it ascribes to nothingness any other existence than in confrontation with God's non-willing. It would be untenable from a Christian point of view to ascribe autonomous existence independent of God or willed by Him like that of His creature.[7] Only the divine

---

7   In this paragraph Barth is opposing any form of metaphysical dualism, wherein evil has self-existence and endures independent of the providential will of God. Elsewhere Barth denies dualism as well: 'Nothingness is radically but not autonomously opposed to the creation and covenant of God' (III/3.332); '[T]he door has been closed on all dualistic views of evil by the eternal resolve of God which became a historical event on Golgotha' (IV/1.409).

non-willing can be accepted as the ground of its existence. Equally untenable from a Christian standpoint, however, is any conception in which its existence in opposition to the divine non-willing is denied and it is declared to be a mere semblance. Within this limit nothingness is no semblance but a reality, just as God's non-willing in relation to it, and the whole strange work of the divine jealousy, wrath and judgment, is no semblance but a reality.

5. The character of nothingness derives from its ontic peculiarity. It is evil. What God positively wills and performs in the proper work of His election, of His creation, of His preservation and overruling rule of the creature revealed in the history of His covenant with man, is His grace – the free goodness of His condescension in which He wills, identifying Himself with the creature, to accept solidarity and to be present with it, to be Himself its Guarantor, Helper and King, and therefore to do the best possible for it. What God does not will and therefore negates and rejects, what can thus be only the object of His strange work, of His jealousy, wrath and judgment, is a being that refuses and resists and therefore lacks His grace. This being which is alien and adverse to grace and therefore without it, is that of nothingness. This negation of His grace is chaos, the world which He did not choose or will, which He could not and did not create, but which, as He created the actual world, He passed over and set aside, marking and excluding it as the eternal past, the eternal yesterday. And this is evil in the Christian sense, namely, what is alien and adverse to grace, and therefore without it. In this sense nothingness is really privation, the attempt to defraud God of His honour and right and at the same time to rob the creature of its salvation and right. For it is God's honour and right to be gracious, and this is what nothingness contests.[8] It is also the salvation and right of the creature to receive and live by the grace of God, and this is what it disturbs and obstructs. Where this privation occurs, nothingness is present; and where nothingness is present this privation occurs, i.e., evil, that which is utterly inimical first to God and then to His creature. The grace of God is the basis and norm of all being, the source and

---

8   In *CD* IV Barth will discuss sin by way of exegeting key biblical stories (e.g. the golden calf in Exodus 32, Ahab and Naboth in 1 Kings 21). These stories are lenses through which Christians can see all their sinful lives: not simply as morally problematic or personally/socially destructive (though sin is all of these things), but fundamentally as idolatry and the failure to give God glory, laud, and honour. Such idolatry locates the creature in the place of the Creator; as Augustine argued: 'All those who wander far away and set themselves up against you are imitating you, but in a perverse way; yet by this very mimicry they proclaim that you are the Creator of the whole of nature and that in consequence there is no place whatever where we can hide from your presence' (*Confessions*, bk. 2, sec. 14). While all sin is idolatry against God, it also takes numerous shapes. So Barth will address three major forms of sin within his doctrine of reconciliation: sloth, pride, and falsehood.

criterion of all good. Measured by this standard, as the negation of God's grace, nothingness is intrinsically evil. It is both perverting and perverted. In this capacity it does not confront either God or the creature neutrally. It is not merely a third factor. It opposes both as an enemy, offending God and threatening His creature. From above as well as from below, it is the impossible and intolerable. By reason of this character, whether in the form of sin, evil or death, it is inexplicable as a natural process or condition. It is altogether inexplicable. The explicable is subject to a norm and occurs within a standard. But nothingness is absolutely without norm or standard. The explicable conforms to a law, nothingness to none. It is simply aberration, transgression, evil. For this reason it is inexplicable, and can be affirmed only as that which is inherently inimical. For this reason it can be apprehended in its aspect of sin only as guilt, and in its aspect of evil and death only as retribution and misery, but never as a natural process or condition, never as a subject of systematic formulation, even though the system be dialectical. Being hostile before and against God, and also before and against His creature, it is outside the sphere of systematisation. It cannot even be viewed dialectically, let alone resolved. Its defeat can be envisaged only as the purpose and end of the history of God's dealings with His creature, and in no other way. As it is real only by reason of God's strange work, the divine negation and rejection, so it can be seen and understood only in the light of God's proper work, only in relation to the sovereign counter-offensive of God's free grace. It 'is' only as the disorder at which this counter-offensive is aimed, only as the non-essence which it judges, only as the enemy of God and His creation. We thus affirm that it is necessary to dismiss as non-Christian all those conceptions in which its character as evil is openly or secretly, directly or indirectly, conjured away, and its reality is in some way regarded or grouped with that of God and His creature. Where God and His creature are known, and His free grace as the basic order of their relationship, nothingness can only be understood as opposition and resistance to this basic order and cannot therefore be regarded or grouped with God and His creature.

6. The controversy with nothingness, its conquest, removal and abolition, are primarily and properly God's own affair. It is true of course, that it constitutes a threat to the salvation and right of the creature, but primarily and supremely it contests the honour and right of God the Creator. It is also true that in the form of sin nothingness is the work and guilt, and in the form of evil and death the affliction and misery, of the creature.[9] Yet in all these forms it is first and foremost the problem of God

---

9   Of course, it is important to remember that Barth locates discussion of nothingness within the
     context of God's providential rule. So he notes earlier (III/3.292) that one can err by treating

Himself. Even the man who submits to nothingness and becomes its victim is still His creature. His care for His creature takes substance as its work and guilt and affliction and misery engender such rebellion and ruin, such disturbance and destruction. It is true, again, that God does not contend with nothingness without allowing His creature a share in the contention, without summoning His creature to His side as His co-belligerent. Yet the contention remains His own. His is the cause at stake, His all the power, His all the wisdom, His every weapon profitable and effectual in the strife. His free grace alone is victorious even where it is given to His creature to be victorious in this conflict. Everything depends upon the performance of His proper work. Only with the operation of His election and grace, and only as its converse, is His strange work also performed, and the sovereign No pronounced by which nothingness is granted its distinctive form and existence. Only within the limit of His No does nothingness have its reality, and in its reality its character as that which is evil, alien and adverse to grace, and therefore without it. And the limit of His No, and therefore of nothingness, is His Yes, the work of His free grace. As God performs this work, espousing the cause of the creature, He engages in controversy with nothingness, and deals with it, as is fitting, as that which is separated, passed over and abandoned, as the eternal yesterday. He exercises the non-willing by which it can have existence, and His jealousy, wrath and judgment achieve their purpose and therefore their end, which is also the end and destruction of nothingness. It is God's proper work, the work of His right hand, which alone renders pointless and superfluous His strange work, the work of His left. This penetration and victory of His free grace as the achievement of the separation already recognisable in creation, and therefore as the destruction of chaos, is the meaning of the history of the relationship between God and His creature. He alone, His activity grounded in His election, can master nothingness and guide the course of history towards this victory. God alone can defend His honour, ensure His creature's salvation, and maintain His own and His creature's right in such a way that every assault is warded off and the assailant himself is removed. God alone can summon, empower and arm the creature to resist and even to conquer this adversary. This is what has taken place in Jesus Christ. But it has taken place in Him as the work of the creature only in the strength of the work of the Creator. The creature as such would be no match for nothingness and certainly unable to overcome it.

nothingness as if it 'derives from the positive will and work of God' or as if it 'derives solely from the activity of the creature, in relation to which the lordship of God can only be a passive permission'. Barth maintains the *concursus* doctrine here, even as he notes an asymmetry in God's providential plan (that is, God more directly ordains the good, though he also – mysteriously – ordains in some way such nothingness).

It is not insignificant that the story of the creature in its relationship to God begins in Gen. 3 with a disastrous defeat, and that in the terrible form of human sin the chaos separated by God becomes a factor and secures and exercises a power which does not belong to it in relation to God but can obviously do so in relation to His creature. The creature had neither the capacity nor the power to effect that separation. It neither could nor should be God, judging between good and evil. It could and should live only by the grace of God and in virtue of the judgment already accomplished by Him. It could not and should not deal with nothingness as God did, nor master and overcome it like God. Only in covenant with God could it and should it confront nothingness in absolute freedom. And even in covenant with God, where God never fails, there could be and has been failure on the part of the creature. It is worth noting that in Gen. 3 the failure of the creature consisted in the fact that, succumbing to the insinuations of nothingness, it desired to be like God, judging between good and evil, itself effecting that separation, unwilling to live by the grace of God and on the basis of the judgment already accomplished by Him, or to persist in the covenant with God which is its only safeguard against nothingness. It did evil by desiring to do in its own strength the good which cannot be done save by God alone and by the creature only in covenant with Him. The creature sinned by thinking, speaking and acting in a way alien and adverse to grace and therefore without it. We are certainly not to say that man was capable of sin. There is no capacity for nothingness in human nature and therefore in God's creation, nor is there any freedom in this direction as willed, ordained and instituted by God. When man sinned he performed the impossible, not acting as a free agent but as a prisoner. We can and must say, however, that the creature in itself and as such did not and does not confront nothingness in such a way as to be exempt from its insinuation, temptation and power. It cannot, then, be secured against it apart from the grace of God, nor is it a match for it in its own strength.[10] If it tries to meet and fight it in its own strength, as in Gen. 3, it has already succumbed to it. This is the disastrous defeat of the creature by nothingness as typically described in Gen. 3.

---

10   Barth firmly insists, though, that nothingness is truly defeated by God; while it is different from God, and while it cannot be defeated or successfully opposed by the creature, God 'can deal with it and has already done so, in accordance with the fact that He transcends it from all eternity in His essence as God' (III/3.303). So Barth's comments here about how creatures cannot defeat death are meant to limit our confidence in human strength, not our confidence that death has been defeated. Elsewhere he will say: 'From the act of atonement which has taken place in Jesus Christ it is clear that in evil we do not have to do with a reality and power which have escaped the will and work of God, let alone with something that is sovereign and superior in relation to it. Whatever evil is, God is its Lord' (IV/1.408).

CHAPTER 11

RECONCILIATION IN CHRIST

The atonement is history. To know it, we must know it as such. To think of it, we must think of it as such. To speak of it, we must tell it as history. To try to grasp it as supra-historical or non-historical truth is not to grasp it at all. It is indeed truth, but truth actualised in a history and revealed in this history as such – revealed, therefore, as history … To say atonement is to say Jesus Christ.[1]

The fourth volume of the *Church Dogmatics* is no doubt its pinnacle. Here the Christological concentration addresses its gospel centre head on. It is also one of the most difficult theological texts to read, in as much as there are multiple layers of exposition (each of which interpenetrates the others, so that an error in exposition or a failure to appreciate an element can lead to distortion and imbalance elsewhere).

Barth's doctrine of reconciliation gathers a number of triads, as he outlines in the thesis statement of §58: 'The content of the doctrine of reconciliation is the knowledge of Jesus Christ who is (1) very God, that is, the God who humbles Himself, and therefore the reconciling God, (2) very man, that is, man exalted and therefore reconciled by God, and (3) in the unity of the two the guarantor and witness of our atonement. This threefold knowledge of Jesus Christ involves the knowledge of the sin of man: (1) his pride, (2) his sloth, and (3) his falsehood – the knowledge of the event in which reconciliation is made: (1) his justification, (2) his sanctification, and (3) his calling – and the knowledge of the work of the Holy Spirit in (1) the gathering, (2) the upbuilding and (3) the sending of the community, and of the being of Christians in Jesus Christ (1) in faith, (2) in love and (3) in hope' (IV/1.79).

The doctrine embraces all these triads, because Jesus Christ is the one Word of God in whom all reality – God as well as created being – can be known (ultimately, because all reality – God and creaturely – is elected or determined in Jesus). Barth's doctrine of election shapes his ontology – Jesus as manifesting what is true of God and humanity – and thus shapes his epistemology – Jesus as *manifesting* what is true of God and humanity. The excerpted text is a

---

1 *CD* IV/1.157.

programmatic discussion that suggests why Barth believes these various aspects must all be addressed in a robust Christology. It concludes a paragraph on 'The Doctrine of Reconciliation (Survey)' (§58) by addressing 'the three forms of the doctrine of reconciliation'.

Bibliography

George Hunsinger, 'Karl Barth's Christology: Its Basic Chalcedonian Character', in *Disruptive Grace: Studies in the Theology of Karl Barth* (Grand Rapids: Eerdmans, 2000), pp. 131–47.

Paul Dafydd Jones, *The Humanity of Christ: Christology in Karl Barth's Church Dogmatics* (London: T & T Clark, 2008).

Bruce McCormack, 'Karl Barth's Historicized Christology: Just How "Chalcedonian" Is It?' in *Orthodox and Modern: Studies in the Theology of Karl Barth* (Grand Rapids: Baker Academic, 2010), pp. 201–3.

The Text (*CD* IV/1.128–137)

If in this sense and with this understanding we return to the being of Jesus Christ as we have briefly defined it, we find at once that there are three 'christological' aspects in the narrower sense – aspects of His active person or His personal work which as such broaden into three perspectives for an understanding of the whole event of the atonement.

The first is that in Jesus Christ we have to do with very God. The reconciliation of man with God takes place as God Himself actively intervenes, Himself taking in hand His cause with and against and for man, the cause of the covenant, and in such a way (this is what distinguishes the event of reconciliation from the general sway of the providence and universal rule of God) that He Himself becomes man. God became man. That is what is, i.e., what has taken place, in Jesus Christ. He is very God acting for us men, God Himself become man. He is the authentic Revealer of God as Himself God. Again, He is the effective proof of the power of God as Himself God. Yet again. He is the fulfiller of the covenant as Himself God. He is nothing less or other than God Himself, but God as man. When we say God we say honour and glory and eternity and power, in short, a regnant freedom as it is proper to Him who is distinct from and superior to everything else that is. When we say God we say the Creator and Lord of all things. And we can say all that without reservation or diminution of Jesus Christ – but in a way in which it can be said in relation to Him, i.e., in which it corresponds to the Godhead of God active and revealed in Him. No general idea of 'Godhead' developed abstractly from such concepts must be allowed to intrude at this point. How the freedom of God is constituted, in what character He is the Creator and Lord of all things distinct from and superior to them, in short, what is to be understood by 'Godhead,' is something which – watchful against all imported ideas, ready to correct them and perhaps to let them be reversed and renewed in the most astonishing way – we must always learn from Jesus Christ. He defines those concepts: they do not define Him. When we start with the fact that He is very God we are forced to keep strictly to Him in relation to what we mean by true 'Godhead.'

This means primarily that it is a matter of the Godhead, the honour and glory and eternity and omnipotence and freedom, the being as Creator and Lord, of the Father, Son and Holy Spirit. Jesus Christ is Himself God as the Son of God the Father and with God the Father the source of the Holy Spirit, united in one essence with the Father by the Holy Spirit. That is how He is God. He is God as He takes part in the event which constitutes the divine being. *the event of Trinity*

We must add at once that as this One who takes part in the divine being and event He became and is man. This means that we have to understand the very Godhead, that divine being and event and therefore Himself as the One who takes part in it, in the light of the fact that it pleased God – and this is what corresponds outwardly to and reveals the inward divine being and event – Himself to become man.[2] In this way,

---

2   Barth argues that the incarnation defines the Godhead, in other words, God is the one who does this sort of thing. It is not a matter of 'though he is God, he became incarnate'; rather, Barth teaches that 'because he is God, he became incarnate'. His deity includes his perfection, but it is a perfection that wills and maintains presence even at great cost (see, e.g., IV/1.159, 179, 199–200). 'It is His sovereign grace that He wills to be and is amongst us in humility, our God, God for us. But He shows us this grace, He is amongst us in humility, our God, God for us, as that which He is in Himself, in the most inward depth of His Godhead. He does not become another God. In the condescension in which He gives Himself to us in Jesus Christ he exists and speaks and acts as the one he was from all eternity and will be to all eternity … The One who reconciles the world with God is necessarily the one God Himself in His true Godhead. Otherwise the world would not be reconciled with God' (IV/1.193).

   Heated debate has arisen amongst Barth scholars about the way in which Barth's theology may have developed (particularly following the shift in his doctrine of election). Bruce McCormack and a number of younger scholars influenced by him argue that Barth's revision of the doctrine of election – to be an election of himself as well as of humans – involves a recasting of his doctrine of God that is never really completed (even in IV/1) but that requires volume IV to be treated as trumping some of the statements found in volume I. Most pointedly, McCormack claims that God determines to be triune in his act of election. For one such argument, see Bruce L. McCormack, 'Election and the Trinity: Theses in Response to George Hunsinger', *Scottish Journal of Theology* 63, no. 2 (May 2010), pp. 203–24. However, George Hunsinger, Paul Molnar, and John Webster have tried to argue that Barth's doctrine of God does not undergo a massive shift with the revision of the doctrine of election. Rather, Barth continues to insist on the fullness of God's eternal being, out of which election flows. For an example of this reading, see George Hunsinger, 'Election and the Trinity: Twenty-Five Theses on the Theology of Karl

in this condescension, He is the eternal Son of the eternal Father. This
is the will of this Father, of this Son, and of the Holy Spirit who is the
Spirit of the Father and the Son. This is how God is God, this is His
freedom, this is His distinctness from and superiority to all other reality.
It is with this meaning and purpose that He is the Creator and Lord of
all things. It is as the eternal and almighty love, which He is actually
and visibly in this action of condescension. This One, the One who
loves in this way, is the true God. But this means that He is the One
who as the Creator and Lord of all things is able and willing to make
Himself equal with the creature, Himself to become a creature; the
One whose eternity does not prevent but rather permits and commands
Him to be in time and Himself to be temporal, whose omnipotence is
so great that He can be weak and indeed impotent, as a man is weak
and impotent. He is the One who in His freedom can and does in fact
bind Himself, in the same way as we all are bound. And we must go
further: He, the true God, is the One whose Godhead is demonstrated
and plainly consists in essence in the fact that, seeing He is free in His
love, He is capable of and wills this condescension for the very reason
that in man of all His creatures He has to do with the one that has fallen
away from Him, that has been unfaithful and hostile and antagonistic
to Him. He is God in that He takes this creature to Himself, and that
in such a way that He sets Himself alongside this creature, making His
own its penalty and loss and condemnation to nothingness. He is God
in the fact that He can give Himself up and does give Himself up not
merely to the creaturely limitation but to the suffering of the human
creature, becoming one of these men, Himself bearing the judgment
under which they stand, willing to die and, in fact, dying the death
which they have deserved. That is the nature and essence of the true
God as He has intervened actively and manifestly in Jesus Christ. When
we speak of Jesus Christ we mean the true God – He who seeks His
divine glory and finds that glory, He whose glory obviously consists,
in the fact that because He is free in His love He can be and actually
is lowly as well as exalted; He, the Lord, who is for us a servant, the
servant of all servants. It is in the light of the fact of His humiliation that
on this first aspect all the predicates of His Godhead, which is the true

Barth', *Modern Theology* 24, no. 2 (April 2008), pp. 179–98. In many ways, this debate turns on
two things: (1) how to take some of Barth's statements that seem to directly and radically link the
contingencies of history with the eternal character of God – whether hyperbolic, analogical, or
otherwise; and (2) how to relate Barth's mature theology to the classical Christian conception of
God's triune character (with a host of attendant attributes: eternity, infinity, immutability, impas-
sibility, etc.). The key essays in the debate – as well as some responses – have been collected in
Michael T. Dempsey (ed.), *Trinity and Election in Contemporary Theology* (Grand Rapids: Eerdmans,
2011).

Godhead, must be filled out and interpreted. Their positive meaning is lit up only by this determination and limitation, only by the fact that in this act He is this God and therefore the true God, distinguished from all false gods by the fact that they are not capable of this act, that they have not in fact accomplished it, that their supposed glory and honour and eternity and omnipotence not only do not include but exclude their self-humiliation. False gods are all reflections of a false and all too human self-exaltation. They are all lords who cannot and will not be servants, who are therefore no true lords, whose being is not a truly divine being.

The second christological aspect is that in Jesus Christ we have to do with a true man. The reconciliation of the world with God takes place in the person of a man in whom, because He is also true God, the conversion of all men to God is an actual event. It is the person of a true man, like all other men in every respect, subjected without exception to all the limitations of the human situation. The conditions in which other men exist and their suffering are also His conditions and His suffering. That He is very God does not mean that He is partly God and only partly man. He is altogether man just as He is altogether God – altogether man in virtue of His true Godhead whose glory consists in His humiliation. That is how He is the reconciler between God and man. That is how God accomplishes in Him the conversion of all men to Himself. He is true man, and altogether man, for in Him we have to do with the manifestation of the glory of the One who is true God and altogether God, and with the conversion to God of the One who is true man and altogether man. Here, too, there is no reservation and no diminution, which would be an immediate denial of the act of atonement made in Him. Jesus Christ is man in a different way from what we are. That is why He is our Mediator with God. But He is so in a complete equality of His manhood with ours. To say man is to say creature and sin, and this means limitation and suffering. Both these have to be said of Jesus Christ.[3] Not, however, according to the standard of general concepts, but only with reference to Him, only in correspondence with His true manhood. As in relation to His Godhead, so also in relation to His manhood, we must not allow any necessary idea of the human situation and its need to intervene. What His manhood is, and therefore true manhood, we cannot read into Him

 3   Barth is at pains in IV/1 to affirm the fullness of Christ's humanity, even going so far as to speak of his assuming a fallen human nature (I/2.152–153; IV/3.166–168). Though Christ is not a sinner in himself, he assumes a humanity suffering the plague of Adam's fall. In fact Barth believes that it is only in the passion of Jesus that we see the fullness of sin's plague upon God's good creation: while we may have premonitions of what sin is, it is fully manifest in the killing of the Son of God (IV/3.1.500–510).

from elsewhere, but must be told by Him.[4] But then we find that it is a matter of the manhood of the eternal Son of God. It is a matter of the real limitation and suffering of the man with whom the high God has ordained and elected and determined to be one, and has therefore humbled Himself. In His limitation and suffering, this is the true man. And that means at once that He is the man exalted by God, lifted above His need and limitation and suffering in and out of His need and limitation and suffering. In virtue of the fact that He is one with God He is free man. He is a creature, but superior to His creatureliness. He is bound by sin, but quite free in relation to it because He is not bound to commit it. He is mortal, and has actually died as we must all die. But in dying He is superior to death, and at once and altogether rescued from it, so that (even as a man like us) He is triumphant and finally alive. As the true God, i.e., the God who humbles Himself, Jesus Christ is this true man, i.e., the man who in all His creatureliness is exalted above His creatureliness. In this He is also exalted above us, because He is different from us, and is given the precedence in the ranks of our common humanity. But He does precede us. As God He was humbled to take our place, and as man He is exalted on our behalf. He is set at the side of God in the humanity which is ours. He is above us and opposed to us, but He is also for us. What has happened in Him as the one true man is the conversion of all of us to God, the realisation of true humanity. It is anticipated in Him, but it is in fact accomplished and revealed. As in Him God became like man, so too in Him man has become like God. As in Him God was bound, so too in Him man is made free. As in Him the Lord became a servant, so too in Him the servant has become a Lord. That is the atonement made in Jesus Christ in its second aspect. In Him humanity is exalted humanity, just as Godhead is humiliated Godhead. And humanity is exalted in Him by the humiliation of Godhead. We cannot regard the human being of Jesus Christ, we cannot − without denying or weakening them − interpret His predicates of liability to sin and suffering and death, in any other way than in the light of the liberation and exaltation accomplished in His unity with God. It is in its impotence that His being as man is omnipotent, in its temporality that it is eternal, in its shame that it is glorious, in its corruptibility that it is incorruptible, in its servitude that it is that of the Lord. In this way, therefore, it is His true being as man − true humanity.

---

4   Jesus Christ is the manifestation of what it means to be God (a lord who serves) as well as what it means to be human (a servant given lordship). Barth eschews all anthropocentric approaches to human knowledge, wherein we assume that we understand the human prior to considering Jesus or the gospel. Rather, Barth argues that Jesus is the true image of the human.

The Evangelists clung to this in their representation of the human being of Jesus Christ. They left no doubt that it was a human being like others, but even less so that as such it was the human being of the true God, and therefore in spite of its likeness to all others distinguished from all others in its freedom in face of limitation and suffering. From the very first they describe it in the light and clear reference of the final thing they have to report concerning Him: His resurrection from the dead as the event in which His exaltation cannot merely be discerned but is openly manifested – lighting up both that which precedes and that which follows. Therefore they describe the man Jesus as the One who, being tempted and suffering and dying as King, overcomes as King, and therefore passes through the midst of all others as King. That is how we must see Him.

In so far as He was and is and will be very man, the conversion of man to God took place in Him, the turning and therefore the reconciliation of all men, the fulfilment of the covenant. And in the light of Jesus Christ the man who is still not free in relation to limitation and suffering, who is still not exalted, who is still lowly (lowly, as it were, in the abstract), can be understood only as false man – just as in the light of Jesus Christ the empty loveless gods which are incapable of condescension and self-humiliation can be understood only as false gods.

Before we pass on to the third christological aspect, we may at this point interpose another discussion concerning the method of treating the doctrine of reconciliation. In considering the first two aspects we brought together in rather an unusual way two elements in traditional Christology: the doctrine of the two 'natures' of Christ, His deity and humanity, and the doctrine of the two 'states' of Christ, His humiliation (state of humiliation) and His exaltation (state of exaltation). We must now consider to what extent this presentation involves a change in traditional Christology and soteriology, and how far that change is right and necessary.

In comparison with older dogmatics, our presentation has undoubtedly the advantage that it does far greater justice to the particular doctrine of the two states.

In the older Lutherans this doctrine forms a great excursus in the doctrine of the human nature of Christ, which as they understood it was not merely exalted in the incarnation but actually divinised, i.e., according to their particular doctrine of the communication of the attributes furnished with all the attributes of Godhead. For them the only significance of the doctrine of the two states was that it answered what was for them the very difficult question how far Jesus Christ could have lived and suffered and died as a real man in time and space and under all the other restrictions of human life. For them humiliation meant that for a time, for the period of His life up to and including death, the God-man denies Himself that divinisation of His humanity (either by concealment or by genuine renunciation), but then reassumes it with the exaltation which begins with His triumphant descent into hell.

The older Reformed writers described the two states rather obscurely as the humiliation and exaltation of the divine Logos, and with them the doctrine is simply left in the air, following that of the work of Christ but not organically related to it. It was brought in for the sake of completeness, but on their presuppositions it had only an incidental application.[5] If our presentation is right, then at least the doctrine of the humiliation and exaltation of Christ does acquire a place and function in line with its scriptural and factual importance. But this necessitates certain decisive innovations in relation to the older dogmatics which we must openly admit and for which we must give our reasons.

Now (1) we have not spoken of two 'states' (*status*) of Jesus Christ which succeed one another, but of two sides or directions or forms of that which took place in Jesus Christ for the reconciliation of man with God.[6] We used the concepts humiliation and exaltation, and we thought of Jesus Christ as the servant who became Lord and the Lord who became servant. But in so doing we were not describing a being in the particular form of a state, but the twofold action of

[handwritten marginal note: Christ's humanity reveals divinity itself]

5   Barth's criticism – whether fair or not surely depends on greater historical argument than he offers in this immediate context – is that the 'older Reformed writers' did not allow the two states to shape their thought about the eternal Logos and the doctrine of God. In other words, the incarnation history was at best a result of the will of the eternal God, but it did not exercise a formal role in shaping thought about the character of that eternal God, namely, why the triune God chose to live and love in this way. Barth unpacks this Christological reflection on the eternal God's character throughout IV (see, e.g., IV/1.177–180, 199–200). Indeed, Barth goes so far as to argue that the obedient faithfulness of the incarnate Son must reveal something eternal about the way Father and Son relate internal to the Trinity (see, e.g., IV/1.208–209): 'Does subordination in God necessarily involve an inferiority and therefore a deprivation, a lack? Why not rather a particular being in the glory of the one equal Godhead ... Why should not our way of finding a lesser dignity and significance in what takes the second and subordinate place (the wife to her husband) need to be corrected in the light of the shared essence (*homoousios*) of the modes of divine being?' (IV/1.202); some have criticized Barth's rather traditional sexual morality (regarding differentiated gender roles) as based on this view of how the economy relates to the immanent trinity (see Paul Dafydd Jones, *The Humanity of Christ: Christology in Karl Barth's Church Dogmatics* [London: T & T Clark, 2008], pp. 212–13).

6   Barth 'actualizes' the doctrine of the two states, arguing that the eternal Word is both humiliated and exalted in character throughout his life. Of course, he does affirm that various events in his human life manifest these characteristics (birth, ministry, death, and resurrection are different sorts of things, and Christmas, Palm Sunday, Good Friday, and Easter Sunday are markedly different liturgical events). Barth's main concern here is to show that the same character chooses to be humbled and then to reign – his reign is that of a servant, even as his humiliation is that of a King.

Jesus Christ, the actuality of His work; His one work, which cannot be divided into different stages or periods of His existence, but which fills out and constitutes His existence in this twofold form. Our question is whether this does not better correspond to the witness of the New Testament concerning Jesus Christ. Where and when is He not both humiliated and exalted, already exalted in His humiliation, and humiliated in His exaltation? Where in Paul, for example, is He the Crucified who has not yet risen, or the Risen who has not been crucified? Would He be the One whom the New Testament attests as the Mediator between God and man if He were only the one and not the other? And if He is the Mediator, which of the two can He be alone and without the other? Both aspects force themselves upon us. We have to do with the being of the one and entire Jesus Christ whose humiliation detracts nothing and whose exaltation adds nothing. And in this His being we have to do with His action the work and event of atonement. That is the first reason for this alteration of the traditional dogmatic form.

But even more penetrating (2) is the fact that understanding the doctrine of the two states in this way we have tried to interpret it in the light of the doctrine of the two natures, and the other way around.[7]

Notice that there can be no question of abandoning the 'truly God, truly man.' If it is a matter of the reconciliation of man with God in Jesus Christ, i.e., the reconciliation of man with God and by God, then obviously we have to do truly and wholly with God and truly and wholly with man. And the more exact determination of the relationship between God and man in the famous Chalcedonian definition, which has become normative for all subsequent development in this dogma and dogmatics, is one which in our understanding has shown itself to be factually right and necessary. But according to our understanding there can be no question of a doctrine of the two natures which is autonomous, a doctrine of Jesus Christ as God and man which is no longer or not yet related to the divine action which has taken place in Him, which does not have this action and man as its subject matter. There is no such doctrine in the New Testament, although we cannot say that the New Testament envisages the being and relationship of God and man in Jesus Christ in any other way than it became conceptually fixed in the doctrine of the two natures.

---

7   In other words, the character of the Son drives the narrative, so that the narrative manifests his character (a Kingly character and, simultaneously, a servant character). Barth opposes the notion that we see a humble human raised from the dead, ascended, and thus treat him as King (an adoptionistic approach based on moving from the states to supposed inferences about his nature; cf. IV/1.162–163).

Similarly, there can be no autonomous doctrine of the humiliation and exaltation which took place in Jesus Christ, especially without a reference to what took place in Jesus Christ between God as God and man as man. There is a humiliation and exaltation – it hardly needs to be demonstrated that in Phil. 2.6f. and indeed all the New Testament Jesus Christ is regarded in the light of these two aspects and concepts. But if there is, it is not something incidental to His being. It is the actuality of the being of Jesus Christ as very God and very man. We cannot, therefore, ascribe to Jesus Christ two natures and then quite independently two states. But we have to explain in mutual relationship to one another what Jesus Christ is as very God and very man and what takes place as the divine work of atonement in His humiliation and exaltation.

But this brings us (3) to what is perhaps the greatest objection which might be brought against our presentation from the standpoint of the older dogmatics. To explain in the light of each other the deity and humanity of Jesus Christ on the one hand and His humiliation and exaltation on the other means that in Jesus Christ God – we do not say casts off His Godhead but (as the One who loves in His sovereign freedom) activates and proves it by the fact that He gives Himself to the limitation and suffering of the human creature, that He, the Lord, becomes a servant, that as distinct from all false gods He humbles Himself – and again, that in Jesus Christ man, without any forfeiture or restriction of His humanity, in the power of His deity and therefore in the power of and thanks to the humiliation of God, is the man who is freed from His limitation and suffering, not divinised man, but man sovereign and set at the side of God, in short, man exalted by God. The humiliation, therefore, is the humiliation of God, the exaltation the exaltation of man: the humiliation of God to supreme glory, as the activation and demonstration of His divine being; and the exaltation of man as the work of God's grace which consists in the restoration of his true humanity. Can we really put it in this way? We have to put it in this way if we are really speaking of the deity and humanity of Jesus Christ, of *His* humiliation and exaltation, of *His* being and *His* work.

For who is the God who is present and active in Him? He is the One who, concretely in His being as man, activates and reveals Himself as divinely free, as the One who loves in His freedom, as the One who is capable of and willing for this inconceivable condescension, and the One who can be and wills to be true God not only in the height but also in the depth – in the depth of human creatureliness, sinfullness and mortality.[8]

---

8   Barth insists that perfection and presence are not contradictory; God's self-sufficient lordship is not competing in a zero-sum game with his investment in the economy of redemption that plays

And who is the man Jesus Christ? He is the One in whom God is man, who is completely bound by the human situation, but who is not crushed by it, who since it is His situation is free in relation to it, who overcomes it, who is its Lord and not its servant.

Conversely, what is the humiliation of Jesus Christ? To say that He is lowly as a man is tautology which does not help us in the least to explain His humiliation. It merely contains the general truth that He exists as a man in the bondage and suffering of the human situation, and is to that extent actually lowly – a general truth which is in fact very forcibly called in question by the humanity of Jesus Christ. But the peculiar thing about the humiliation of Jesus Christ, the significant thing, the effective thing, the redemptive thing, is that it is the work of atonement in its first form. In Him it took place that while maintaining His true deity God became man, in Him to make His own the cause of man. In Him God Himself humiliated Himself – not in any disloyalty but in a supreme loyalty to His divine being (revealing it in a way which marks it off from all other gods). That is the secret of Christmas and Good Friday and the way which leads from the one to the other. Jesus Christ is the Reconciler of all men of all times and places by the fact that in Him God is active and revealed as the One who in His freedom, in His divine majesty, so loves that in Him the Lord became a servant, a servant like all of us, but more than that, the servant of us all, the man who did for us what we ourselves would not and could not do.

Again, what is the exaltation of Jesus Christ? To say that as God He is transcendent, free, sovereign, above the world, and therefore above the limitation and suffering of the human situation is again tautology which does not help us to understand His exaltation. God is always free in His love, transcendent God. He does not cease to be God transcendent when He makes it His glory to be in the depths, in order to make peace on earth to the men of His goodwill. In His Godhead, as the eternal Son of the Father, as the eternal Word, Jesus Christ never ceased to be transcendent, free, and sovereign.[9] He did not stand in

out over a long human history. Rather, 'God gives Himself, but He does not give Himself away. He does not give up being God in becoming a creature, in becoming man' (IV/1.185). Note that this shapes the way Barth approaches the so-called *kenosis* of the Son (the 'self-emptying' of the Son referenced in Phil. 2.7). While many Lutheran theologians of his era focused on this as a divestment of divine being or a determination not to exercise divine prerogatives or power while incarnate, Barth interpreted the *kenosis* in a traditional Reformed fashion, as the assumption of human life rather than the divestment of divine life (see *The Epistle to the Philippians* [trans. James W. Leitch; Louisville: Westminster John Knox, 2002], p. 64).

9   It is worth highlighting here that Barth does affirm the doctrine of the *logos asarkos* and its corollary, the so-called *extra Calvinisticum*, namely, the belief that the incarnation of the Son does not exhaust the personality of the Son; rather, while the Son is located in one physical place as Jesus of Nazareth, that same Son (and not another or a more numinous figure) also fills the entire

need of exaltation, nor was He capable of it. But He did as man – it is here again that we come up against that which is not self-evident in Jesus Christ. The special thing, the new thing about the exaltation of Jesus Christ is that One who is bound as we are is free, who is tempted as we are is without sin, who is a sufferer as we are is able to minister to Himself and others, who is a victim to death is alive even though He was dead, who is a servant (the servant of all servants) is the Lord. This is the secret of His humanity which is revealed in His resurrection and ascension and therefore shown retrospectively by the Evangelists to be the secret of His whole life and death. It is not simply that He is the Son of God at the right hand of the Father, the *kyrios*, the Lord of His community and the Lord of the cosmos, the bearer and executor of divine authority in the Church and the world, but that He is all this as a man – as a man like we are, but a man exalted in the power of His deity. This is what makes Him the Mediator between God and man, and the One who fulfils the covenant.

If we have correctly related these four considerations concerning the deity, the humanity, the humiliation and the exaltation of Jesus Christ, we not only can but must speak as we have done on this matter. The doctrine of reconciliation in its first two forms will then necessarily begin with a discussion of the God who humbles Himself in Jesus Christ and of the man who in Jesus Christ is exalted.

In the light of this we shall have to consider the whole event of atonement twice over, examining it in detail. The correct titles for these first two sections will be 'Jesus Christ, the Lord as Servant' and 'Jesus Christ, the Servant as Lord.' We shall still follow the traditional path to the extent that in content and meaning this division corresponds exactly to what earlier dogmatics worked out as the doctrine of the high-priestly and kingly office of Christ (in the framework of that doctrine of the threefold office of Christ in which they used to picture His work). I prefer the first two titles as more precise and also more comprehensive (since they also include the earlier doctrine of the person of Christ).

The third christological aspect to which we must now turn is at once the simplest and the highest. It is the source of the two first, and it comprehends them both. As the God who humbles Himself and therefore reconciles man with Himself, and as the man exalted by God

cosmos and upholds it by his Lordly power. For the classic articulation of this doctrine in Calvin, see his *Institutes of the Christian Religion*, II.viii.4. Barth is not satisfied, though, to speak of a *logos asarkos* without specifying that this is the same Word who willed to become incarnate; though exceeding the flesh, he is nonetheless of the same character and known only by the fleshly Christ. Barth eschews any notion of a 'God behind the incarnate God'. So Barth said that 'the man Jesus is in [the] genuine and real yesterday of God's eternity' (III/2.484; II/2.104).

and therefore reconciled with Him, as the One who is very God and very man in this concrete sense, Jesus Christ Himself is one. He is the 'God-man,' that is, the Son of God who as such is this man, this man who as such is the Son of God.

The New Testament obviously speaks of Jesus Christ in both these ways: the one looking and moving, as it were, from above downwards, the other from below upwards. It would be idle to try to conclude which of the two is the more original, authentic and important. Both are necessary. Neither can stand or be understood without the other. A Christ who did not come in the flesh, who was not identical with the Jesus of Nazareth who suffered and died under Pontius Pilate, would not be the Christ Jesus – and a Jesus who was not the eternal Word of God, and who as man was not raised again from the dead, would not be the Jesus Christ – of the New Testament. The New Testament, it is true, knows nothing of the formulæ of later ecclesiastical Christology, which tried to formulate the two aspects with conceptual strictness. But it knows even less of the docetic and ebionite abstractions, the attempts to make absolute either the Godhead or the manhood, which it was the concern of the later Christology to rebut. In fact the one aspect is given the greater prominence at this point, the other at that. But it knows only the one person, Jesus Christ Himself, who without division or distinction is both God and man. We remember: both, not in a general and arbitrarily determined sense of the concepts, but in that sense which has been specifically filled out and made concrete.[10] We must never lose sight of Him in the (often very abstract) content given to the concepts in the fathers and later development. The One who is both in this concrete sense is the Jesus Christ of the New Testament. To understand, we must emphasise the phrase: the One who is both – both, and not a third between God and man or a mixture of the two. The Judaic and Hellenistic environment of the New Testament did know such mixtures. The New Testament speaks the language of this environment, but it does not speak of this kind of third. The concrete views of God and man which it has before it in Jesus Christ cannot be mixed but can only be seen together as the forms of a history: the reconciling God and the man reconciled by Him. In face of the history which took place in Jesus Christ the New Testament says that these two elements of the one grace, the divine and the human, are one in Him, not in one form but in two. For that reason its statements concerning Him always move in either the one direction or the other, from above

---

10 Again, Barth insists on moving from the concrete (actual) to the conceptual (possible). In this case, God's lordship is defined as compatible with, nay, as consisting in his lordly embrace of service and suffering.

downwards or from below upwards. The only statement in the New Testament which brings together both in one is properly the name of Jesus Christ, which forbids and makes quite impossible any separation of the one from the other or any fusion of both in a third. When, therefore, the later Christology safeguarded against any confusion or transmutation of the two natures the one into the other and therefore into a third, the innovation was not one of substance but only of theology, and one which the substance itself demanded.

There can be no question of our trying to see a third thing in what we have called the third christological aspect.[11] Everything that can be said materially concerning Jesus Christ and the atonement made in Him has been said exhaustively in the twofold fact – which cannot be further reduced conceptually but only brought together historically – that He is very God and very man, i.e., the Lord who became a servant and the servant who became Lord, the reconciling God and reconciled man. The third aspect can be only the viewing of this history in its unity and completeness, the viewing of Jesus Christ Himself, in whom the two lines cross – in the sense that He Himself is the subject of what takes place on these two lines. To that extent the reconciliation of the world with God and the conversion of the world to God took place in Him. To that extent He Himself, His existence, is this reconciliation. He Himself is the Mediator and pledge of the covenant. He is the Mediator of it in that He fulfils it – from God to man and from man to God. He is the pledge of it in that in His existence He confirms and maintains and reveals it as an authentic witness – attesting Himself, in that its fulfilment is present and shines out and avails and is effective in Him. This is the new thing in the third christological aspect. Jesus Christ is the actuality of the atonement, and as such the truth of it which speaks for itself. If we hear Jesus Christ, then whether we realise it or not we hear this truth. If we say Jesus Christ, then whether we realise it or not we express and repeat this truth: the truth of the grace in which God has turned to the world in Him and which has come to the world in Him; the truth of the living brackets which bring and hold together heaven and earth, God and all men, in Him; the truth that God has bound Himself to man and that man is bound to God. The One who bears this name is Himself this truth in that He

---

11 There is no third nature or state, but there is a third aspect to Christology. So Barth moves from considering 'Jesus Christ, the Lord as Servant' to 'Jesus Christ, the Servant as Lord', and eventually to 'Jesus Christ, the True Witness'. The third aspect focuses on the oneness of the one who encompasses these two natures and two states in his one act of atonement. Barth identifies each aspect with one of the offices of Jesus Christ (for lengthier analysis of the *munus triplex* ['threefold office'], see IV/3.1.13–18): 'Lord as Servant' refers to his priestly work, 'Servant as Lord' refers to his kingly work, and 'True Witness' refers to his prophetic work (see IV/1.137–138).

is Himself this actuality. He attests what He is. He alone is the pledge of it because He alone is the Mediator of it. He alone is the truth of it. But He is that truth, and therefore it speaks for itself in Him. It is not in us. We cannot produce it of ourselves. We cannot of ourselves attest it to ourselves or to others. But it encounters us majestically in Him – the promise of the truth which avails for us as the atonement – of which it is the truth – took place for us and as ours, the truth which for that reason can and should be heard and accepted and appropriated by us, which we can and should accept as the truth which applies to us. It encounters us in Him as the promise of our own future. It is He, and therefore the actuality of our atonement, who stands before us. It is to Him, and therefore to the revelation of this actuality, that we move. He is the Word of God to men which speaks of God and man and therefore expresses and discloses and reveals God and ourselves – God in His actual relationship to us and us in our actual relationship to God. He is the Word of God by which He calls us in this relationship and therefore calls us to Him and therefore calls us also to ourselves. He was and is the will of God to speak this Word – this Word of His act. And it is our destiny to hear this Word, to live under and with and by this Word. That is the third christological aspect.[12]

Of the doctrine of reconciliation as such we must now say that in the light of this aspect a third and concluding section will be necessary in our presentation: concluding, but at the same time opening up and forming a transition to the doctrine of the redemption or consummation, the 'eschatology' in which all dogmatics culminate. It is easy to find a title for this third section: 'Jesus Christ the Guarantor.' 'Jesus Christ the Witness' would also be possible and impressive, but it might be understood too formally, whereas the neutral concept 'guarantor' expresses more clearly what we are trying to say – that He who is Himself the material content of the atonement, the Mediator of it, stands security with man as well as God that it is our atonement – He Himself being the form of it as well as the content.

---

12 George Hunsinger has argued that these three aspects can be aligned with three elements of Barth's Chalcedonian Christology, namely, that he (1) affirms that both natures enjoy full integrity in their own right, (2) insists that both natures pertain to one person and thus exist in the closest possible intimacy, and (3) confesses consistently that the divine nature precedes and assumes the human nature in an eternal asymmetry (see 'Karl Barth's Christology: Its Basic Chalcedonian Character', in *Disruptive Grace: Studies in the Theology of Karl Barth* [Grand Rapids: Eerdmans, 2000], pp. 131–47). More recently, Bruce McCormack has disputed Hunsinger's contention that Barth's Christology remains Chalcedonian, preferring to see it as bursting the ontological framework of Chalcedon with its historicist and actualist emphases (see 'Karl Barth's Historicized Christology: Just How "Chalcedonian" Is It?' in *Orthodox and Modern: Studies in the Theology of Karl Barth* [Grand Rapids: Baker Academic, 2010], pp. 201–33). This debate is linked tightly to the issues mentioned in fn 2.

CHAPTER 12

JUSTIFICATION AND SANCTIFICATION

There is always something wrong and misleading when the faith of a man is referred to as his way of salvation in contrast to his way in wicked works, or his true way of salvation in contrast to his way in the supposed good works of false faith and superstition. Faith is not an alternative to these other ways. It is not the way which – another Hercules at the crossroads – man can equally well choose and enter, which he can choose and enter by the same capacity by which he might go any other way. Even in the action of faith he is the sinful man who as such is not in a position to justify himself, who with every attempt to justify himself can only become the more deeply entangled in his sin.

Barth addresses three aspects of salvation: justification, sanctification, and vocation. He does not view these as temporally successive parts, but as three aspects of the one work of God. He will argue for a logical sequence (for example, sanctification flowing from and out of justification), but the logical need not equal the chronological. In fact, he links each aspect of reconciliation to the life of Christ, arguing (as we saw in the last chapter) that humiliation and exaltation – every aspect of the life of Christ – should be viewed as occurring at every state of his experience, not in successive stages (see, e.g., IV/1.516).

Barth opposes both 'cheap grace' (of pietism) and 'illusory activism' (of liberalism) in this section from a paragraph on 'The Sanctification of Man' (§66), arguing that the 'one grace of Christ' genuinely is gracious (it is not earned or merited) yet it effectively is gracious (it accomplishes something vital by raising us from the dead). In this paragraph he will address a host of topics: 'justification and sanctification', 'the Holy One and the saints', 'the call to discipleship', 'the awakening to conversion', 'the praise of works', and 'the dignity of the cross'.

He means to affirm the importance of the traditional doctrine of the Protestant, specifically the Reformed, churches regarding justification by faith alone, though

1   *CD* IV/1.616.

he wants to accent the way in which this justification necessarily brings with it sanctification. They necessarily come together, because they are both received given in union with the same Jesus Christ. Barth distances justification from psychological analysis (often put forward under the guise of pneumatology) and relocates it in more objective terms (drawing on Calvin's doctrine of union with Christ). He also speaks of sanctification by union with Christ. Their objective nature in Jesus provides a way of showing how they are distinct yet never apart. This excerpt – from the section on 'justification and sanctification' – seeks to explain their logical connection. As Barth will say later: 'Faith is not obedience, but as obedience is not obedience without faith, faith is not faith without obedience. They belong together, as do thunder and lightning in a thunderstorm' (IV/2.538).

Bibliography

George Hunsinger, 'A Tale of Two Simultaneities: Justification and Sanctification in Calvin and Barth', in *John Calvin and the Interpretation of Scripture: Calvin Studies X and XI* (ed. Charles Raynal; Grand Rapids: CRC Product Services, 2006), pp. 223–45.

Bruce McCormack, '*Justitia aliena*: Karl Barth in Conversation with the Evangelical Doctrine of Imputed Righteousness', in *Justification in Perspective: Historical Developments and Contemporary Challenges* (ed. Bruce McCormack; Grand Rapids: Baker Academic, 2006), pp. 167–96.

Bruce McCormack, 'Participation in God, Yes; Deification, No: Two Modern Protestant Responses to an Ancient Question', in *Orthodox and Modern: Studies in the Theology of Karl Barth* (Grand Rapids: Baker Academic, 2008), pp. 235–60.

The Text (*CD* IV/2.499–509)

Under the title 'sanctification' we take up the theme which constitutes the particular scope of this second part of the doctrine of reconciliation. The divine act of atonement accomplished and revealed in Jesus Christ does not consist only in the humiliation of God but in and with this in the exaltation of man. Thus it does not consist only in the fact that God offers Himself up for men; that He, the Judge, allows Himself to be judged in their place in this way establishing and proclaiming among sinners, and in defiance of their sin, His divine right which is as such the basis of a new right of man before Him. It does not consist, therefore, only in the justification of man.[2] It consists

---

2   Barth summarizes his approach to justification in §61 by saying: 'The right of God established in the death of Jesus Christ, and proclaimed in His resurrection in defiance of the wrong of man, is

also in the sanctification which is indissolubly bound up with his justification, i.e., in the fact that as He turns to man in defiance of his sin, He
also, in defiance of his sin, turns man to Himself. The reconciliation of
man with God takes place also in the form that He introduces as a new
man the one in relation to whom He has set Himself in the right and
whom He has set in the right in relation to Himself. He has introduced
him in the new form of existence of a faithful covenant-partner who
is well-pleasing to Him and blessed by Him. 'I will be your God' is the
justification of man. 'Ye shall be my people' is his sanctification. It is
not the final thing that has to be said concerning the alteration of the
human situation which has taken place in the reconciliation achieved
and revealed in Jesus Christ. In a third part of the doctrine of reconciliation we shall have to consider the whole in relation to the provisional
goal of the covenant newly and definitively established in Jesus Christ
and therefore in relation to the calling of man. But our present problem
is that of his sanctification – his reconciliation with God from the standpoint of his conversion to Him as willed and accomplished by God.[3]

What is meant by sanctification (*sanctificatio*) might just as well be
described by the less common biblical term regeneration (*regeneratio*)
or renewal (*renovatio*), or by that of conversion (*conversio*), or by that of
penitence (*poenitentia*) which plays so important a role in both the Old
and New Testaments, or comprehensively by that of discipleship which
is so outstanding especially in the synoptic Gospels. The content of
all these terms will have to be brought out under the title of sanctification.[4] But there is good reason to keep the term sanctification itself

as such the basis of the new and corresponding right of man. Promised to man in Jesus Christ,
hidden in Him and only to be revealed in Him, it cannot be attained by any thought or effort
or achievement on the part of man. But the reality of it calls for faith in every man as a suitable
acknowledgement and appropriation and application' (IV/1.514).

3   Barth summarizes the argument of this §66 – The Sanctification of Man – as follows: 'The
exaltation of man, which in defiance of his reluctance has been achieved in the death and declared
in the resurrection of Jesus Christ, is as such the creation of his new form of existence as the faithful
covenant-partner of God. It rests wholly and utterly on his justification before God, and like this it
is achieved only in the one Jesus Christ, but effectively and authoritatively for all in Him. It is self-
attested, by its operation among them as His direction, in the life of a people of men who in virtue
of the call to discipleship which has come to them, of their awakening to conversion, of the praise
of their works, of the mark of the cross which is laid upon them, have the freedom even as sinners
to render obedience and establish themselves as the saints of God in a provisional offering of the
thankfullness for which the whole world is ordained by the act of the love of God' (IV/2.499).

4   It is important to note that Barth here moves from the domain of discourse known as biblical
studies to the domain of discourse known as Christian doctrine. In saying this, we cannot
imagine that he views the two as separate or disparate, rather they are intimately related and
mutually interdependent. But he is clearly saying that terms are used one way in the Bible (note
the multiplicity: conversion, regeneration, etc.) and yet are brought under one doctrinal heading
(sanctification as a concept inclusive of these other topics).

in the foreground. It includes already, even verbally, the idea of the 'saint,' and therefore in contradistinction to the other descriptions of the same matter it shows us at once that we are dealing with the being and action of God, reminding us in a way which is normative for the understanding of the other terms as well of the basic and decisive fact that God is the active Subject not only in reconciliation generally but also in the conversion of man to Himself. Like His turning to man, and man's justification, this is His work, His doing. But it is now seen and understood, not as his justification, but as his sanctification.

In the Bible God Himself is the One who is originally and properly holy, confronting man in his creatureliness and sinfullness, and the whole created cosmos, with absoluteness, distinctness and singularity, with inviolable majesty. 'I am God, and not man' (Hos. 11.9). The seraphim proclaim Him (Is. 6.3) as the One who is thrice holy – 'holy as it were to a threefold degree' (Proksch in *Kittel*, I, p. 93) – in this sense, in this uniqueness and superiority. But in this as in other respects the biblical teaching about God is not theoretical. It is given in the context of accounts of God's action in the history inaugurated by Him. Nowhere, then, does it look abstractly to this One who confronts us, in His own inner being. He is indeed holy in and for Himself. But he demonstrates and reveals Himself as such in His establishment and maintenance of fellowship with man and his world.[5] The prophet Hosea was the first and, in the Old Testament, the only writer to understand and describe this Holy One as specifically the One who loves His people. But this equation is the implicit declaration of the whole of the Old Testament. In it we have to do with the Holy One who encounters the man who is so very different from Himself, and who does so in that unapproachable majesty, and therefore effectively, but who demonstrates and reveals Himself as the Holy One in the fact that He sanctifies the unholy by His action with and towards them, i.e., gives them a derivative and limited, but supremely real, share in His own holiness. The reference is to the Holy One of Israel, to use the term which dominates both parts of the Book of Isaiah. 'God that

---

5   If creaturely holiness is a participation in God's own holiness (on the notion of 'participation', see IV/2.511; as well as the differentiation between participation and deification described by Bruce McCormack, 'Participation in God, Yes; Deification, No: Two Modern Protestant Responses to an Ancient Question', in *Orthodox and Modern: Studies in the Theology of Karl Barth*, pp. 235–60), and if God's own holiness is not merely distinction from but also fellowship with creatures, then Barth will argue later that human sanctification involves human vocation (service amongst others). Thus he will dispute any monastic model of sanctification, arguing that heavenly participation in Jesus (union with Christ by the Spirit) involves earthly activity. He seeks to illustrate this by concluding each volume of the doctrine of reconciliation with ethical implications. For example, this part volume on sanctification concludes with his lengthy discussion of love (IV/2.727–840).

is holy shall be sanctified in righteousness' (Is. 5.16). It is by His acts of judgment and grace among and to this people that He sanctifies it as its Lord (Ez. 37.28) 'before the heathen' (Ez. 20.41), 'before their eyes' (Ez. 36.23) – and in so doing sanctifies Himself in the world, i.e., activates and reveals Himself in His majesty in the forms and circumstances of human history. This people may and shall and must be 'holy to me' (Lev. 10.3), i.e., enabled to worship Me, the Holy One, and therefore to attest Me as the Holy One in the world. To use the classical definition of Lev. 19.2 (cf. 11.44, 20.7) quoted in 1 Pet. 1.16: 'Ye shall be holy: for I ... am holy.' The holiness of this God demands and enforces the holiness of His people. It requires that His own divine confrontation of the world and all men should find a human (and as such very inadequate, but for all its inadequacy very real) correspondence and copy in the mode of existence of this people. It requires this already in and with the election and calling of this people, in and with the fact that He has made Himself the God of this people and this people His people. The imperative: 'Ye shall be holy,' is simply the imperative indication of the irresistible dynamic of the indicative: 'I am holy,' i.e., I am holy, and act among you as such, and therefore I make you holy – this is your life and norm. It is not the glory of any man or creature, not even of Israel, but that of Yahweh Himself, which sanctifies the tent of meeting (Ex. 29.43). And at the central point in the New Testament – in spite of all the appeals and exhortations to holiness of life, or rather as their presupposition – there is set as the primary petition (Mt. 6.9; Lk. 11.2): 'hallowed be Thy name.' The 'name' of God is the holy God Himself, who is present as such in His holiness, present to His people as the Lord, to sanctify it, and in so doing to sanctify Himself. 'The name of God is as little hallowed by men as His kingdom comes or His will is done by them' (Proksch, *op. cit.*, p. 113). 'It is God Himself who proves His name holy' (p. 91). He proves it in and to men. He sanctifies men. His sanctifying involves a modification of their situation and constitution. They have to deduce the consequences of it. But the sanctifying by which He claims and makes them and their actions usable in His service and as His possession is 'a manifestation of His own divine power' (E. Gaugler, *Die Heiligung im Zeugnis der Schrift*, 1948, p. 13), and as such it is wholly and exclusively His own act, and not theirs. 'And the very God of peace sanctify you wholly' (1 Thess. 5.23). He it is who wills and accomplishes, not only His own turning to man, but man's conversion to Him, the claiming of man for His service. And He wills that we should call upon Him daily that this may happen. 'I am the Lord which sanctify you' (Lev. 20.8). In everything that we have to say further on this subject we must exert ourselves always to start from this point.

We must begin, and this is our task in the present sub-section, by glancing back at the first part of the doctrine of reconciliation and making some clarifications concerning the mutual relationship of justification and sanctification as roughly outlined.

For what follows, cf. Alfred Göhler, *Calvins Lehre von der Heiligung*, 1934, p. 81 f., 107 f., and G. C. Berkouwer, *Faith and Sanctification*, 1952, with which I am particularly happy to record my general agreement.

1. As we now turn to consider sanctification in and for itself, we are not dealing with a second divine action which either takes place simultaneously with it, or precedes or follows it in time. The action of God in His reconciliation of the world with Himself in Jesus Christ is unitary. It consists of different 'moments' with a different bearing. It accomplishes both the justification and the sanctification of man, for it is itself both the condescension of God and the exaltation of man in Jesus Christ. But it accomplishes the two together. The one is done wholly and immediately with the other. There are also different aspects corresponding to the different 'moments.' We cannot see it all at once, or comprehend it in a single word. Corresponding to the one historical being of Jesus Christ as true Son of God and true Son of Man, we can see it only as the movement from above to below, or the movement from below to above, as justification or sanctification. Yet whether we look at it from the one standpoint or the other our knowledge can and may and must be knowledge of the one totality of the reconciling action of God, of the one whole and undivided Jesus Christ, and of His one grace.

In its later stages the older Protestant dogmatics tried to understand justification and sanctification as steps in a so-called order of salvation, preceded by a vocation and illumination, and followed by the separate processes of regeneration and conversion, and then (in the Lutherans) by a mystical union and glorification. For the most part this order of salvation was thought of as a temporal sequence, in which the Holy Spirit does His work here and now in men – the outworking of the reconciliation accomplished there and then on Golgotha. This temporal sequence corresponded only too readily to that of the temporal relationship between the humiliation and exaltation of Christ as it was viewed in the Christology of the older dogmatics. A psychologistic pragmatics in soteriology corresponded to the historicist pragmatics of Christology. Psychologistic? This was not the primary intention, and it was indeed the fear of slipping into psychology, into a mere recording of the spiritual experience of the Christian, which for a long time restrained the older orthodoxy from constructing an order of salvation in the sense of a temporal sequence. The original aim was to describe the order of the gracious application of the Holy Spirit, of the appropriation to the needy human subject of the salvation objectively accomplished in

Jesus Christ – that which is summed up in the title of the third book of Calvin's *Institutes*: 'On the means of obtaining the grace of Christ, the benefits for us which proceed therefrom, and the effects resulting from it.' But if this obtaining consists in a series of different steps, how can it better be made apprehensible than as a series of spiritual awakenings and movements and actions and states of a religious and moral type? The greater and more explicit the emphasis on the order of salvation understood in this way – and this was the tendency in the 17th century – the more clearly it was revealed by the uncertainties, contradictions and exegetical and conceptual arbitrariness and artificiality in which those who espoused it were entangled, that they were on the point of leaving the sphere of theology. And the nearer drew the time – the time of the Enlightenment which dawned already with Pietism – in which a religious and moral psychology would take over the leadership and suppress theology, first at this point, and then everywhere. Certainly there are rays of light, as when we suddenly read in Quenstedt (*Theol. did. pol.*, 1685, III, *c*. 10, *th*. 16) that all these works of Jesus Christ and the Holy Spirit, and particularly justification and sanctification, take place at one and the same time, and as in any mathematical point, they cohere too closely to be divided or separated. This is inevitable if we are really thinking of the act of God as it comes to man in Jesus Christ by the Holy Spirit. If Quenstedt and that whole theology had taken this insight seriously, it would have meant that they could not have understood that order as a series of different divine actions, but only as the order of different 'moments' of the one redemptive occurrence coming to man 'at the same time' of the one event. This would perhaps have led to a collapse of the historicist pragmatic, and even perhaps to the dualism between an objective achievement of salvation there and then and a subjective appropriation of it here and now, in favour of a recognition of the simultaneity of the one act of salvation whose Subject is the one God by the one Christ through the one Spirit – 'more closely united than in a mathematical point.'[6] The God who in His humili-

---

6   Note that Barth finds any strong distinction between objective and subjective moments to be false. He does not deny a distinction between objectivity and subjectivity, but he argues that justification involves both (Christ's objective work for us, and our faith appropriating it) as does sanctification (Christ's holiness, our faith conforming to it). Surely there is some tension here between places where Barth does seem to suggest that there is no necessary element involved in justification (e.g. in places where he sounds more 'universalist' by arguing that Jesus is the only ground or even the only condition for justification – e.g., in IV/2 alone: pp. 275–6, 281, 433, 516, 520, 702, 756), though he speaks here and elsewhere (see, e.g., IV/1: 514) of the needed creaturely instrument: faith. Barth scholars rightly debate the possibility of resolving these seemingly divergent strands of his thought. See, for example, Oliver Crisp, '"I teach it, but I also do not teach it": Karl Barth (1886–1968) on Universalism', in '*All Shall be Well*': *Explorations in Universalism and Christian Theology* (ed. Gregory Macdonald; Eugene, OR: Cascade Books, 2010), pp. 305–24.

ation justifies us is also the man who in His exaltation sanctifies us. He is the same there and then as He is here and now. He is the one living Lord in whom all things have occurred, and do and will occur, for all. Unfortunately, however, the recognition of this 'at the same time' did not lead even to a serious consideration of the relationship between justification and sanctification, let alone to any general advance in this direction. We cannot escape to-day the task of taking this recognition seriously.

When, however, we speak of justification and sanctification, we have to do with two different aspects of the one event of salvation. The distinction between them has its basis in the fact that we have in this event two genuinely different moments. That Jesus Christ is true God and true man in one person does not mean that His true deity and His true humanity are one and the same, or that the one is interchangeable with the other. Similarly, the reality of Jesus Christ as the Son of God who humbled Himself to be a man and the Son of Man who was exalted to fellowship with God is one, but the humiliation and exaltation are not identical. From the Christological 'inconfusably' and 'immutably' of Chalcedon we can deduce at once that the same is true of justification and sanctification. As the two moments in the one act of reconciliation accomplished in Jesus Christ they are not identical, nor are the concepts interchangeable. We are led to the same conclusion when we consider the content of the terms. In our estimation of their particular significance we must not confuse or confound them. Justification is not sanctification and does not merge into it. Sanctification is not justification and does not merge into it. Thus, although the two belong indissolubly together, the one cannot be explained by the other. It is one thing that God turns in free grace to sinful man, and quite another that in the same free grace He converts man to Himself. It is one thing that God as the Judge establishes that He is in the right against this man, thus creating a new right for this man before Him, and quite another that by His mighty direction He claims this man and makes him willing and ready for His service. Even within the true human response to this one divine act the faith in which the sinful man may grasp the righteousness promised him in Jesus Christ is one thing, and quite another his obedience, or love, as his correspondence, to the holiness imparted to him in Jesus Christ. We shall speak later of the indestructible connexion between these. But it is a connexion, not identity. The one cannot take the place of the other. The one cannot, therefore, be interpreted by the other.

It is a twofold grace that we receive in the participation in Christ

(Calvin, *Instit.*, III, 11, 1).[7] Similarly, its reception in faith and penitence is twofold; even if they cannot be separated, they ought nevertheless to be distinguished. Although they cohere with one another by a perpetual bond, nevertheless they should be more joined than confused. (3, 5). For: If the light of the sun cannot be separated from its heat, should we then say that the earth becomes warm by its light, and is illuminated by its heat? (11, 6)?

Sanctification is not justification. If we do not take care not to confuse and confound, soteriology may suffer, allowing justification (as in the case of much of Roman Catholicism in its following of Augustine, but also of many varieties of Neo-Protestantism) to merge into the process of his sanctification initiated by the act of the forgiveness of sins, or by allowing faith in Jesus Christ as the Judge judged in our place (this is in my view the most serious objection to the theology of R. Bultmann) to merge into the obedience in which the Christian in his discipleship has to die to the world and himself.[9] The 'I am holy' is not merely a kind of preface or unaccented syllable introducing the really important

7   For a historical study of the 'twofold grace' (*duplex gratia*) in Calvin's theology, see Todd Billings, 'John Calvin's Soteriology: On the Multifaceted "Sum" of the Gospel', *International Journal of Systematic Theology* 11, no. 4 (2009), pp. 428–47. On Barth's relation to Calvin regarding this issue, see the penetrating essay by George Hunsinger, 'A Tale of Two Simultaneities: Justification and Sanctification in Calvin and Barth', in *John Calvin and the Interpretation of Scripture: Calvin Studies X and XI* (ed. Charles Raynal; Grand Rapids: CRC Product Services, 2006), pp. 223–45.

8   One biblical example of the distinction-within-unity and unity-within-distinction of faith and repentance is found in Isaiah 30.15 – 'in returning and rest we shall be saved'. 'Return' involves a turning away from idols and sin; 'rest' involves trust and belief in Jesus. So Barth will say: 'Faith is not obedience, but as obedience is not obedience without faith, faith is not faith without obedience. They belong together, as do thunder and lightning in a thunderstorm' (IV/2: 538). The unity-within-distinction is illustrated in Barth's earlier exposition of the double love command (I/2.371–456).

9   Barth is suggesting that both Roman Catholicism and many varieties of Neo-Protestantism (modern liberal Christianity) try to encourage moral action by merging sanctification into justification, by making moral change a necessary condition or cause of justification (reconciliation with God). Barth believes they undercut both justification and sanctification in so doing. He argues that justification is radically free and fully in Christ, and he then argues (in the next paragraph) that sanctification is motivated by delight in the radically free justification we are given (so that, ironically, attempts to legislate moral change as a constitute part of our acceptance with God actually undercut the effectiveness of sanctification). For more on Barth's reflections on the Roman Catholic doctrine of justification, see IV/1.621–626. The Roman Catholic dissenter Hans Küng has argued that Barth effects *rapprochement* between Protestantism and Roman Catholicism: 'Protestants speak of a declaration of justice and Catholics of a making just. But Protestants speak of a declaring just which includes a making just; and Catholics of a making just which supposes a declaring just. Is it not time to stop arguing about imaginary differences?' (*Justification: The Doctrine of Karl Barth and a Catholic Reflection* [Louisville: Westminster John Knox, 2004], p. 221). While Barth was hesitant to disagree (stating that Küng understood his approach well), it must be noted that Barth's writings clearly suggest that he perceived an enduring difference on this matter.

statement: 'Ye shall be holy.' In all the thinking along these lines about the justifiable emphasis on the existential relevance of the atonement, where is the regard for the God who accomplishes it, the bowing before the freedom of His grace, the adoration of the mystery in which He really says an unmerited No to sinful man, the joy of pure gratitude for this benefit? Where is the presupposition of a Sanctification worthy of the name? Is it not better to make justification, even in its significance for Sanctification, genuinely justification, instead of trying to understand it from the very outset merely as the beginning of sanctification?

On the other hand, justification is not sanctification. If we do not take care not to confuse and confound, soteriology may also suffer by allowing sanctification to be swallowed up in justification. It may be because of the overwhelming impression of the comfort of the grace which is effective and has to be understood as justification. It may be in view of the true consideration that justification is in any event the dominating presupposition of sanctification. It may be with the correct insight that even in his best works the sanctified man still stands in continual need of justification before God. It may be in a justifiable anxiety that under the name of sanctification a prior or subsequent self-justification may creep in to the detriment of the sovereignty of grace. These are all legitimate considerations which can be traced back to the younger Luther and Zinzendorf and H. F. Kohlbrügge; and with the help of some of the more pointed statements of these writers, and an exaggeration (and therefore distortion) of their basic teaching, they can easily lead to a monism of the theology of the cross and the doctrine of justification. In this monism the necessity of good works may be maintained only lethargically and spasmodically, with little place for anything more than rather indefinite talk about a life of forgiveness, or comforted despair, or Christian freedom, or the love active in faith. If we do not give any independent significance to the problem of sanctification, do we not necessarily obscure in a very suspicious way the existential reach of the atonement, the simple fact that justification always has to do with man and his action, and that faith in it, even though it is a work of the Holy Spirit, is still a decision of man? Can we ignore the fact that in the Bible the work of the sovereign grace of God as a work of Jesus Christ and the Holy Spirit includes the sanctification of man as distinct from his justification? Is it not a serious matter to miss the sovereignty and authority of grace in this form? If we do not understand it as sanctifying grace, we not only do despite to its richness, but far too easily, and indeed inevitably, we begin to look for the indispensable norm of the Christian way of life elsewhere than in the Gospel (in which we think we have only the consoling word of justifying grace), and are forced to seek and grasp a law formed either by considerations drawn from the Bible or natural law, or by historical convenience. But this means that we are involved in double book-keeping, and either tacitly or openly we are subjected to other lords in a kingdom on the left as well as to the Lord Jesus Christ whose competence extends only, as we think, to the forgiveness of sins. Is it not advisable to make sanctification, even in its connexion with justification, genuinely sanctification, instead of trying to understand it from the very outset merely as a paraphrase of justification?

3. Yet it is even more important to remember, and the warning we have to give in this respect must be correspondingly sharper, that since justification and sanctification are only two moments and aspects of one and the same action, they do belong inseparably together. We have had to draw attention to the unavoidable dangers of confusion which threaten on both sides, and which have actually overwhelmed the Church and theology with very serious consequences. But we have to say that to ignore the mutual relationship of the two can only lead at once to false statements concerning them and to corresponding errors in practice: to the idea of a God who works in isolation, and His 'cheap grace' (D. Bonhoeffer), and therefore an indolent quietism, where the relationship of justification to sanctification is neglected; and to that of a favoured man who works in isolation, and therefore to an illusory activism, where the relationship of sanctification to justification is forgotten.[10] A separation of justification and sanctification can have its basis only in a separation within the one actuality of Jesus Christ and the Holy Spirit; in an isolation of the self-humiliating Son of God on the one side, and of the exalted Son of Man on the other. If we have also to accept the 'indivisibly' and 'inseparably' of Chalcedonian Christology, justification and sanctification must be distinguished, but they cannot be divided or separated.[11] We have only to ask ourselves:

---

10   A failure to appreciate the 'inseparabl[e]' relation between these two aspects of the one grace in Christ can lead to one of two errors: (1) a 'cheap grace' or quietism that promises peace when there is no peace and fails to honour the transforming, exalting work of Christ – Barth addresses this error in his description of sloth (IV/2.378–498), or (2) an 'illusory activism' that busies itself with work in personal and social transformation – human exaltation – and does so apart from a reliance on Christ's work in one's place – Barth addresses this error in his description of pride (IV/1.358–513). Both quietism and moralism err in failing to perceive the links between justification and sanctification.

11   George Hunsinger's three explanatory glosses on 'Chalcedonian Christology' – what he calls the 'Chalcedonian pattern' – can be employed helpfully here. (1) Justification and sanctification are both affirmed in their individual, full integrity. (2) Justification and sanctification are both affirmed in the closest possible intimacy, as two sides of the same coin and two aspects of the 'one grace'. (3) Justification and sanctification are related in a logical – though not temporal – fundamental asymmetry, with the work of Christ outside us actually bringing about the work of Christ within us.

What is the forgiveness of sins (however we understand it) if it is not directly accompanied by an actual liberation from the committal of sin? What is divine sonship if we are not set in the service of God and the brethren? What is the hope of the universal and definitive revelation of the eternal God without striving for provisional and concrete lesser ends? What is faith without obedience? And conversely: What is a liberation for new action which does not rest from the very outset and continually on the forgiveness of sins? Who can and will serve God but the child of God who lives by the promise of His unmerited adoption? How can there be a confident expectation and movement in time without the basis of eternal hope? How can there be any serious obedience which is not the obedience of faith? As God turns to sinful man, the conversion of the latter to God cannot be lacking. And the conversion of man to God presupposes at every point and in every form that God turns to him in free grace. That the two are inseparable means that the doctrine of justification has to be described already as the way from sin to the right of God and man, and therefore as the way from death to life, which *God* goes with him. And it means for the doctrine of sanctification that it has to show that it is really with *man* that God is on this way as He reconciles the world with Himself in Jesus Christ.

It was Calvin who saw and expressed this point with particular clarity. There is hardly a passage in which we have any doubt whether the reference is to justifying or sanctifying grace, and yet he everywhere brings out the mutual relationship of the two moments and aspects. His primary statement and starting-point is as follows: Just as it is not possible to divide Christ into parts, so also there are two inseparable aspects, which we perceive at the same time, joined in him: righteousness and sanctification. Therefore, whomever God receives into his grace, at the same time he gives the Spirit of adoption, by whose power he restores them to his own. (*Inst.*, III, 11, 6).

There is thus no justification without sanctification. Man is justified by faith alone, and by pure forgiveness, but real (so to speak) holiness of life is not to be separated from the free imputation of righteousness. The proclamation of forgiveness has as its aim in order that the sinner may be freed from the tyranny of Satan with its yoke of sin, and the miserable slavery of vice, and cross over into the Kingdom of God. Thus no one can apprehend the grace of the Gospel without the meditation of repentance (3, 1). It is certainly not in virtue of our holiness that we enter into fellowship with God. We have to stand in this already if, engulfed by His holiness (*eius sanctitate perfusi*), we are to follow where He calls. But it belongs to His glory that this should take place, for there can be no *consortium* between Him and our iniquity and impurity (6, 2). We cannot, therefore, glory in God without by definition – and this is for Calvin the basic act of penitence and the new life – renouncing all self-glorying and thus beginning to live to God's glory (13, 2). Thus the righteousness of God calls for a reflection, a *consensus*, which must be actualised in the obedience of the believer. It calls for a confirmation of our adoption to divine sonship (6, 1). For this reason the one grace of God is necessarily sanctifying grace as well.[12] In the participation in Christ, by which we are justified, sanctification is contained no less than justification ..., Christ holds each inseparably in himself ..., Therefore Christ justified no-one whom he does not at the same time sanctify (16, 1, and we find the same *simul* in 3, 19). While we admit ..., God reckons us whom he has given free forgiveness of sins as righteous, that his goodness is at the same time conjoined with mercy, because by his Holy Spirit he lives in us, by whose power we are sanctified, that is, we are consecrated to the Lord for true purity of life (14, 9). There can thus be no doubt that, as Calvin saw it, the Reformation did not wish to give to the problem of the life of the Christian man, of penitence and good works, any less but a much greater and more serious and penetrating attention than was done either by the Humanists (who followed Erasmus) on the one side or contemporary Romanists on the other. In the context in which it was set by him the 'by faith alone' obviously could not become a comfortable kiss of peace.

On the other hand, of course, there is no sanctification without justification. Or could true repentance exist without faith? By no means! (3, 5). There is no duration of time between the two in which the man who is righteous before God in faith is not also h o l y and obedient to Him. But it is only this man who can and will be obedient and holy. How could he be seriously penitent if he did not know: that he belonged to God? But no-one is truly persuaded that he belongs to God, unless he has beforehand grasped his grace. (3, 2). How can there be a free and happy conscience towards God in penitence and therefore in the life of the Christian without the certainty of the righteousness before God which he is given, and has to be given continually, by God? (13, 3). Even the obedient and holy and loving man who penitently lays hold of this righteousness still lives in the flesh and therefore as a sinner before God. Hence it follows: There has not been one work of a pious man which, if examined by the severe

---

12   In as much as justification is by faith, it necessarily involves the simultaneous work of sanctification by faith. The very same faith that looks away from oneself to Christ is the faith that looks away *from oneself* to Christ. Sanctification and justification are both by faith; in fact, in looking to Jesus for satisfaction, the believer is at the same time looking away from their own devices and from creaturely methods of satisfaction. So repentance is looking away from other things; faith is looking to Jesus in faith. They are two sides of the same coin; justification and sanctification are 'the one grace of God' and not discrete and disparate gifts.

justice of God, would not be damnable (14, 11) and: not one work goes forth from the saints which, if considered in itself, would not merit the righteous recompense of reproach (14, 9). Even the regenerate and converted stand in absolute need of forgiveness and justification in all their works of penitence and obedience, which of themselves cannot possibly justify them (14, 13). Good works, which God has promised to reward (18, 1f.), in which we have to progress, and in the doing of which we may find confidence (14, 18f.), can be present only as God of His free goodness justifies not only our persons but also our works (17, 5f.), as by a constant forgiveness of sins (14, 10; 12) He assesses and recognises and accepts as good, on the basis of the righteousness of Jesus Christ ascribed to us, that which we do in supreme imperfection and even guilt and corruption (14, 8f.).[13] There can be no doubt that Calvin — the reformer at the time of the reconstruction of the Evangelical Churches and the developing Counter-Reformation, and therefore with different interests from Luther — stands squarely on the basis of his predecessor. The notion of twofold grace was not his own. Even the older Luther (cf. *CD.*, IV, 1, p. 525 f.), in passages which are, of course, rather remote and obscure, had referred in the same sense as Calvin, and with the same conjunction and distinction, to justification and sanctification, healing, purification, etc. And Calvin for his part had not surrendered one jot of the decisive insight of Luther concerning justification. The only distinctive features — and they were not really un-Lutheran, or prejudicial to the content and function of the doctrine of justification — were the formal consistency with which he spoke of this twofold grace and the material emphasis which he laid on the doctrine of the newness of life based on justification.

4. It remains only to ask whether there is perhaps an order (of salvation) in the relationship of justification and sanctification and therefore a superiority and subordination, a before and after, in the one event of grace and salvation. We presuppose that there is no such order in the temporal sense. The 'at the same time' of the one redemptive act of God in Jesus Christ cannot be split up into a temporal sequence, and in this way psychologised.[14] The justification and sanctification of man,

---

13   Barth argues that justification is continually necessary — and continually given — even to the lifelong Christian. Furthermore, not only their person but also their pious works require justification from outside, that is, for the sake of Jesus Christ.

14   Note that Barth's main concern is the psychologization of salvation. He believes a temporal sequence implies a sequence of psychological or emotive acts or experiences, creating a typecast character ('the Christian') from which there can be no faithful psychological or experiential deviation. Bruce McCormack has argued that while Barth agrees with the thrust of the older Protestant consensus on justification, he wants to shift its focus from pneumatology to Christology (or from psychologically accessed experience to union with the objective Christ);

manifest in the resurrection of Jesus Christ and effective in the Holy Spirit, are an event in this 'at the same time,' and not therefore in such a way that his justification first takes place separately (as though it could be his justification by God if it did not also include his sanctification), and then his sanctification takes place separately (as though it could be his sanctification by God if at all its stages and in all its forms it were not based upon and borne by the event of his justification). No, they both take place simultaneously and together, just as the living Jesus Christ, in whom they both take place and are effective, is simultaneously and together true God and true man, the Humiliated and the Exalted. Yet this does not mean that we can lay aside the question of their order. It has to be raised and answered because it is necessary that we should dissipate the last remnants of the monistic and dualistic thinking which occupied us under (2) and (3). If there can be no question of a temporal order, the only order can be that of substance. And it is not quite so easy to answer the question of this order as might at first sight appear.

From our deliberations under (2) and (3) it is clear in what sense justification has to be understood as the first and basic and to that extent superior moment and aspect of the one event of salvation, and sanctification as the second and derivative and to that extent inferior. It is indeed in virtue of the condescension of God in which the eternal Word assumed our flesh that there takes place the exaltation of man in the existence of the royal man Jesus. It is in virtue of the forgiveness of his sins and his establishment as a child of God, both fulfilled in the gracious judgment and sentence of God, that man is called and given a readiness and willingness for discipleship, for conversion, for the doing of good works, for the bearing of his cross. It is in virtue of the fact that he is justified in the presence of God by God that he is sanctified by Him. Surely it is obvious that if we ask concerning the structure of this occurrence justification must be given the priority over sanctification.

Yet is this the end of the matter? Do we not have to recognise that the existence of the royal man Jesus, and therefore the true answering of the question of obedience, the summoning and preparing of man for the service of God, have a radiance and importance in the Bible which are not in any way secondary to those of justifying grace? Is the first the only possible answer? In the question of the material order of this whole event do we not have to take into account – irrespective of the question of its inner movement – its meaning and purpose and goal? And does it not seem that that which is second in execution (*executione posterius*),

---

see '*Justitia aliena*: Karl Barth in Conversation with the Evangelical Doctrine of Imputed Righteousness', in *Justification in Perspective: Historical Developments and Contemporary Challenges* (ed. Bruce McCormack; Grand Rapids: Baker Academic, 2006), pp. 167–96.

i.e., sanctification, is first in intention (*intentione prius*)? What is it that God wills and effects in the reconciliation of man with Himself? By the incarnation of His Word does He not will and effect the existence of the royal man Jesus and His lordship over all His brothers and the whole world? By His humiliation to be the Judge judged for us, and therefore by the justification of man before Him, does He not will and effect the existence of a loyal and courageous people of this King in covenant with Himself, and therefore the sanctification of man? And even this may not be the ultimate, or penultimate, word concerning the *telos* of the event of atonement. Yet in relation to the relationship between justification and sanctification are we not forced to say that teleologically sanctification is superior to justification and not the reverse? It is obvious that we cannot help putting and answering the question in this form too.

Yet there are still good reasons for the first answer; and it is not without its significance. This being the case, is it really necessary or wise to choose between them at all? In so doing, might we not be encroaching on the actuality of the one grace of the one Jesus Christ? And this is something which cannot be permitted merely out of a desire to systematise. In any case, are we not asking concerning the divine order of the divine will and action revealed and effective in Jesus Christ? Might it not be that in this – in this particular function and respect – the before is also the after and *vice versa*? This would mean that both answers have to be given with the same seriousness in view of the distinctive truth in both – intersecting but not cancelling one another. In the 'at the same time' of the one divine will and action justification is first as basis and second as presupposition, sanctification first as aim and second as consequence; and therefore both are superior and both subordinate.[15] Embracing the distinctness and unity of the two moments and aspects, the one grace of the one Jesus Christ is at work, and it is both justifying and sanctifying grace, and both to the glory of God and the salvation of man. Where else does God (the God known in Jesus Christ) seek and create His glory but in the salvation of man? And yet who can say that the glory of God to the salvation of man is greater or smaller in man's justification or sanctification? Again, where is the salvation of man (the man known in Jesus Christ) to be found but in the glory which God prepares for Himself in His action to and with man? Yet who is to say

15   In other words, there is superiority in terms of being either a basis or a telos. Depending on which factor one views as determinative, either the first or the second is superior. So Barth finds justification the ground of sanctification, and sanctification the purpose of justification. If being the relational basis for something is viewed as being superior, then justification is superior. But if being the telos of something is considered superior, then sanctification is superior. Both statements have their importance.

that the salvation of man to the glory of God is greater or smaller in the fact that man is justified by God or sanctified by Him? If we start at this point, and therefore at the grace of the covenant effective and revealed in Jesus Christ, we have the freedom, but we are also bound, to give to the question of the order of the relationship between justification and sanctification this twofold answer. There is no contradiction. As a twofold answer, it corresponds to the substance of the matter.

CHAPTER 13

THE LIVING CHRIST AND THE PROMISED SPIRIT

Jesus Christ is the same yesterday and today and forever.[1]

Because of his Christological concentration, Karl Barth has suffered criticism regularly for a failure to affirm adequately the importance of the Holy Spirit's work. Of course, it would be to ask Barth to be an entirely different theologian for him to address any topic in anything but a Christ-centred way, but we can do well to ask what a Christ-centred doctrine of the Holy Spirit would look like.

Barth addresses the doctrine of the Holy Spirit as part of his account of the threefold advent (*parousia*). In other words, the Holy Spirit is sent by the Son, as an auxiliary and advocate of his ministry of reconciliation and revelation. As such, pneumatology follows Christology. In particular, Barth re-locates pneumatology under the sign of the Ascension and heavenly session of Jesus, with Pentecost being the public manifestation of the Spirit's advocacy on behalf of the enthroned Son. We could describe this dogmatic manoeuvre as a thorough-going attempt to avoid any dualism in relating Christ and the Spirit. Many say that this suggests a primacy to the Son and a subordination of sorts to the Spirit. Barth's exegesis and dogmatic analysis, however, seek to show that the Spirit is personally distinct from the Son and, further, that one such distinction is the Christ-centred shape of the Spirit's life.

These excerpts come from a paragraph entitled 'The Glory of the Mediator' (§69), of which there are four sections: 'the third problem of the doctrine of reconciliation', 'the light of life', 'Jesus is victor', and 'the promise of the Spirit'. Both excerpts come from that final section on pneumatology. 'The glory of the Mediator consists in the fact that He not only is what He is as such, and does what He does as such, but that He is also revealed, i.e., reveals Himself, as the One He is and in what He does' (IV/3.275). These particular excerpts address 'the self-declaration of Jesus Christ … and therefore the revelation of the reconciliation of the world with God, the immediate and perfect prophecy, by a new and specific divine act, of the divine-human High-priest and King' (IV/3.290).

1   Hebrews 13.8 (ESV).

These excerpts address the 'threefold advent' of this revelatory prophecy of Jesus Christ by the promised Holy Spirit.

Bibliography

Karl Barth, 'Concluding Unscientific Postscript on Schleiermacher', in *The Theology of Schleiermacher* (ed. Dietrich Ritschl; trans. Geoffrey Bromiley; Grand Rapids: Eerdmans, 1982), pp. 261–79.

Andrew Burgess, *The Ascension in Karl Barth* (Barth Studies; Aldershot: Ashgate, 2004), part 1.

George Hunsinger, 'The Mediator of Communion: Karl Barth's Doctrine of the Holy Spirit', in *Disruptive Grace: Studies in the Theology of Karl Barth* (Grand Rapids: Eerdmans, 2000), pp. 148–85.

John Webster, '"Eloquent and Radiant": The Prophetic Office of Christ and the Mission of the Church', in *Barth's Moral Theology: Human Action in Barth's Thought* (London: T & T Clark, 1998), pp. 125–50.

The Text (*CD* IV/3.291–296, 356–362)

Our first and unconditional objective must be to see and know what the Easter message no less unconditionally says.

In a first and very general formulation of its declaration, we venture the statement that the Easter event, as the revelation of the being and action of Jesus Christ in His preceding life and death, is His new coming as the One who had come before. As is made quite clear by the accounts in the Gospels, the One who now comes afresh and appears to His disciples is none other than the One who had come before. He is 'Jesus Christ yesterday' (Heb. 13.8), the One who yesterday acted and suffered and was finally crucified in His existence as temporally limited by His birth and death, with all the power and range and significance of this event for the whole world, but still enclosed yesterday within the limits of His existence, concealed and unknown in the world reconciled to God in Him, not yet exercising the latent power and range and significance of His presence and therefore putting into effect what was done in Him for all men and for the whole created order. This One who came before now comes afresh in the Easter event. He is 'Jesus Christ to-day,' in all His being and action of yesterday, and its whole power for the world, new in the fact that to-day, His death and the empty tomb behind Him, He moves out from the latency of His being and action of yesterday and from the inoperativeness of His power, appearing to His disciples and in them potentially to all men and the whole cosmos, declaring Himself, making known His presence and what has been accomplished in Him for all men and for the whole created order, putting it into effect. With its manifestation and self-declaration, the fact of there and yesterday now becomes the factor of here and to-day. And in virtue of this event, newly come in His self-revelation as the One who came, Jesus Christ will not cease to be this factor and to work as such. Hence 'Jesus Christ for ever' (Heb. 13.8). As this factor, as the Prophet, Witness and Preacher entered into the world, as the light of His mediatorship, of the atonement made in Him, shining from this place, He is the living Jesus Christ, who has death behind Him, the light which shines in the world and can never be extinguished. And the world for its part is what it is enabled to be in the presence of this factor, in encounter with Him, in the shining of His light, in the determination given it by Him.

The citation in 1 Tim. 3.16 from what is probably a liturgical text old even at the time of the composition of the Epistle should be allowed to speak for itself in this connexion: 'He was manifest in the flesh, justified in the Spirit, seen of angels, preached unto the Gentiles, believed on in the world, received up into glory.' The passage is introduced into the Epistle as a comprehensive definition of what is 'by agreed confession' (ὁμολογουμένως) the one great 'mystery of (Christian) godliness' (μέγα τὸ τῆς εὐσεβείας μυστήριον). Its six clauses can hardly be understood as a list of successive saving events such as we have in the oldest versions of the Christian creed. They are rather six references from different standpoints to a single event which can only be that of the resurrection or self-declaration of the living Jesus Christ as the divine act. All the references apply to this. If the passage is really a hymn, it must surely be an Easter hymn, or part of such a hymn.

It is not merely possible but imperative that what took place in the Easter event, the fresh coming of Jesus Christ as the One who came before, should be summed up under the New Testament concept of the coming of Jesus Christ. However the New Testament writers may apply the term in other respects, or refer to it without application, the concrete perception with which they do so is that of the resurrection of Jesus Christ, just as conversely their notion of the resurrection is strictly identical with the full range of content of the concept of coming.

The word 'coming' (cf. for what follows the article by A. Oepke in Kittel) derives from Hellenistic sources and originally means quite simply 'effective presence.' A coming might be a military invasion, or the visitation of a city or district by a high dignitary who, as in the case of the emperor, might sometimes be treated so seriously that the local calendar would be dated afresh from the occasion. The term was also applied sometimes to the helpful intervention of such divine figures as Dionysius or Aesculapius Soter. What is signified by the term, if not the term itself, is familiar and important in the thinking of the Old Testament. From His place, whether Sinai, Sion or heaven, Yahweh comes in the storm, or enthroned over the ark of the covenant, or in His Word or Spirit, or in dreams or visions, or simply and especially in the events of the history of Israel. To the men of His people He comes finally as universal King in the unfolding of His power and glory. The coming of 'one like the Son of man with the clouds of heaven' (Dan. 7.13); the coming of the righteous and victorious Messiah-King abolishing war and establishing peace (cf. Zech. 9.9f.); above all the recurrent Old Testament picture of the coming God of the covenant Himself manifesting Himself in movement from there to here – all these constitute materially the preparatory form of what in the New Testament is called παρουσία in the pregnant technical sense, namely, the effective presence of Jesus Christ.

What is formally meant by the word is best seen from the fact that in the later New Testament (especially the Pastorals, yet also as early as 2 Thess. 2.8) it is found in close proximity to, and sometimes replaced by, the term 'manifestation.' In its Hellenistic origin at least manifestation denotes the making visible of concealed divinity. In 2 Thess. 2:8 both terms appear in a way which is not just plerophoric (so W. Bauer) but materially instructive. With the breath of His mouth the Lord Jesus will slay a hidden but one day manifested lawless one, destroying him at the appearance of his coming. What else can this genitive conjunction mean but that the epiphany of Jesus Christ is the manifestation of His coming or effective presence, or conversely that His coming takes place in His epiphany and therefore His manifestation?

As far as I can see, there are no passages (not even 2 Tim. 1.10) where either term refers abstractly to the first coming of Jesus Christ as such, i.e., to His history and existence within the limits of His birth and death, of Bethlehem and Golgotha. In relation to these there would be no point in speaking either of manifestation or of coming (effective presence). In them He is not even 'manifest in the flesh' (1 Tim. 3.16), and none of the other references in this passage can really apply to His pre-Easter existence as such. To be sure, the Word then became flesh, and His whole work was done in all its dimensions. But the incarnate Word was not yet revealed and seen in His glory (Jn. 1.14). This took place in the event of Easter. In this event we certainly have the coming of the One who came before in that sphere. But it is now His coming in effective presence, because in visible manifestation in the world. It is now His coming in glory as the active and dominant factor within it. It is thus His new coming as the One who came before. It is now His 'coming again,' and in spite of Oepke I do not see how we can avoid this expression as we have provisionally and generally explained it.

We must now continue that, as concerns the scope and content of this event, the New Testament knows of only one coming again of Jesus Christ, of only one new coming of the One who came before, of only one manifestation of His effective presence in the world corresponding to His own unity as the One who came before. This does not exclude the fact that His new coming and therefore His manifestation in effective presence in the world takes place in different forms at the different times chosen and appointed by Himself and in the different relationships which He Himself has ordained. Everything depends, of course, upon our seeing and understanding the one continuous event in all its forms. But in the time of the community and its mission after the Easter revelation it also takes place in the form of the impartation of the Holy Spirit, and it is with this that we are particularly concerned in this sub-section. It will also take place in a different and definitive form (of which we shall have to speak in eschatology), as the return of Jesus Christ as the goal of the history of the Church, the world and each individual, as His coming as the Author of the general resurrection of the dead and the Fulfiller of universal judgment. In all these forms it is one event. Nothing different takes place in any of them. It is not more in one case or less in another. It is the one thing taking place in different ways, in a difference of form corresponding to the willing and fulfilment of the action of its one Subject, the living Jesus Christ. Always and in all three forms it is a matter of the fresh coming of the One who came before. Always and in different ways it is a matter of the coming again of Jesus Christ.[2]

The Easter event is only the first form of this happening. From the standpoint of its substance, scope and content, it is identical with its occurrence in the forms which follow. It is no less significant than these, nor is it to be depreciated in relation to them. On the contrary, the one and total coming in its other forms has its primal and basic pattern in the Easter event, so that we might well be tempted to describe the whole

---

2   The one yet threefold coming of Jesus Christ carries with it both ontological and epistemological ramifications. §69, of which this section is a part, is summarized as such (quoting the opening lines of the Theological Declaration of Barmen): 'Jesus Christ as attested to us in Holy Scripture is the one Word of God whom we must hear and whom we must trust and obey in life and in death' (IV/3: 3). This is a claim about the unity of the Word (person, with ontological implications) as well as the unity of the Word (revelation, with epistemological implications). The 'oneness' of the Word and his reconciling, revealing work is articulated throughout volume four (IV/1.763; IV/2.5; IV/3.293; IV/4.29). While each stage or form is different, 'there can be no question ... of understanding the alteration as more real and complete in its final form and less real and complete in its provisional' (IV/1.328).

event simply as one long fulfilment of the resurrection of Jesus Christ. There are, of course, similar temptations in relation to the second and third forms of the event. We shall not attempt to reduce it in this way, since in so doing we should wander too far not only from the speech and terminology but also the material outlook of the New Testament. Thus, there can be no question that in all its forms the one totality of coming again does really have the character, colours and accents of the Easter event. There can also be no question that this is only the first if also the original form of this one totality.

If we allow the New Testament to say what it has to say, we shall be led in this matter to a thinking which is differentiated even in its incontestable unity, formally corresponding to that which is required for an understanding of the three modes of being of God in relation to His one essence in triunity: one substance in three persons, three persons in one substance.

When the matter is usually spoken of in the New Testament under the terms *parousia* or epiphany, the reference is usually or chiefly to the third and final form, to the eschatological form in the narrower traditional sense, of the return of Jesus Christ, i.e., to His manifestation and effective presence beyond history, the community, the world and the individual human life, and as their absolute future. But reference to this climax of His coming dominates New Testament thought and utterance even where it is materially concerned with the subject without using these particular terms. We can hardly deny or explain this away in such typical passages as the Coming passages in the Synoptics, or the Thessalonian Epistles of Paul, or 1 Cor. 15, or the Apocalypse with its final 'come, Lord Jesus' (22.20). Even the Gospel of John, which seems particularly to invite us to do this with its placing of both the gift of eternal life and the judgment in the present, resists it inasmuch as it is rather strangely the only book in the whole of the New Testament to speak of the last day (ἐσχάτη ἡμέρα) when Jesus will awaken the dead (6.39, 40, 44, 54) and His Word spoken to men will judge them (12.48); and it is advisable not to solve the implied difficulty of interpretation by critical amputation. According to the New Testament, the return of Jesus Christ in the Easter event is not yet as such His return in the Holy Ghost and certainly not His return at the end of the days. Similarly, His return in the Easter event and at the end of the days cannot be dissolved into His return in the Holy Ghost, nor the Easter event and the outpouring of the Holy Spirit into His last coming. In all these we have to do with the one new coming of Him who came before. But if we are to be true to the New Testament, none of these three forms of His new coming, including the Easter event, may be regarded as its only form. The most that we can say is that a particular glory attaches to the Easter event because here it begins, the Easter event being the primal and basic form in which it comes to be seen and grasped in its totality.

Yet, as we must plainly distinguish the resurrection, the outpouring of the Spirit and the final return of Jesus Christ, so we must understand and see them together as forms of one and the same event.[3] A no less sharp warning must be issued against an abstract separation of the three forms of the new coming of Jesus Christ for which there is no basis in the New Testament. How else could we distinguish them except within the unity of the whole and therefore on the assumption of one event in these three forms?

Oepke is surely right when he says of the so-called last discourses in John that in them the 'coming of the Resurrected, the coming in the Spirit and the coming at the end of the days merge into one another,' and when he also says of the Synoptic Jesus that it is impossible to decide to what extent He made a clear distinction between His resurrection and His Coming in its final form. Yet may it not be that we can very definitely decide that He, or the Synoptic and also the Johannine tradition concerning Him, did not in fact make any absolute distinction between them at all in respect of either matter or form? What do we learn from the well-known passages (considered in detail in *C.D.*, III, 2, pp. 499 ff.) in which Jesus unmistakeably prophesies the manifestation of the kingdom of God 'in power' (Mk. 9.1f.), the coming of the Son of Man (Mt. 10.23, 26.64), or at least the sign which directly precedes (Mk.13.30 and *par.*) within the lifetime of those around Him? If we may eliminate in advance what is in its way the greatest triviality of any age, what are we to make of the assumption which underlay a particular school of Neo-Liberal theology, and which is unfortunately encountered only too often outside the narrow circle of this school, namely, that Jesus was deluded? If we find in the coming of the Resurrected, His coming in the Holy Spirit and His coming at the end of the age three forms of His one new coming for all their significant differences, there need be no artificiality in explaining that these passages refer to the first and immediate form in which His coming did really begin in that generation as the Easter event and in which the two remaining forms are plainly delineated and intimated. We are then forced to accept the statement of W. Michaelis which Oepke contests: 'The

---

3   Saint Bernard of Clairvaux: 'We have come to know a threefold coming of the Lord ... his first coming was in the flesh and in weakness, this intermediary coming is in the spirit and in power, the last coming will be in glory and majesty' (cited in Pope Benedict, *Jesus of Nazareth: Holy Week: From the Entrance into Jerusalem to the Resurrection* [San Francisco: Ignatius, 2011], p. 290). Bernard bases this reflection on John 14.23.

resurrection ... is the Coming,' or again the statement of R. Bultmann (with particular reference to John's Gospel): 'The Coming has already taken place,' although we must be careful to make the proviso that these statements are not to be taken exclusively but need to be amplified by the recollection that this is not the whole story. The outpouring of the Holy Spirit is also the coming. In this it has not only taken place but is still taking place to-day. And as it has taken place in the resurrection and is taking place to-day in the outpouring of the Holy Spirit, it is also true that it will take place at the end of the days in the conclusion of the self-revelation of Jesus Christ.[4]

It is thus impossible to relate a concept of the eschatological which is meaningful in the New Testament sense merely to the final stage of the coming. Eschatological denotes the last time. The last time is the time of the world and human history and all men to which a term is already set in the death of Jesus and which can only run towards this appointed end. In the Easter event as the commencement of the new coming of Jesus Christ in revelation of what took place in His life and death, it is also revealed that the time which is still left to the world and human history and all men can only be the last time, i.e., time running towards its appointed end. In this sense the Easter event is the original because the first eschatological event. The impartation of the Holy Spirit is the coming of Jesus Christ in the last time which still remains. As we shall see, it is the promise, given with and through the Holy Spirit, by which the community, and with it the world in which it exists and has its mission, may live in this time which moves towards its end. Hence the new coming of Jesus Christ has an eschatological character in this second form too. If the coming is an eschatological event in its third and final stage as well, this means specifically that in it we have to do with the manifestation and effective presence of Jesus Christ in their definitive form, with His revelation at the goal of the last time. It will consist again in a coming of Jesus Christ, and at this coming this last time, too, will reach the end which is already set for it in His death

---

4   Barth chastises an over-realized eschatology, that is, a belief that the great hope has arrived. He will later say: 'They are Christians as or to the extent that they are really on the move as pilgrims' (IV/3.343). A long line of spiritual and theological reflection characterizes the Christian as a pilgrim (e.g. John Bunyan's famous allegory, *The Pilgrim's Progress*, or a long host of post-Reformation Protestant theology which spoke of itself as theology for pilgrims). Of course, the New Testament suggests the importance of such imagery in texts like 1 Corinthians 10 and Hebrews 3–4, 12–13, where the church is likened to the journeying Israelites in the wilderness. A pilgrim life befits the provisional time of the present. It is all provisional: not our new creation and regeneration as accomplished on the cross and resurrection of Jesus Christ, but its present manifestation; not our justification, but its present form; not the being of Jesus Christ in us and our being in him, but the form in which we are now with him, raised and quickened and resurrected with him (IV/1.330).

and revealed in His resurrection. The happening of the coming is thus eschatological throughout its course. And it is this, as already indicated from the very first by the Easter event, because already and particularly in this event the term set to time in the death of Jesus Christ is revealed and the character and stamp of the last time is given to all the time which remains.

When we treat of the unity of the three forms or stages of the one event of the return of Jesus Christ, it is perhaps worth considering and exegetically helpful, again in analogy to the doctrine of the Trinity, to think of their mutual relationship as a kind of *perichoresis* (cf. *CD.*, I, 1, p. 425).[5] It is not merely that these three forms are interconnected in the totality of the action presented in them all, or in each of them in its unity and totality, but that they are mutually related as the forms of this one action by the fact that each of them also contains the other two by way of anticipation or recapitulation, so that, without losing their individuality or destroying that of the others, they participate and are active and revealed in them. As the Resurrected from the dead Jesus Christ is virtually engaged already in the outpouring of the Holy Spirit, and in the outpouring of the Holy Spirit He is engaged in the resurrection of all the dead and the execution of the last judgment. The outpouring of the Holy Spirit obviously takes place in the power of His resurrection from the dead, yet it is already His knocking as the One who comes finally and definitively, and it is active and perceptible as such. Similarly His final coming to resurrection and judgment is only the completion of what He has begun in His own resurrection and continued in the outpouring of the Holy Spirit.

To be sure, this is a view which is never systematised in the New Testament or presented in the form of instruction. But this does not mean that we are false to the Bible, or obscure its statements concerning the coming, by adopting this view. Are we not more likely to throw light on them if we advance it with the necessary prudence yet also

5   *Perichoresis* refers to the mutual interpenetration of things, persons, or, as suggested here, events. They are mutually implicated: the resurrection involves the new life that will bring the Spirit and the kingdom; the giving of the Spirit flows from resurrection and to the kingdom; the kingdom culminates the trajectory of resurrection and outpouring. While Barth argues that the order of being flows one way (from resurrection onward), he elsewhere suggests that the order of exposition could differ. For example, he spoke at two points in his career about 'the possibility of a theology of the third article, … a theology predominantly and decisively of the Holy Spirit' ('Concluding Unscientific Postscript on Schleiermacher', in *The Theology of Schleiermacher* [ed. Dietrich Ritschl; trans. Geoffrey Bromiley; Grand Rapids: Eerdmans, 1982], p. 278; *Protestant Theology in the Nineteenth Century: Its Background and History* [trans. Brian Cozens and John Bowden; Grand Rapids: Eerdmans, 2002], pp. 458–60). Such a theology would have to take the form of perichoretically relating the Spirit's ministry to the risen Christ, but it could begin with the third article of the Apostles' Creed nonetheless.

[handwritten margin note: Is this how (one can speak of the "terrible beauty" of the cross?]

boldness? Are there not many passages in the New Testament which with their apparent contradictions cannot be satisfactorily explained except on the assumption of such a view? This is not a key to open every lock. But it is one which we do well not to despise.[6]

We have now tried to understand the distinctive feature of the Easter event in the great context in which it stands and from which it must not be wrested. May we not say even in this respect that to a large degree it has not been taken with the seriousness appropriate to it, being hardly at all, or only very partially, seen and understood in this context? But after this attempt to clarify and enlarge the horizon, we must now return to this distinctive feature as such. What is specifically contributed in the resurrection of Jesus Christ as the commencement of His new coming as the One who came before, and therefore in the revelation of His reconciling being and action in its primal and basic form as the entry into His prophetic office?

[...]

This, then, is the new coming in our historical sphere of the Jesus Christ who once came in His own time as very God and very man. This, then, is His new coming in the glory and revelation of His mediatorial act, as the light and Word of life, in His prophetic office. In correspondence with the fact that it is the form of His coming between the commencement and the goal, and in correspondence with our historical place between, it is His coming as the hope of all men. We say this when we say that it is His universally relevant coming in the Holy Spirit and in the promise of the Holy Spirit. As He comes here and now in this form to us and all men, His second coming, His prophetic work, proceeds here and now without a break or pause, without the arising of a vacuum in which nothing happens and we and all men are left to ourselves without Him, in another sphere than that of His light and Word, being referred simply to recollection and expectation. As we have seen, the Easter event, which initiated His coming again in glory, His self-declaration, as the One who came before, was limited by His ascension, which in the language of the Bible speaks of His exit from the sphere which death limits for all creatures and His corresponding

---

6   Barth seems to suggest that the various triune actions and eschatological events ⟨resurrection, Pentecost, and return/judgement/kingdom⟩ will seem contradictory unless we ask intertextual questions about their interpenetration. Many modern biblical scholars – committed to reading Matthew independent of Paul and Revelation – would juxtapose the apocalyptic preaching of Matthew 25 with the early sermons regarding Pentecost in Acts or the teaching of Paul to the Thessalonians about the return of Jesus. Barth believes that a Trinitarian commitment to the interpenetration of these various eschatological moments allows us to (1) honour the diversity of moments while (2) acknowledging their unity.

entry into the mystery of the living God. In this transition He appeared then and there to His disciples. Anticipating it in His own person, He indicated to them then and there the goal of His self-declaration as the Mediator between God and the world and therefore the ultimate future of the relationship and intercourse between God and the world, i.e., the redemption and consummation. In this form in which He was then and there present and manifest to His disciples. He is not now present and manifest to the world or to us who exist between this event and the ultimate future indicated by it. The form in which He is here and now present and manifest to the world in the time between these two times, the form in which He comes to us here and now, is the power of His coming in that first form, of the light which from it shines into this world of ours.[7] It is the form of His coming in which He is the hope of all men, namely, the promise of His Holy Spirit.

There are many old and new prejudices and reservations in respect of the meaning and character of this new coming which takes place here and now in our sphere. These are shortsighted and restrictive because they weaken the material content. They are thus to be dispelled.

In this form (1) it is no less genuinely His own direct and personal coming, His coming, presence and revelation, than was His coming there and then to His disciples in the Easter event, or than will be one day His coming in its final and conclusive form as the Judge of the quick and the dead. He is in heaven. He has entered the mystery of the living God. He is not present, then, as He was once as the One who came before, or as He was in the Easter event, at a specific and limited point in creaturely space. Nor is He extended over all points in creaturely space as maintained by the original Ubiquitarianism of the Lutherans[8] He is to be sought in heaven 'at the right hand of God the Father Almighty' and therefore up above (Col. 3.1). This does not

---

7   Though Barth employs the notion of light here and elsewhere, he follows the Reformed tradition broadly in emphasizing the verbal nature of revelation. Thus he will regularly mix and mingle visual with vocal terminology (following the suggestion of Exodus 34, where God's visual appearance to Moses is depicted as speech). See the following quotes with italicized terms referencing revelation via visual and verbal terminology: 'Reconciliation is not a dark or dumb event, but *perspicuous* and *vocal*' (IV/3: 8, italics mine); '*statement, word, kerygma, light*' (IV/3.221, italics mine); 'with all the *clarity* and urgency of a *Word*, which whether it is received or not, is *spoken* here today' (IV/3.224, italics mine). For Barth the verbal nature of revelation accentuates its actualist and event-oriented nature: it is never the possession of humans but always the free gift of the triune God.

8   *Ubiquity* is the notion of the divine and human natures sharing properties. In particular Lutheran Eucharistic theology maintained that the divinity of the Son enabled him to be present in multiple places at one time as a human being; thus, Jesus could be in, with, and under the bread and wine as a human being. Barth joins with other Reformed theologians in arguing that ubiquity cannot be squared with a genuine humanity.

mean, however, that He is imprisoned there (for we remember that this is indeed the mystery of the living God). It does not mean that He is prevented from being and working and revealing Himself here too. How can He who is there not also be willing and able to be here too, and to do His work here? The fact that He is there at the right hand of God means that He is in full possession and exercise of the freedom of action, the authority of rule and the disposal of grace of God Himself. It means that He exercises them here and now, in the sphere of existence left to us, on this side of the fulfilment of His prophetic work and in its progress to its goal, in the form of the power of His resurrection and the promise of His Spirit. Yet He does exercise them truly and properly and not improperly. In this form we have to do with His own direct and personal coming even though we still await the final form. In this form we are concerned in the full sense of the words with His coming, presence and revelation.

In this form of His coming (2) He is no other, but the Son of God and Man, the Mediator between God and the world, in the totality and not merely a part of His being and existence. That He comes to us here and now in the promise of the Spirit does not mean then (as is rather incautiously maintained by *Qu.* 47 of the *Heidelberg Catechism*) that He comes only in the power of His pure deity, His humanity being left in heaven.[9] In His presence and activity in the promise of the Spirit, if it is really His promise of His Spirit and the power of His resurrection, there can be no question of a restitution of the separation between divine and human being which was done away in His incarnation. It was not in such separation, but in the unity of His divine and human natures, that He went to heaven, and entered the mystery of the living God, and now lives at the right hand of God the Father Almighty. When He came again in the Easter event, having crossed the frontier of death imposed on all creatures, He did not appear to His disciples as another and purely divine being, but as the One who had come before and lived among them and died on Golgotha. His coming in its final form will be His coming as this One. And in exactly the same way His coming in the promise of the Spirit between these two times is His new coming as this One who came before. In this form of His coming, presence and self-revelation, He is in this mode the One who came before, very God and very man, the One whose unique life and death are attested in the New Testament, on the basis of the Easter event, as the reconciliation of

---

9   Heidelberg Catechism Q. 47. Is not Christ then with us even to the end of the world, as he has promised? A. Christ is very man and very God; with respect to his human nature, he is no more on earth; but with respect to his Godhead, majesty, grace and spirit, he is at no time absent from us.

the world to God accomplished in Him. As this One in His totality He is here and now the hope of all men. How would He or could He be this if His presence and action in the promise of the Spirit were those of another, of a Word of God without and apart from the flesh assumed by Him? Even in the promise of the Spirit, however, He is this One, and as such the hope of the world. He is the incarnate Word of God, not abandoning this flesh of ours, not leaving it behind somewhere (even in heaven, in the mystery of God), but acting, speaking and revealing His glory in the flesh.

His working in this form of His coming (3) is qualitatively no less than it was in the first form and will be in the last.[10] The promise of the Spirit is no more but also no less than the power of the resurrection of Jesus Christ operating in the time between the times.[11] This power, however, is absolutely His power as Son of God and Man. It is the power of the atonement made in Him, which in its revelation, and in every form of its revelation, is no less but in the full sense just as powerful as it is in itself. For the prophetic work of Jesus Christ is no mere appendage or echo of His high-priestly and kingly work. It is an integral element in the whole occurrence. Hence if the promise of the Spirit is one of the forms of the prophetic work of Jesus Christ, then quite apart from the dignity to be ascribed to the Holy Spirit on a sound doctrine of the Trinity, we cannot possibly think less of His work than we do of that of Jesus Christ Himself. The Spirit is His Spirit, and therefore the Spirit of the Father, and therefore without any reservation or diminution the Spirit of God. His promise is, then, in both its senses

10 Jesus Christ continues as the primary actor in this provisional time. As he says earlier: 'As He lives, Jesus Christ speaks for Himself ... He is His own authentic witness ... of Himself He grounds and summons and creates knowledge of Himself and His life' (IV/3.46); 'In short, it is not in the first instance the world, or the Church, or an individual man suffering under and either rebelling against or in some way enduring the conflict, but He Himself, the Resurrected, who is still on the way, still in conflict, still moving towards the goal which He has not yet reached' (IV/3.329). Barth believes the continuing agency of Jesus has serious polemical repercussions for addressing both Roman Catholicism and liberal Protestantism, both of which he sees as co-ordinating or replacing the current agency of Jesus with creaturely – whether churchly or culturally construed, respectively – agency (IV/3.349). On his approach to the prophetic office of Christ, see John Webster, '"Eloquent and Radiant": The Prophetic Office of Christ and the Mission of the Church', in Barth's Moral Theology: Human Action in Barth's Thought (London: T & T Clark, 1998), pp. 125–50.

11 For a wonderful analysis of Barth's doctrine of the Holy Spirit and his role in mediating the presence of Christ, see George Hunsinger, 'The Mediator of Communion: Karl Barth's Doctrine of the Holy Spirit', in Disruptive Grace: Studies in the Theology of Karl Barth (Grand Rapids: Eerdmans, 2000), pp. 148–85. Hunsinger's study is especially important, because it addresses a consistent criticism raised against Barth, namely, that his Christological focus renders his theology of the Spirit insufficient. Barth himself was not unaware that his emphasis on the objective might be read as rendering the subjective moot (I/1.453; IV/2.297; IV/3.10).

the work of God. As the Spirit of the Lord (2 Cor. 3.17), the Spirit is Himself the Lord. To restrict His dignity or depreciate His work is thus to question God Himself. To reject Him in this time between is to reject God, i.e., the God who in this time acts and speaks in the Son by the Holy Ghost. Hence the famous hard saying in Mt. 12.31 about the sin of blasphemy against the Holy Ghost which cannot be forgiven because it denies the presence of God as the source of a life of forgiveness. The coming, presence and revelation of Jesus Christ in the promise of the Spirit are not confronted by another coming, promise and revelation distinguished by the fact that they are more divine, more glorious, more effective to salvation, and therefore to be taken more seriously and valued more highly. If we do not have here the only form of the prophecy of Jesus Christ, but only the second and middle form, in this form the prophecy is the total proclamation of the total love of God and the total salvation of man. It is not because of the form, but of the men who may be and become the recipients of the Spirit and His promise, that the impression or notion arises that what is addressed and given us in this time between by God through the Spirit is less valuable, less helpful and even perhaps inadequate. The 'sufferings of this present time' (Rom. 8.18); the fact that in this time we and all creation look forward with groaning (Rom. 8.19f.) to the redemption and consummation and therefore to the coming of Jesus Christ in His final form; the cry: 'O wretched man that I am!' in face of the contradiction in which even the Christian and apostle continually finds himself entangled (Rom. 7.24) – these cannot mean that Christians have cause to complain of an inadequacy of the Spirit who is given them as the pledge and firstfruits of the ultimate future, or of His eternal and temporal promise, or of the lights and powers and gifts which are bestowed with it. The promise of the Spirit gives us no grounds for sighing. On the contrary, it is the power of the resurrection of Jesus Christ. There is repeated in it the anticipation of His final revelation. In it all things are already given to us and the world. From the standpoint of the Holy Spirit and His promise, of His presence and action, of the Giver and the gift, there can be nothing lacking here and now to those to whom it is addressed and given, unless it be the progress of the prophecy of Jesus Christ from its present to its future fullness, 'from glory to glory.' And indeed, according to 2 Cor. 3.18, even this is the work of the Lord who is Spirit, so that it can throw no shadow on the perfection of His work. This contention is indispensable to a right understanding of the human situation in this time of ours. The idea that it is a vacuum must be completely dispelled even in the form which suggests that it may be regarded and therefore accepted and endured as a 'day of small things.' If it really is this or worse, if our existence in it may be represented with some reason as sojourn or pilgrimage in a vale of tears, this is not because it is no longer the time of Easter and not yet the time of the end, but 'only' the time of the Holy Ghost. For what could 'only' mean in such a context? If it is the time of the Holy Spirit given to Christians with His sure and powerful pledges, and promised to non-Christians with His equally sure and powerful pledges, then this settles the fact that in it, even on the assumption of the conditions set and obtaining for us men in the transition and therefore the limitation, vulnerability and weakness in which we now exist, even within world-occurrence moving to this goal and end, everything is of God and is therefore in order, i.e., in the special yet divinely ordained order appropriate to this time of transition. If we can and should long for the new order of the future world – and the Spirit Himself makes this unavoidable in His great promise for the last days – then we can and should also rejoice with unstinted gratitude in the order which is present already, being established by the presence and action of Jesus Christ in the promise of the Spirit. Not only was God glorious in the past, and not only will He be glorious in the final fulfilment of His promise, but He is glorious here and now in the promise of His Spirit, He Himself being present and active yesterday, to-day and to-morrow. In relation to Him there is no cause to bemoan or bewail or reject our present, but rather to extol and accept it from the heart. How can the joyful call to advance which we hear in it and which we should observe give to it a tragic aspect? If it were really tragic, there would be a serious threat that we should not hear this call, but that in our expectant longing for the coming new world and its order we should be disillusioned rather than genuinely comforted and encouraged. If we do not honour the little, penultimate pledge as seriously given to us here and now by the present and living Christ, we cannot appreciate or make much of the great and ultimate pledge for the eternal there and then. In these circumstances, have we really received the Spirit and His twofold pledge, the temporal as well as the eternal, the eternal as well as the temporal? If we have, how can we help being merry even here and to-day? It is no contradiction to us that in the one hope in Jesus Christ our time is given us only for eternity and eternity only for our time.

Yet the question which we have already posed and answered once arises again. Why is it, in what sense, and on the basis of what higher necessity, that a history of the prophecy of Jesus Christ must arise at all in these three forms, and must still be in progress for us in this middle form? Why must there be, between the Easter time and the definitive end time, this intervening time, the time of the promise of the Holy Spirit, the time of Jesus Christ as our hope? Why was not the beginning immediately the goal, the goal already the beginning, the appearance of the living Jesus Christ to His disciples His coming, presence and revelation to the eyes and ears of all creation and therefore their redemption and consummation? We can no longer restrict ourselves to our previous answer that it was and is the goodness of God that to His own glory and the salvation of the creature He does not overlook the latter, but wills to give and gives it time and space and opportunity for the expression of its freedom within the context of His work.[12] This is true. But we can now give the better and deeper answer that the return of Jesus Christ in this middle form, that His prophecy in its extension as ongoing history, that the reconciliation of the world to God as it is not yet concluded as revelation but still moves forward to its goal, has its own specific glory. We do not forget or depreciate the provoking and even dreadful riddle, indeed, it is daily and hourly before us both in great things and small, that in the form of the promise of His Spirit, Jesus Christ is dealing both in Christians and non-Christians with men who are not yet redeemed and perfected in a world which, while it is reconciled to God, is still wrapped in such thick darkness. Now this riddle is not as such solved or set aside. Yet supposing that it has a bright and perhaps luminous side on which it necessarily does not appear so dreadful but may be tolerated with unbroken joy? Supposing that the great regime of the transition which characterises the 'still' and 'not yet' that cause so much human questioning and longing and sighing, which characterises our time and situation and our existence in them, is not at all negative as His regime, nor a mere burden which has to be cast off as quickly as possible, but a specific form of the greatness of the pitying love of God, a specific demonstration of the reconciliation of the world as it is accomplished in Jesus Christ? Is it then something negative, or does it include a lack, that Jesus Christ is here and now the hope of us all, or that He is thus present in the promise of the

---

12   Earlier Barth says: 'He Himself who is alone the Head and Lord will naturally speak the last and decisive Word in this respect too. But first He allows the creation reconciled in Him to speak. He has not yet spoken His last and decisive Word because in this respect, too, He does not will to be alone or without us, because He does not will to go over our heads, because He wills to give us a share in His work in our independence as the creatures of God summoned to freedom, as those who are justified and sanctified in Him. And so He wills to give us time and space for this participation in His work. He wills to preserve the world, to cause it to persist, in its present and provisional form, in order that it should be the place where He can be perceived and accepted and known and confessed by the creature as the living Word of God' (IV/3.332). It is not only time for people to receive him, though, but for him as well: 'the provisional nature of our situation has its true basis and determination in the fact that it is the good will of Jesus Christ to move from the commencement of His revelation to its completion, not causing the commencement and the completion to coincide, but Himself *first to be provisionally who He is and to do provisionally what He does, giving Himself time and place for combat*' (IV/3.330, italics mine).

Spirit? We have seen that in this way He is no less real, that He is not another, that He is no less the One He was and is and will be. How can it be burdensome or a matter of embarrassment and unsettlement that He is present in this way? Why should we not have here a particular, and in its particularity a necessary, indispensable and true development of His glory, which deserves our praise and thanksgiving, so that instead of doubting and murmuring we should joyfully accept it? Can we reckon as a demonstration of the glory and humanity of God only the great final promise whose recipients, bearers and possessors we may now be, and not in like manner, according to its own truth and power, the enclosed, little, penultimate promise according to which He is on the way with us and we may be on the way with Him? Will the faithfullness of God only begin to be His total and as such effective faithfullness when this great and ultimate promise is fulfilled? Or does it not encounter us in its totality and power even in the fulfilments of the little, penultimate promise in which Jesus Christ is with us here and now, our Companion on the way through time, the Mediator, Saviour and Lord that He is, our Leader present all the days in the power of His leadership? What basis is there for the speculative wish or postulate that the first form of the coming, presence and revelation of Jesus Christ should also have been its last? This would imply the impossible and blasphemous assumption that there ought not to have been the particular development of the grace, the deity and humanity of God in which Jesus Christ is the hope of all and therefore in the promise of the Spirit, but that God should have withheld from Himself and us His presence and action in the form of His provisional promise in time, and the demonstration of His power in our present, under the conditions and in the limitations and problems of our present, and in the vulnerability of our existence, refraining from being our God or having us as His people in this way. We have only to realise how great God is in the fact that He did not refrain from willing to give, and giving, and continuing to give the history of His dealings and fellowship with the world and us men, i.e., the history of salvation, this form as well, and we shall see at once how empty is this postulate, and be kept from raising this idle question even in dilettante fashion. The bright and luminous side of the riddle of our existence in transition, in the time of the 'still' and 'not yet,' is the fact that Jesus Christ Himself is in transition, living, acting, speaking and working under the same sign, and that this is not even partially to His shame but to His distinctive glory, so that it cannot be to our hurt that He is present in the form of the promise of the Spirit, but to our full salvation. To Him there is really to be ascribed praise and thanksgiving even from the depths and in and under all the sighing for the progress and conclusion of His work.[13] Unreservedly joyful praise and sincere thanksgiving must be given Him for the fact that He willed and arranged that we should have time and place and opportunity not merely for the expression of our creaturely freedom but for life in hope in Him as the hope of all men, for life under the promise of God and in the power of this promise.

13   For thoughtful reflection on Barth's analysis of the ascension and heavenly session of Jesus – 'the progress ... of His work' for which he is 'to be ascribed praise and thanksgiving' – see Andrew Burgess, *The Ascension in Karl Barth* (Barth Studies; Aldershot: Ashgate, 2004), part 1.

CHAPTER 14

VOCATION AND WITNESS

Where it is believed and acknowledged in the Holy Spirit, the revelation of God creates men who do not exist without seeking God in Jesus Christ, and who cannot cease to testify that He has found them.[1]

The doctrine of the church appears throughout volume four of the *Church Dogmatics*. At the beginning of this volume, Barth laid out his plan to consider the 'knowledge of the work of the Holy Spirit in (1) the gathering, (2) the upbuilding and (3) the sending of the community (IV/1.79). Like his pneumatology, Barth's ecclesiology has been much maligned. As exemplified by Mangina (see below), many advocates of ecclesiologies tethered primarily to the practices of the church and the *communio* metaphysics of the Roman Catholic *nouvelle théologie* (e.g. exemplified by Roman Catholics as significant as Henri de Lubac, Hans Urs von Balthasar, Pope John Paul II and Pope Benedict XVI, and Protestants like Robert Jenson) find Barth's ecclesiology to be rather ethereal and idealist. His critics suggest that too little attention is devoted to the concrete shape of the church's practices and the natural media employed by the Spirit's grace in the life of the church.

Barth is not opposed to creaturely agency and churchly action. But he is committed to the distinction between uncreated and created being, and thus he always wants to distinguish divine and human action and, further, to relativize the latter by means of the former. In addition, he strongly maintains the need to distinguish between the person of Christ and the people of Christ. So, for example, he opposes language of 'incarnational ministry', saying 'Thus to speak of a continuation or extension of the incarnation in the Church is not only out of place but even blasphemous. Its distinction from the world is not the same as His; it is not that of the Creator from His creature. Its superiority to the world is not the same as His; it is not that of the Lord seated at the right hand of the Father. Hence it must guard as if from the plague against any posturing or acting as if in relation to world-occurrence it were another Christ, or a vicar of Christ, or a co-redemptress, or a mediator of all graces, not only out of fear

1   CD I/2.362.

of God, but also because in any such behaviour, far from really exalting itself or discharging such functions, it can only betray, surrender, hazard and lose its true invisible being, and therefore its true distinction from the world and superiority to world-occurrence' (IV/3.729).

This selection comes from Barth's consideration of the 'sending of the Christian community' (IV/3.681–901). This paragraph (§72) addresses 'the people of God in world-occurrence', 'the community for the world', 'the task of the community', and 'the ministry of the community'. This excerpt comes from the fourth section, where it unpacks the particular service fulfilled by the church, namely, that the church is 'ordained for its part to confess Him before all men, to call them to Him, and thus to make known to the whole world that the covenant between God and man concluded in Him is the first and final meaning of its history, and that His future manifestation is already here and now its great, effective, and living hope' (IV/3.681).

Bibliography

Karl Barth, 'The Real Church', *Scottish Journal of Theology* 3, no. 3 (1950), pp. 337–51.

Michael Allen, 'The Church and the churches: A Dogmatic Essay on Ecclesial Invisibility', *European Journal of Theology* 16, no. 2 (2007), pp. 113–19.

Eberhard Busch, *Karl Barth and the Pietists: The Young Karl Barth's Critique of Pietism and Its Response* (trans. Daniel Bloesch; Downers Grove, IL: InterVarsity, 2004).

Joseph Mangina, 'Bearing the Marks of Jesus: The Church of the Economy of Salvation in Barth and Hauerwas', *Modern Theology* 52 (1999), pp. 269–305.

John Webster, '"Life from the Third Dimension": Human Action in Barth's Early Ethics', in *Barth's Moral Theology: Human Action in Barth's Thought* (Edinburgh/Grand Rapids: T & T Clark/Eerdmans, 1998), pp. 11–40.

The Text (*CD* IV/3.830–840)

The ministry of the community is very definite, and therefore limited, but also full of promise. This must be our next theme.

It is definite (1) because it consists quite simply in the fact that as the community of Jesus Christ it has to exist actively for the world, as we saw in the second sub-section, and therefore to execute its task within it by attesting to it the Word of God, as we saw in the third. It is for this that it is sent by God to men. It is in this, in its whence and whither, that it has its specific basis of existence. There took place there the gracious work of God, as there still takes place its disclosure in His gracious self-revelation. And there exist here the men for whom it took place and to whom it is revealed, but who have not yet received it, who do not yet know that it took place for them and is revealed to them, for whom it seems to this extent to have taken place and to be revealed in vain. Between the two, in the service of God and serving men, there strides Jesus Christ in His prophetic office and work. As the living Word of God in the calling, enlightening and awakening power of the Holy Spirit, He marches through the history of humanity which hastens to its goal and end, continually moving from our yesterday, through our to-day into our to-morrow.[2] Yet He does not do so alone. He is accompanied by the community gathered, built up and sent by His attestation. He is surrounded by the people established and characterised by the ministry laid upon it. Thus the ministry of this people also takes place in the course, in the constantly changing stages and situations, of ongoing human history. And its ministry of witness, ordered in relation to that of Jesus Christ, is also both a ministry to God and a ministry to man: a ministry to God in which it may serve man; and a ministry to man in which it may serve God; and therefore a ministry to the God who speaks to man in His Word, and to the man who is already called and now summoned to hear, perceive and accept the Word of God.

The ministry of the community is given this concrete definiteness as a ministry to God and man by its institution and ordination as such in the discipleship of Jesus Christ. He, or the Gospel which He proclaims and which proclaims Him, is the content of the witness which is alone at issue in its ministry: He as very God and very Man; He as Mediator between the two; He as the Executor of the divine work of grace accomplished for men; He as the man in whom it has already reached its goal and is already valid for all; He as the one Word of God and its one Hearer, Witness and Guarantor in advance of all others. Other service can be offered both to God and man, some of it real and some only apparent. But the mark which distinguishes all other such service from the ministry of the community is the lack of necessity and certainty with which it is genuine service of

---

2   This section addresses the prophetic office of Jesus as well as the sending of the Spirit to the church (the 'Christian community'). It is summarized earlier: 'The Holy Spirit is the enlightening power of the living Lord Jesus Christ in which He confesses the community called by Him as His body, i.e., as His own earthly-historical form of existence, by entrusting to it the ministry of His prophetic Word and therefore the provisional representation of the calling of all humanity and indeed of all creatures as it has taken place in Him. He does this by sending it among the peoples as His own people, ordained for its part to confess Him before all men, to call them to Him and thus to make known to the whole world that the covenant between God and man concluded in Him is the first and final meaning of its history, and that His future manifestation is already here and now its great, effective and living hope' (IV/3.681).

both God and man, the latter as the irresistible consequence of the former and the former as the root of the latter. On the one side, it may perhaps be merely genuine service of God, and only apparently so in this abstraction. On the other side, it may perhaps be merely genuine service of man, and only apparently so in the corresponding abstraction. Or the connexion in virtue of which it either is or pretends to be both is perhaps on the one side or the other so slight, contingent or arbitrary that it cannot really and truly be either the one or the other. The ministry of the great, primary and true Minister Jesus Christ is with clear and indissoluble unity both service of God and of man, and both truly and properly. Now the community ministers, however imperfectly, in His school and discipleship. It is orientated by His ministry. It continually orientates itself by it. And inasmuch as it does so, its service of God and man is distinguished by its recognisable and basic unity from all other true or pretended service. Executed in the name of Jesus Christ, it is thus a definite ministry in this concrete sense. Executed by it as His community, it cannot fail to be in movement wholly from God and wholly to man. More clearly in some cases and less clearly in others, but always at least in outline, the essential and characteristic action of Christendom in all the forms and formations of its history is always distinguished in this way from all other human action and indeed from all other creaturely occurrence.

As concerns its definiteness more specifically as the service of God, it is to be noted that it can be discharged as such (in the service of man) only as it continually becomes this, i.e., only as the community does not cease to pray, and so does not cease to be granted, that its ministry, which it can execute only in very human fashion, may continually acquire the character of service of God without which it cannot be true service of man, and that it may be acceptable to God as such. It cannot be taken for granted that it really has and does not merely seem to have this character. It cannot count on this as a given factor. If and when it has it, this is always the gift of free grace which God has certainly promised and always does promise to His community, but which He does not owe it, which it has rather the responsibility of continually seeking from Him and receiving at His hands. That its ministry as true service of man should primarily and supremely become service of God is something which can only happen in its ongoing encounters with the source of its knowledge and confession, in its vitally necessary listening to the voice of the Good Shepherd, which means in practice its constant listening to the prophets and apostles called by Him, and therefore its constant investigation of Scripture and instruction by it.[3] Because the Spirit which enlightens the community is not its own spirit but the Holy Spirit, what matters is that there should be heard the sigh which it must never neglect at any stage or at any turn of the way: Come, Creator Spirit! God Himself, His presence and action, are required if its service of man is not to be only this and therefore not very good as such, but is to take place with the character of service of God which is decisive for its soundness as service of man, i.e., if it is to be really on the way from God to man in its witness.

As concerns its definiteness more specifically as service of man, it is to be noted that there can be no doubt that it is true service of man if it is true service of God. It may be pointed out, however, that as true service of man and therefore true ministry of witness it will be addressed first and supremely to the men who do not share the knowledge of the community and are thus strangers to it, but then necessarily in this connexion to those who do share its knowledge and thus belong to it. It is thus a ministry both outside of itself and within, and the two in a very definite order. In the light of what we have said in the previous sub-sections concerning its existence and task, it need hardly be established that it is comprehensively and decisively a service of mission and therefore a ministry outside of itself. It has to be light to those who in some way are still in darkness, drawing their attention to the light of life which shines for them. It has to call them to knowledge and obedience, attesting to them the Word of God. In principle it stands in this service and therefore in the service of unbelievers and rebels of all kinds, from lapsed or dead Christians at home to pure heathen abroad, from practical and crude atheists and enemies of the race to theoretical and refined. It stands in the service of those who in fact live in the world without God and their fellows, and therefore in forfeiture of their own true selves. To such it is sent. When active in this field it is what it truly is. Yet its resolute outward service has necessarily an inner dimension. Its witness must also be addressed to its own members and continually made perceptible to them. None of the Christians united in it so shares in its knowledge and confession that he does not need every day to be

---

3   Barth highlights the listening nature of the church's vocation, even when it must itself be a speaker to the world. Earlier he spoke of 'the vocation of man': 'The Word of the living Jesus Christ is the creative call by which He awakens man to an active knowledge of the truth and thus receives him into the new standing of the Christian, namely, into a particular fellowship with Himself, thrusting him as His afflicted but well-equipped witness into the service of His prophetic work' (IV/3.481). The Christian is 'afflicted' (dependent and daily needy) but 'well-equipped' (promised and delivered grace in the gospel) – Jesus acts now to ensure this in an ongoing way through his speech by the Spirit. Barth emphasizes the present activity of *the Son* through the Spirit, reflecting the emphasis of Jesus' words that he will lose none of those given him by his Father (John 6.39).

enlightened and awakened afresh to this participation, and therefore nourished, comforted and admonished as a living Christian.)The same Word which the community has to attest to the world will and must be continually heard afresh by it to its own constant gathering, upbuilding and sending.[4] In this sphere as well, therefore, its witness must never cease. If it were to fail here, its outer witness might be compared to the empty bed of a stream which has been sealed at its source, or to the sowing of bad or shrivelled seed. Christians can obviously be serviceable in the ministry of the Word to those without only if they find themselves constantly placed under the same Word. This relationship is not to be reversed. The indispensable ministry of the community must not become, as has happened and still happens on innumerable occasions, an end in itself, the true and dominant purpose of the service to be rendered by it. If its inward service is not to become an institution for private satisfaction in concert, or a work of sterile inbreeding, it must accept the priority of its sending to the world, of its task in relation to those without. Yet for the sake of the execution of this task, in order that the missionary community may be the living and authentic Christian community which is able and willing to execute it, its witness must also be directed inwards to its own members.[5] In this respect we may think of the circular motion of the heart which in order to pump blood through the whole organism not only goes out in the diastole but also has to return in the systole, yet only to go out again in the renewed diastole. In this relationship of outward and inward action, the ministry of the community will always be both true service of God and true service of man. We need not waste words in showing how seldom this relationship between its outer and its inner ministry has been correctly perceived, understood and achieved by Christianity in our hemisphere right up to our own times. It is to be hoped that it may be led to a fresh realisation by the existence and example of the so-called young churches of Asia and Africa, assuming that the latter do not age too quickly and come to be churches with a decisive inward and only an occasional outward orientation.

In this definiteness, the ministry laid on the community has (2) its

---

4   Barth believes the gospel must be preached to Christians daily even as it must also be proclaimed to non-Christians. The gospel must confront the fickle fears of the Christian with the promise of Jesus. There is a progression here – 'gathering, upbuilding, sending' (and only in that order) – but it is not a progress beyond or around the gospel, rather it is a progress deeper into the gospel.

5   The church must be refreshed by the gospel, so that she may proclaim the gospel to others. Barth sees two dangers: either that the church would stop its mission to others (and thus become an institution akin to a religious country club; cf. IV/3.655–656) or that she would attempt such a mission without constantly being sustained by the gospel herself (and thus become a self-righteous institution proclaiming life in Jesus and practising life in her own power).

limitation. We shall consider this from two angles. It is determined by the fact that it is ministry, and more specifically by the fact that it is ministry of witness.

It is ministry – ministry to God and to man, no less, no more, no other. It is no less, and therefore in no conceivable form is it either a neutral co-existence with God and man or a domination and control on the one side or the other. Ministry means active subordination.[6] As the ministry of the community, this means its active subordination to God from whom it derives and therefore to man to whom it turns and whom it is to serve if it serves God. God demands, and man may expect of it, no less than faithfullness in this active subordination. That which it has to do in obedience to its mission and task must not sink below this level.

Yet no more is demanded nor to be expected. It can only serve God and man. It can neither carry through God's work to its goal nor lead men to the point of accepting it. It transgresses the limits of its mission and task, is guilty of culpable arrogance and engages in a futile undertaking if it makes this the goal and end of its activity, assuming responsibility both for the going out of the Word of God and its coming to man. If this takes place at all, it does so in the power of the Holy Spirit over whom it has no power. Its task is simply to serve this happening, i.e., to assist both God and man. This task is serious and difficult enough. It can and should be grateful that it is committed to it and that it is spared anything more. It can and should be humble enough to be content with it. It is called and engaged to faithfullness in service and not to mastery.

Finally, it is not commanded to do anything other than render its specific service to God and man, and therefore it is not commanded to pursue fooling about which, quite irrespective of its possibility, importance or necessity, cannot be its concern and can only disturb and confuse the action demanded of it.[7] It can, of course, be said of

6 Active subordination highlights the nature of ministry (*diakonia*) as 'service' of a particularly active sort (cf. IV/3.833). One serves a master, seeking to meet his or her needs and wants. One does so, not by losing oneself or ceasing to act, but by being thoroughly attentive to his or her directives and signals and acting accordingly. Barth radically defines the church *vis à vis* Jesus Christ: 'The community is the earthly-historical form of the existence of Jesus Christ Himself' (IV/1.661). The Christological concentration of his thoughts on ecclesiology impel him to speak of its invisibility as well as its visibility in faith (for exposition of the often misunderstood doctrinal topic in conversation with Barth, see Michael Allen, 'The Church and the churches: A Dogmatic Essay on Ecclesial Invisibility', *European Journal of Theology* 16, no. 2 [2007], pp. 113–19).

7 In this paragraph the distinctive role of the church (the 'Christian community') is limited by its commission by God. He draws from Calvin and the Reformed heritage an emphasis on defining the meaning of ministry in concert with the limitations of ministry (see *Institutes of the Christian Religion*, IV.i.6). This is a formal limitation: there are many good things to do in life, but that the

all organic and inorganic creation that secretly but very really it stands in the service of both God and man, and that it probably does so in its own way far more effectively and gloriously than the poor Christian community. Yet in the context of this great and comprehensive ministry of all creation the Christian community has its own specific function and service. In this context it is indeed distinguished to the extent that in it and in it alone is it a matter of the service of reconciliation, and this in the direct and concrete following of the prophetic work of the One in whom God has accomplished it. It is also distinguished to the extent that as such it does not take place secretly like that of the rest of creation, to be manifested in its reality only in and with the final revelation of Jesus Christ, but that even in its weakness and corruption, in anticipation of the disclosure of the secret of all creation, it is already revealed to be service of God and man here and now in time and space. It is as well for the community to keep to the ministry assigned it. If it is the creature of God in exemplary fashion, it is not the only creature. If its ministry has central significance for the whole, it cannot comprehend or replace or even transcend and improve all that takes place as the quiet service of God and man offered by creation in nature and history. And if the measure of what is required of it certainly cannot be foreseen and fixed in advance and in general, because new and very unexpected tasks might constantly be asked of it within the sphere of its service, what is demanded will never be immeasurable, but always measurable. In no time or situation is the Church called to do anything and everything, but always and everywhere there are other things which do not fall within the sphere of its service and which it is well advised to leave alone if it is rightly to do what it should. One constant criterion for distinguishing other things from what is demanded is perhaps as follows. Where it is not clear in a given case that it has to render service of both God and man in that strict connexion, where under any title it is a matter of a supposed service of God to which the character of service of man is totally alien, or where under any title there is question of a supposed service of man which has nothing to do with the service of God, there a plain warning is given, and, as in the case of the 'too little' and the 'too much,' it is clearly shown the limit of its ministry which it must not transgress.

Its ministry is also limited, however, by the fact that it is materially determined as a ministry of witness. For the sake of comprehension, and in order not to overlook anything of importance, we may again say

church is not called to engage them all (cf. IV/3.676). In the next paragraph Barth will move to consider the limitation materially – as a call to witness and none other.

that it is no less, no more and no other than the ministry of witness required of it and constituting it.[8]

It is no less. The community is the people of Christians who even as individuals are decisively and essentially witnesses. It is the company of those who could and can hear the Word of God spoken in the existence of the great, active and primary Witness in His prophetic office, of the Mediator between God and man. It is the company of those who could and can hear His Word of the atonement made in Him, of the divine covenant concluded and sealed in Him, of the divine lordship established in Him, and therefore of the new and true world reality. It is the company of those who could and can hear it in order to represent it to all other men. Their ministry consists in causing this divine Word of this divine work to be heard in the world, and therefore in confession to the world as His witnesses that Jesus Christ is the One in whom it has taken place and is revealed. Beneath the level of the witness determined by its origin, theme and content the ministry of the community must never sink if it is to be true and genuine service of both God and man. The matter in which it is engaged is no less than this.

It must not happen, for example, that it should have to propose only a particularly radical criticism of human existence and the human situation in its disintegration and destruction. What it has to attest is the light which has broken into the world in Jesus Christ, not the darkness into which it falls in order to dispel it. For the same reason its concern cannot be merely with human questions, longings and hopes for an expected alteration of the world, but only with that which is already accomplished in Jesus Christ, which is already reality, and which hastens towards its full and definitive manifestation.[9] For the same reason again

---

8   Witness is the key term to describe the church's ministry. John the Baptist is the key paradigm. Barth kept a portrait over his desk of the Isenheim altarpiece by Matthias Grünewald, where John the Baptist is in the foreground pointing to the crucified Jesus in the background and saying: 'He must increase; I must decrease' (John 3.30). Barth regularly employs the Baptizer as a paradigm for the church's role in testifying to Jesus (IV/3.836, 854). Confession is the synonym often employed to highlight the character of the church's witness and testimony. 'Why "confession" as the basic act of the church's ministry? Partly in order to retain the primacy of that which is confessed in its sheer reality as self-positing glory. But partly also to ensure that the church's prophecy does not do anything other than indicate the prophetic work and word of Jesus himself' (John Webster, '"Eloquent and Radiant": The Prophetic Office of Christ and the Mission of the Church', in *Barth's Moral Theology: Human Action in Barth's Thought* [Edinburgh: T & T Clark, 1998], p. 145). Witness takes the form of word and then deed, that is, of announcing the gospel and then adorning the gospel (IV/3: 862–864).

9   Here Barth opposes any anthropological interpretation of the Christian faith (cf. IV/3.676). Surely he has the modern liberal Protestants in view. As John Webster says, 'His emphasis on transcendence, otherness, the "higher order", is clearly not designed to exclude social action but to relativize it' ('"Life from the Third Dimension": Human Action in Barth's Early Ethics', in *Barth's Moral Theology: Human Action in Barth's Thought* [Edinburgh: T & T Clark, 1998], p. 22).

it cannot be concerned only with abstract doctrines, principles, ideas and ways of salvation. It has to attest the crucified and risen Jesus Christ who in His person is salvation and its self-declaration. Certainly God and man might be served by critical analyses of existence, by the expression of serious human questions and longings, by the proclamation of correct ideas of salvation. Nor is there any reason why such undertakings with all their doubtful features should not be secondarily accepted by God in His grace along with many other human thoughts and words and works, and therefore sanctified and made helpful to men. The only thing is that these things are too small in relation to the witness required of the community. The community of Jesus Christ cannot rest content with them. It must not transgress the lower limit marked by them.

Again, however, no more is demanded or expected than this definite witness. The reconciliation of the world to God, the divine covenant, the kingdom of God, the new reality of the world, cannot be its work. Nor can the manifestation of these things. It is not itself Jesus Christ either acting for the world or speaking to it.[10] It is only the particular people which on the basis of His gracious self-declaration may know about Him, believe in Him and hope in Him. It has to confess Him, therefore, according to the knowledge granted to it. It has to attest Him to the world as the work of God accomplished for it and the Word of God going out to it. What is demanded and expected therewith is glorious enough to render superfluous any grasping at higher possibilities. It is also serious and difficult enough to claim all its attention, fidelity, courage and resources. But it is not commanded to represent, introduce, bring into play or even in a sense accomplish again in its being, speech and action either reconciliation, the covenant, the kingdom or the new world reality. It is not commanded even in the earthly-historical sphere to take the place of Jesus Christ. In so doing it would only arrogate to itself something which is absolutely beyond its capacity, in which it could achieve only spurious results, and which would finally involve it in failure. In so doing it would do despite to Jesus Christ Himself as the one Doer of the work of God and the primary and true Witness of this work, becoming a hindrance to what He Himself wills to do and accom-

---

10   Barth is zealous to guard the distinction between the Reconciler and the reconciled. There is a connection, of course, owing to the commission of the reconciled to the ministry of reconciliation (see 2 Corinthians 5–6), but it is always a ministry (not a lordship) and one by grace (not by nature). Barth has major concerns, then, about ecclesiologies that seem to relate directly the Incarnation and Atonement with their witness (cf. IV/3.543, 603, 768). The church is trusted as a minister, but it is not itself the object of trust for it is not itself the Reconciler (IV/3.786), a claim no doubt influenced by Calvin's famous reflections on the creedal statement: 'I believe the holy catholic church' (*Institutes of the Christian Religion*, IV.i.2).

plish. Its prophecy would in so doing become false, unauthorised and misleading prophecy. It lives as true prophecy by the fact that it remains distinct from His, that it is subject to it, that it does not try to replace it, but that with supreme power and yet with the deepest humility it points to the work of God accomplished in Him and the Word of God spoken in Him, inviting to gratitude for this work and the hearing of this Word, but not pretending to be claimed for more than this indication and invitation, nor to be capable of anything more.

In the sphere of Romanism and Eastern Orthodoxy we have examples of the transgression of this upper limit of the ministry of the community to the extent that in them the Church ascribes to itself, to its life and institutions and organs, particularly to its administration of the sacraments and the means of grace entrusted to it, and in Romanism to its government by the teaching office, certain functions in the exercise of which it is not only not subordinate to Jesus Christ but is ranked alongside and in practice even set above Him as His vicar in earthly history, its ministry of witness being left far behind as it shares with Him an existence and activity which are both human and divine, and human in divine reality and omnipotence.[11] Yet even outside these particular historical spheres there is no lack of notions and enterprises in which Christendom inclines more or less clearly and definitely to what is attempted along these lines, trying to give to its resolutions the character of semi-divine decisions, to its offices a semi-divine dignity, to its proclamation the quality of semi-divine revelation, to its sacraments the nature of once-for-all established channels of grace, to its efforts outside of itself the character of the establishment and extension of the kingdom of God, and in short seeking to understand and set up itself, the Church, as a direct representation of Jesus Christ, its existence as a vicariate, its action as a direct repetition and continuation of His.[12] This

11   Barth's criticism of Roman Catholicism especially, but also Eastern Orthodoxy, involves the need and their failure (in his assessment) to maintain the distinction between Reconciler and reconciled. For a contemporary account engaged with Roman Catholicism and much influenced by Barth's reflections on Christ's prophetic office, see John Webster, 'On Evangelical Ecclesiology', in *Confessing God: Essays in Christian Dogmatics II* (London: T & T Clark, 2005), pp. 153–94.

12   Barth here addresses the liberal Protestant manoeuvre, similar to Roman Catholicism and Eastern Orthodoxy in his eyes, of identifying itself with the kingdom of God. Whereas Barth sees the Roman error largely in identifying sacramental and magisterial action too closely with God's actions, he sees the liberal Protestants as identifying their cultural endeavours too closely with the kingdom of God. The clearest exposition of this remains his 'Concluding Unscientific Postscript on Schleiermacher', in *The Theology of Schleiermacher: Lectures at Göttingen, Winter Semester of 1923/1924* (ed. Dietrich Ritschl; trans. Geoffrey Bromiley; Grand Rapids: Eerdmans, 1982), pp. 261–79. Barth argues that Schleiermacher – and with him most of liberal Protestantism – has spoken 'as if pneumatology were anthropology; that is, as if God's Spirit was identified with the efforts of modern men and women (p. 279).

is the very thing which it must not do whether on a large scale or a small, or indeed the very smallest.

The community does not achieve less but more, i.e., it fulfils the truly high ministry required of it, if it observes the limit set for it by the fact that, like John the Baptist, it is not worthy to loose the shoes' latchets of Him who comes, being willing to shine, not as itself the light, but as its witness and therefore in the brightness of the one true light. On the other hand, it does not accomplish more but less, and is indeed in danger of serving darkness instead of light, if it will not follow this example and observe this upper limit.

We may again conclude by saying that it is not commanded to do other than render this definite ministry of witness. Alongside Jesus Christ and the world reality renewed in Him there may well be other realities demanding to be recognised, acknowledged, confessed and attested. There may well be spiritual and natural forces which also, and to some degree perhaps with good reason, claim our notice and will to be proclaimed in their dignity and importance. This may and perhaps must be done, though we must be careful to see that they deserve it and also to consider the consequences if we do hear and obey them. It is indisputable, however, that in the ministry of the community there can never be any question of the attestation of these other realities and forces even in the sense of an ancillary task subordinate to the main one. This work is to be left to their own authorised or unauthorised prophets. They may, of course, be significant to the community and worthy of its consideration. Nothing human can be wholly out of place in the sphere of its own task. According to the circumstances of the case all the factors and lights which under God's providence are operative in the sphere of His creation and important to man deserve its serious and even zealous attention. But it does not stand in the service of any of the factors or lights in question. It cannot combine the witness to which it is engaged with the attestation of the reality, dignity and significance of these other lights and factors.

Alongside its proclamation of the message of Jesus Christ, it cannot, for example, work also for the dissemination of the knowledge of this or that higher or lower world, nor for a particular understanding of nature or culture, nor for the establishment of this or that western or eastern philosophy of history, society or the state and the corresponding ethics. It cannot attach itself to any world-view, nor can it produce, propagate and defend any supposed Christian world-view of its own. It can accompany all efforts in this direction sympathetically and more or less hopefully, but in no circumstances may it make common cause with them. It can respectfully acknowledge their results. But it cannot accept any responsibility for them. It cannot appropriate them nor inscribe them on its own banner.[13]

Why not? Because in so doing, even though there might be occasional and temporary success, or at least not total failure, yet it would squander the time and energy which are demanded by its own task with its call for the strictest concentration and the most strenuous effort. Again, in so doing it would enter uncertain ground on which, for the sake of the trustworthiness of its own witness it might be compelled to revoke to-morrow what it maintains to-day or maintain to-morrow what it thinks it should deny to-day. Again, in so doing, by linking its witness with the attestations of such conceptions, however good in themselves, it would make it suspect to those who are perhaps quite disposed to hear it but who for solid or less solid reasons cannot accept the conception in question. Again, in so doing, it would forget or even deny that whatever is true or enduring in these conceptions is much better expressed and honoured in its own witness if this is given its full scope and content than by their proclamation as a subsidiary task outside the context of its witness. Finally, in the service of the attestation of Jesus Christ it cannot even with the best intentions serve two different lords, no matter who the second may be. It can serve Him only whole-heartedly or not at all.[14] In this respect as well it must thus observe the limit of its ministry of witness.

In its definiteness and therefore limitation as witness and ministry of witness, however, it has also (3) its promise. It needs it. The community, feeble people that it is, needs the assurance that as it undertakes and seeks to fulfil its ministry its cause is righteous, that as it discharges it according to the measure of its knowledge and resources it is not left to

13   Barth argues for an *ad hoc* use of philosophy, suggesting that the church ought to travel light when it comes to metaphysical schemes, worldviews, and philosophies. Of course, he is not denying that such projects are necessary for living, but they are not the purview of the church (which has a strictly defined and limited commission). The church can 'accompany' and 'respectfully acknowledge' such projects, but she cannot take up the task of attaching, producing, propogating, and defending any of them. While there are particular metaphysical and philosophical implications of the gospel, there is still a multitude of ways that they may be teased out in a full metaphysical scheme or worldview or philosophy. Thus, Christians cannot act as if such a thing has descended from heaven. In many ways, Barth is maintaining the classical Reformed emphasis on the regulation of the church's authority and the parallel claim of Christian liberty to discern truth in areas where Scripture remains silent (see, e.g., the Westminster Confession of Faith, ch. 22; for fuller exposition, see Michael Allen, 'Culture and Eschatology', in *Reformed Theology* [Doing Theology; London: T & T Clark, 2010], pp. 156–177).

14   Here Barth makes use of biblical language about idolatry. He sees idolatry as a constant theological temptation: the ever-present allurement of 'both … and' over against the gospel's call for 'alone' (see his 'The First Commandment as Theological Axiom', in *The Way of Theology in Karl Barth: Essays and Comments* [ed. Martin Rumscheidt; Allison Park, PA: Pickwick, 1986], pp. 63–78).

its own knowledge and resources, and that it does not finally act in vain. It stood and stands so isolated in relation to the world, to the godless, the indifferent and the pious, to the ancient and the modern, to the western and the eastern, to the middle-class, proletarian and bohemian world. In the exercise of its ministry it sees itself confronted by so many unmistakeable positions of power and not altogether illegitimate claims that it might be genuinely assailed by anxiety as to the justice of its own cause when it is called in question and even contested by so many. In addition it is troubled by the modest and unassuming and even pitiable nature of its own ability and the means at its disposal, and especially by the almost irresistible temptations which come to it and the resultant failures and distortions. Again, it has to face the question whether its whole concern for the witness borne by it, whatever the effects of its activity in this ministry, is not after all a crying in the storm, a writing in the sand or even the water, a futile running up against a cliff. What can it oppose to these many and varied anxieties? How can it keep its courage and the power to endure under this pressure? Is there not cause for astonishment that, with all the defeats and failures and mistakes which it has made in its history and still makes at every point to-day, Christianity has not completely strayed from its ministry and given up the struggle? Is there not cause for astonishment that there have always been new men and generations ready and willing to take up its ministry with new courage and pursue it along new ways, all sooner or later oppressed by the same anxieties, all followed yet again by others who notwithstanding have still been ready and plainly constrained to take up the same cause, but all obviously needing the assurance to make it possible? A powerful counter-pressure is needed if the ministry of the community is not to prove impracticable and to crumble under the pressure of these not unfounded anxieties, if it is to be continually sustained and renewed in the work of its ministry and therefore in its existence.

Nor is this counter-pressure lacking. It is, in fact, stronger than the pressure of the anxieties. It is strong enough to make it possible for the community to discharge its ministry, continually sustaining and renewing this ministry and therefore itself. We refer to the promise which is no less characteristic of its ministry in its definiteness than is the limitation.[15]

---

15   The community is sustained by the divine promise, that is, by the gospel of Jesus Christ. It is important to remember that this section on vocation and witness is embedded within Barth's account of the prophetic office of Jesus. The prophetic office of Jesus relates to the threefold form of the Word of God, as described at length in volume one (IV/3.114; cf. I/1.120–124, 132–143). The main thesis of this volume is found earlier: 'We have now laid down our main Christological thesis that the life of Jesus Christ is as such light and His reconciling work a

It is not proper to it in the sense of a security which it possesses as it discharges its ministry, or a quality inherent to it, like the great or small position in the world, the members and institutions, the codified or uncodified historical traditions, which it thinks it possesses, as though all these things, too, were not really on loan to it. What is true of all these things, however, is particularly true of the promise which sustains, protects and renews it. It is not a state in which its ministry is automatically and once and for all protected against and superior to the questioning which assails it on every hand. It is rather the mystery of the history of its ministry which is free and always remains free. It characterises it as it is given to the community and received by it. Its ministry of witness is neither divine nor semi-divine. It is the unequivocally human speech and action of a people like all others. It stands always in supreme need of assurance. It never shows itself in any respect to be assured in advance. If the question is raised what it has to set against all the anxieties, the answer is that it has nothing of its own to set against them. Of itself it could only be hopelessly defeated by and subjected to them. What it needs, but what it is also given, is the promise which marks its ministry. It is to be noted and grasped that as a free promise it is the needed assurance which actually comes and is therefore proper to its ministry. Nor is it a purely verbal and external assurance. It is a supremely real and internal. This is shown by the fulfilments which it brings with it. Yet it is a free promise which comes to characterise the ministry of the community only in the form of a gift, so that it can never have it at its disposal but only hope for it as it discharges its ministry. Yet it is really proper to it just because it is free and can never be more than the subject of its prayer and thanksgiving. In its very freedom it does in fact secure the ministry of the community, protecting it against all those threats and the consequences of the insecurity in which alone it can discharge it in relation to the world and especially itself. It thus exerts the counterpressure which is more than a match for the pressure under which the community discharges it.

The promise which always does this, and by which the ministry of the community is thus always assured, is, however, quite simply the origin, theme and content of its witness, namely, that which is said and entrusted to the community in and with its gathering, upbuilding

---

prophetic Word ... Positively, this means that He is the light of life in all its fullness, in perfect adequacy; and negatively, it means that there is no other light of life outside or alongside His, outside or alongside the light which He is' (IV/3.86). Jesus is the light and the Word – this is a promise that sustains the church now. There is no ancillary or accompanying luminescence or voice – this is the limit that shapes the church now. The gospel says that Jesus speaks today as the Prophet, so the church can be hopeful. The law provides shape to this hope, so the church will be modest and faithful.

and sending in order that it may repeat it to the world to which it is sent according to the measure of its knowledge. What is said to it, i.e., the Word of God concerning reconciliation, the covenant, the kingdom and the new reality of the world as spoken to it in and by Jesus Christ in the truth and power proper to Him in every dimension, is as such the promise and assurance given to the community, sustaining its witness, and victoriously encountering the pressure under which it stands. The risen and living Jesus Christ Himself, who is the origin, theme and content of its witness, who is indeed the Word of God to be attested by it, gives it this promise and assurance. It will be seen that it is truly free because it is His personal promise. It cannot say to itself what is said to it and entrusted to it to repeat. It can only allow it to be said to it, and in its ministry of witness repeat it as that which is said to it. Similarly it cannot give to itself the promise and assurance in the power of which it may and should attempt its ministry of witness. Nor can it seize it as its own even when it is given. It cannot dispose of it as though it were its own possession and under its own control. It does not have it institutionally. It does not have it even in the power of its own faith and knowledge, its own love and inspiration, or indeed its own prayer.[16] It has it as it is given to and received by it in the power of the Holy Spirit as the power of the personal Word of Jesus Christ. It does receive and have it, however, as the promise and assurance of the living Jesus Christ coming to it in all its incommensurability as the work and Word of God. As such it characterises its ministry from one day and century to another. Hence it can and should know that it is held and carried by it, and be of good courage in the execution of its ministry. The promise which marks its ministry guarantees that, no matter how threateningly they may open up on every hand, the gates of hell (Mt. 16.18) shall not swallow it up.

---

16   Here Barth addresses a pietistic danger, namely, that human spirituality would be viewed as independent of God's promised grace. At times Barth views pietism as prone to anthropocentrism in parallel fashion to Roman Catholicism and liberael Protestantism (see Eberhard Busch, *Karl Barth and the Pietists: The Young Karl Barth's Critique of Pietism and Its Response* [trans. Daniel Bloesch; Downers Grove, IL: InterVarsity, 2004]).

CHAPTER 15

THE CHRISTIAN LIFE

Grace that is not disruptive is not grace ... Grace, strictly speaking, does not mean continuity but radical discontinuity, not reform but revolution, not violence but nonviolence, not the perfecting of virtues but the forgiveness of sins, not improvement but resurrection from the dead. It means repentance, judgment, and death as the portal to life. It means negation and the negation of the negation. The grace of God really comes to lost sinners, but in coming it disrupts them to the core. It slays to make alive and sets the captive free. Grace may of course work silently and secretly like a germinating seed as well as like a bolt from the blue. It is always wholly as incalculable as it is reliable, unmerited, and full of blessing. Yet it is necessarily as unsettling as it is comforting. It does not finally teach of its own sufficiency without appointing a thorn in the flesh. Grace is disruptive because God does not compromise with sin, nor ignore it, nor call it good. On the contrary, God removes it by submitting to the cross to show that love is stronger than death ... grace in its radical disruption surpasses all that we imagine or think.[1]

If it is really true that a man, however timidly and uncertainly, may be a Christian, and that even with the greatest qualifications he may be seriously addressed as such, this means that even as the man he was, is, and will be, he cannot be the same man but has become a very different man. He now lives with a new character in which he is strange to himself and his fellows. For all his identity with himself, he is also different from himself. He has become the bearer of a new name. The compass of what it means for a man to become faithful to the faithful God is not merely underestimated but completely missed if one does not ultimately stand before this fact with helpless astonishment.[2]

---

1   George Hunsinger, *Disruptive Grace: Studies in the Theology of Karl Barth* (Grand Rapids: Eerdmans, 2000), pp. 16–17.
2   *CD* IV/4.3.

This final section of the *Church Dogmatics* was left unfinished and unpublished for some time. Barth ceased writing his *magnum opus* upon his retirement as Professor of Systematic Theology at the University of Basel in 1961, and he was only able to prepare one paragraph of his lecture notes (§75) for publication before his death in 1968. This material – as well as various fragments – have been published under the title *The Christian Life*. While he did lecture on parts of the Lord's Prayer, and he intended to address the Lord's Supper, the only section revised for publication regarded the doctrine of Christian baptism.

Barth's doctrine of baptism has been quite controversial. He follows his son, Markus Barth, in denying the validity of infant baptism. Barth's main concern regards the possible confusion or identification of water baptism with Spirit baptism, in other words, the failure to honour the distinction between uncreated and created being and, thus, the distinction between divine and human action. In fact, this section on 'The Foundation of the Christian Life' (§75) is divided into a discussion of 'baptism with the Holy Spirit' and 'baptism with water'. Barth insists that Jesus Christ is the only sacrament of God. Indeed, many Barth *aficionados* find his approach to be inconsistent with his broader theology, arguing that Barth's doctrine of revelation (with the idea of the threefold Word of God: revelation, Scripture, proclamation) might be used as a template or parallel for a healthier doctrine of baptism.

The selected excerpt introduces Barth's discussion of baptism by asking 'concerning the origin, beginning, and initiation of the faithfullness of man which replies and corresponds to the faithfullness of God'. He does 'assume that there is such a thing as the event of the Christian life', and here he endeavors to clarify its nature and generating, sustaining force in Jesus (IV/4: 3).

Bibliography

Karl Barth, *The Christian Life. Church Dogmatics IV/4. Lecture Fragments* (trans. Geoffrey W. Bromiley; Edinburgh/Grand Rapids: T & T Clark/Eerdmans, 1981).

Karl Barth, *The Holy Spirit and the Christian Life: The Theological Basis of Ethics* (trans. R. Birch Hoyle; Library of Theological Ethics; Louisville: Westminster John Knox, 1993).

George Hunsinger, 'Double Agency as Test Case', in *How to Read Karl Barth: The Shape of His Theology* (New York: Oxford University Press, 1991), pp. 185–224.

Matthew Rose, *Ethics with Barth: God, Metaphysics, and Morals* (Barth Studies; Surrey: Ashgate, 2011), ch. 4.

T. F. Torrance, 'The One Baptism Common to Christ and His Church', in *Theology in Reconciliation* (Grand Rapids: Eerdmans, 1976), pp. 82–105.

John Webster, *Barth's Ethics of Reconciliation* (Cambridge: Cambridge University Press, 1995).

The Text (*CD* IV/4.4–23)

We do not know what we are talking about if in this matter of the awakening and origin of a human faithfullness corresponding to God's faithfullness, in this matter of the foundation of Christian life, we count upon some other possibility than that which is with God alone because it is subject only to His control. So great is the mystery and dignity of this event! But what kind of a divine possibility is this? We have to be clear that the faithfullness to God here at issue must be understood as a human act, the Christian life as the life of a man. The question is how this man himself becomes the subject of this event, of faith in God, love for Him, of hope in Him, a man who wills and acts in this positive relation to Him, a friend instead of an enemy, one who is alive for Him instead of dead for Him.[3] To be an adequate answer to this question, a description of that divine possibility cannot evade the fact that man himself is at issue. It is not enough, then, to describe this possibility as one whose actualisation, while it affects man supremely by setting him in the light of a new, gracious, and consequently positive divine judgment, does not do more than affect him, simply touching him from without, or strictly speaking not touching him at all, since he is as it were sealed off against it, and is not touched and altered by it in his inner being. On this view, how can one claim man seriously

---

3   The summary of this section on 'The Foundation of the Christian Life' goes as follows: 'A man's turning to faithfullness to God, and consequently to calling upon Him, is the work of this faithful God which, perfectly accomplished in the history of Jesus Christ, in virtue of the awakening, quickening, and illuminating power of this history, becomes a new beginning of life as his baptism with the Holy Spirit. The first step of this life of faithfullness to God, the Christian life, is a man's baptism with water, which by his own decision is requested of the community and which is administered by the community, as the binding confession of his obedience, conversion, and hope, made in prayer for God's grace, wherein he honours the freedom of this grace' (IV/4.2). The key issue is how it comes to be that 'He has become the bearer of a new name'; indeed, 'the compass of what it means for man to become faithful to the faithful God is not merely under-estimated but completely missed if one does not ultimately stand before this fact with helpless astonishment' (IV/4.3). The answer for Barth is an actuality that is possible only on the divine side; as he says elsewhere, 'God does not let man go' (III/2.34). Of course, this is not an issue that arises only at the tail end of his *Church Dogmatics*; indeed, Barth argued that dogmatics 'has the problem of ethics in view from the very first' (III/4.3). John Webster has offered a helpful study on the cogency with which Barth offers an ethical dogmatics (*Barth's Ethics of Reconciliation* [Cambridge: Cambridge University Press, 1995]), investigating the ethical drive behind volumes 1–3 as well as a study of the unpublished material which would have formed the conclusion to volume 4. While the ethical arises at various points throughout each of the volumes, it does gain a particular prestige here.

– and this is our theme – as one who for his part is a faithful partner in the covenant of grace? Again, it is not enough to refer simply to the divinely effected actualisation of certain moral impulses in man. There are such. As God's creature man has by nature and creation his own determination which is not destroyed or even damaged by his conflict with God, his fellow-man and himself. When he is faithful to God, he is certainly set on the path to fulfilment of this determination. Nevertheless, this is not what makes a man a Christian. Our question, however, is how a man becomes a Christian, how it comes about that a man is faithful to God, what is the divine possibility in which this takes place. Finally, the view is inadequate that God's possibility here consists in what can only be called the magical infusion of supernatural powers by whose proper use man can do what he cannot do in his own strength, namely, be faithful again to the faithful God. We are not asking concerning natural or supernatural powers which, assuming that man has or receives them, and that he begins the Christian life by using them, might be helpful and serviceable to this end. We are asking how man, for whom it is impossible to begin the Christian life by human judgment, is nevertheless enabled by divine judgment, on the basis of a divine possibility, to will, commence and do this. The mystery and miracle of the event of which we speak consists in the fact that man himself is the free subject of this event on the basis of a possibility which is present only with God. But what kind of a divine possibility is this?

At this point we may set aside three views which have become classical in the history of Christian theology, since we cannot regard as satisfactory their answers to this question. The first equates the divine possibility with God's power to make a man faithful to Himself, to make him a Christian, by blessing him in the form of an infusion of supernatural powers. Exercising the caution demanded by modern investigation we might call this the popular Roman Catholic view.[4] The second view locates the possibility in God's power to be gracious to man by summoning and spurring him on to the fulfilment of his natural religious and moral impulses. A revival of ancient Pelagianism, this is undoubtedly the understanding of Neo-Protestantism, which emerged at the end of the 17th century, which then attained to virtual

---

4   Barth even found the Augustinian – that is, anti-Pelagian – version of Roman Catholic anthro-
     pology and soteriology lacking, in as much as Augustine relied too much on the notion of the
     infusion of grace. Barth launched this attack as early as his 1929 lecture 'The Holy Spirit and
     the Christian Life' (now published as *The Holy Spirit and the Christian Life: The Theological Basis of
     Ethics* [trans. R. Birch Hoyle; Library of Theological Ethics; Louisville: Westminster John Knox,
     1993], p. 22). For a thoughtful and appreciative reply from a Roman Catholic contemporary, see
     Hans Urs von Balthasar, *The Theology of Karl Barth: Exposition and Interpretation* [trans. Edward T.
     Oakes; San Francisco: Ignatius, 1992], pp. 326–80).

dominance (not without parallels in the Roman Catholic world), which has declined somewhat to-day, but which is still powerful and can still bring forth belated fruits – I refer to theological existentialism in all its varied forms. The third view, in contrast to popular Roman Catholicism, restricts the possibility to God's power to introduce a man who has been judged afresh and with grace, but who is in himself unaltered. This is the form which the Reformation doctrine of justification received – incorrectly but in a way which had more than contemporary influence – at the hands of Melanchthon and the Lutheran orthodoxy which followed.[5] If only there had been a happier alternative to the Roman Catholic view and to isolated anticipations of the Neo-Protestant conception! Or if only the (counter-) reforming Council of Trent had been able to offer a happier alternative to the teaching of Melanchthon, and perhaps in advance to the Neo-Protestant understanding! Or if only, might one say, the Neo-Protestant view had transcended and overcome the other two in a happier way! As things were, the three views were from the very first no more than complementary to one another. Each in its particular over-emphasis bore some responsibility for producing and hardening the other two. Hence one can hardly award the palm to any of them. Different though they were and are, they share the common feature that from the standpoint which we have here adopted they are all deficient, since none of them makes it clear how there comes into being the Christian, the man who responds to God's faithfullness with faithfullness, the man who as a free subject is

---

5   Note that Barth argues that the Reformational response to Rome was 'incorrectly' moving on from Luther and Calvin. The path is set for Barth to sketch out his own proposal as a more faithful and, thus, a 'happier alternative' to this malformation (cf. III/2.181). As Timothy Gorringe summarizes Barth's response to this Christomonist approach: 'Grace establishes reality, it does not deny it' (*Karl Barth Against Hegemony* [Oxford: Oxford University Press, 1999], p. 173 fn. 35). Historical debates swirl around the way in which divine freedom and human freedom are related. While later Reformed and Lutheran theologians spoke of a contrastive view between them and, thus, denied true human freedom as (what they took to be) a necessary condition of real divine freedom and sovereignty (e.g. Jonathan Edwards in his work on *The Freedom of the Will*), such was not the case with the early Reformed and Lutheran theologians (see, e.g., *Reformed Thought on Freedom: The Concept of Free Choice in Early Modern Reformed Theology* [ed. Willem J. van Asselt *et al*; Texts & Studies in Reformation & Post-Reformation Thought; Grand Rapids: Baker Academic, 2010]). Barth clearly prefers the earlier Reformed view to the later approach. Thus Barth defines the theological enterprise as such: ' "Theology," in the literal sense, means the science and doctrine of God. A very precise definition of the Christian endeavour in this respect would really require the more complex term "The-anthropology." For an abstract doctrine of God has no place in the Christian realm, only a "doctrine of God and of man," a doctrine of the commerce and communion between God and man' ('Evangelical Theology in the Nineteenth Century', in *The Humanity of God* [trans. Thomas Wieser; Louisville: Westminster John Knox, 1960], p. 11).

God's true partner in the covenant of grace.[6] None of them can show in what sense the existence of this man is grounded in the great possibility of God, in this alone, but in this truly. Hence we must set them all aside and return to the central question: What is this great possibility of God?

The answer which Holy Scripture gives to this question ignores all these views and refers us to the decisive point, to the change which comes on man himself in the freedom of the gracious God, the change in which he himself is free to become what he was not and could not be before, and consequently to do what he did not and could not do before, i.e., be faithful to God. Neither in thought nor utterance should we turn aside from this point. Our gaze must be focused upon it. To be sure, if a man is to be faithful to God, there must be an actualisation of his creaturely determination and consequently of his natural powers. To be sure, all kinds of unsuspected powers, hitherto alien to himself and others, so that for once we can call them 'supernatural,' might well be given him. To be sure, even at best he will always stand in need of the gracious judgment of God. One cannot deny that in each of the three views there is a grain of truth. The real question, however, is that of the reality of man's opening up to this new and strange and different thing, the reality of his free entry into the kingdom of God which has drawn near for him and to him too, the reality of the origin of his free partnership with God in God's covenant of grace which embraces him too because it was instituted for him too. The divine possibility of which Holy Scripture speaks refers to this reality. Man himself, man in his own most proper subjectivity, ceases to stand without as a stranger. He approaches and comes inside to the place where all things are ready for him too, for him specifically. The possibility of God consists in the fact that man – eye of a needle or not – is enabled to participate not just passively but actively in God's grace as one who may and will and can be set to work too.[7] It is God's power to draw and turn, so that this man will voluntarily and by his own decision choose that which God in His grace has already chosen for him, and in this choice he will be one who is converted to God instead of apostate from Him, one who confesses God instead of one who denies Him, a friend instead of an enemy, a man who is no longer unserviceable but serviceable, a witness to God instead of one who brings shame upon Him, in short, a man

6   Barth argues that polemical distinctions forced each of these three views to dogmatic narrowness.

7   Note that Barth affirms the active life of the Christian – involving a real faithfulness to God – but he bases this upon a 'divine possibility' and no human capacity itself. Thus, theologians speak of both an active and a passive nature of Christianity: it is active and involved, but it is passively dependent on God's free grace. Passivity guards the unconditionality of God's free turning to the human, while activity maintains the real life that is conferred by God. For further analysis, see Paul T. Nimmo, 'Part Two: Ontic Aspects of Being in Action', in *Being in Action: The Theological Shape of Barth's Ethical Vision* (London: T & T Clark, 2007), pp. 87–168.

who is no longer unfaithful to God but faithful to Him. The Christian life has its true source in this change which God brings about in man. It begins with it. Of what avail to a Christian are his natural or even supernatural powers, of what avail is even the most gracious judgment of God, if he does not have his origin in this divine turning with its result in his own free decision, if he himself has not first become a Christian therein?

To grasp the meaning, nature, mystery and miracle of this divine turning one must collect and compare the very different but obviously converging ways in which Holy Scripture speaks of it.[8]

The figure of the new garment which is given to the Christian and which he has to put on and wear does not mean that man himself can adopt the distinctive being of a Christian, dressing up as it were in it. Nor does it mean that what is given him is no true Christian being but only something external, not to speak of a mere Christian appearance, a hood which is pulled over him and under the concealment of which he can be the same as he always was. The festive garment in which those who are invited from the streets and lanes take their places at the marriage board of the king is an essential part, indeed, *the* essential part of the gift which is given them along with the invitation. For this reason it would be no mere fault of etiquette (Mt. 22.11f.) but something which from the very first barred them from the table, if they were to try to seat themselves, not in this garment, but in their old rags or even in prelapsarian purity. Similarly, the elect and called are not arbitrarily or autonomously clothed in the white robes which they are said to wear in Revelation (3.4, 5; 6.11; 7.9). These white garments are the official robes along with which — clothes make the man — they receive a new being and are both empowered for and engaged to a corresponding new activity. Above all, the armour (armour of God) which the Christian is to take and put on according to 1 Thess. 5.8 and Eph. 6.13f. is a freedom and power which is neither proper nor available to man by nature, which surpasses him in all its aspects, but which is appropriated to him as a freedom and power which he must

---

8 Barth sketches out three types of passages now. He argues that they fundamentally speak of the same reality, but they have varying emphases. First, he addresses texts that speak of clothing or covering the self; he argues that such imagery is not mere extrinsicism but really changes the name and the self of the Christian. Second, he addresses texts that speak of real moral change and Spirit-wrought obedience; he says that such change is rooted in the work of God, not the capacity of humans. Third, he addresses texts that identify a point of conversion or regeneration, what can only be called a second birth; this divine work, he says, serves as a fulcrum between the emphases of the first two types of texts. Christians are not only given a new name, but the giving of this name actually accomplishes a change of character by the Spirit's work. The three emphases could be identified with key phrases: Christ *outside* us (clothing us with himself), Christ *for* us (changing us morally), Christ *in* us (converting us in new birth).

put into effect as resistance in the evil day. What a man puts on when he
becomes a Christian is according to Col. 3.10 and Eph. 4.24 no more
and no less than – after the putting off of the old – the new man who is
created as godly or according to the image of the one who created him
for the knowledge of God, and in the knowledge of God for agreement
with His will, and consequently for a life in true righteousness and
holiness; the inner man who (Rom. 7.22) delights in the Law of God
as described in Ps. 119, who certainly stands in need of continual
strengthening (Eph. 3.16), but who (2 Cor. 4.16), while the outward
man perishes, is in fact renewed day by day; the hidden man of the
heart (1 Pet. 3.4); the man of God as he is briefly and excellently called
in 2 Tim. 3.17, the man who is fully equipped for every good work.
If a man can put on this man, this wedding garment, the white robe,
the armour of God, this obviously means that he himself (the reference
in every case is to the man) can and should affirm, accept, grasp and
express himself in a form which is prepared for him, which is radically
changed, but which is also adapted and consequently peculiar to him,
that he should do this in his true reality which absolutely transcends
and completely overshadows all that he was before or otherwise is. He
has become (Rev. 2.14) the bearer of a name which corresponds to this
true reality of his, which is thus new, 'which no man knoweth saving he
that receiveth it,' but under which (Rev. 3.5; 13.8; 17.8) he is indelibly
entered in the book of life.

We find the same teaching in other terms in the description which
Paul gives in Rom. 2 of certain notable men whom, to the shame of
the Jews, yet also as examples, he contrasts with the Jews, who have
not let themselves be brought to conversion by God's goodness (v. 4).
Rather surprisingly in view of the context of the chapter, we read here
that there are people (v. 7) who 'by patient continuance in well doing
seek for glory and honour and immortality,' and whom God rewards
therefore with eternal life. These men (v. 13) are justified as doers
of the Law, and they will stand in the judgment. They are 'Gentiles'
(ἔθνη, v. 14), and as such they are people who in an astonishing way
do what is demanded 'by the Law' (τὰ τοῦ νόμου); without having the
Law, they are law to themselves. They give evidence (v.15) that the
work of the Law (not the Law, but the work of the Law) is written in
their hearts (doing this work is characteristic of them and hence self-
evident). This is confirmed by their conscience and by the conflict of
inner thoughts – we are reminded of the later description in Rom.
7 – which distinguishes a man who knows the Law from one who
does not. Though uncircumcised, these men, by keeping the Law,
show (v. 26) that they are truly circumcised. For (v. 28f.) a man is
not a Jew who is one outwardly (a physical and legal member of the

covenant people), nor is that the true circumcision which is outward and corporal. He is a Jew who is so in secret (where only God, but God in very truth, knows him), and the circumcision which counts is that of the heart by the Spirit and not the letter, the being of a man who has praise and honour with God. Paul knows such men; he refers to them. Whom does he have in mind? According to an ancient and almost universally accepted exegetical tradition, though not a tradition which is to be respected merely on this account, his reference is to outstanding Gentiles. On this view we have in Rom. 2 a compelling proof-text for an effective natural revelation of God and knowledge of God. Shortly afterwards (3.9), however, Paul says unmistakably that both Jews and Gentiles collectively and individually live under sin, that none is righteous, no, not one (3.10), that the whole world is guilty before God (3.19), that all have sinned and have no glory with God (3.23). How, then, can he assume in Rom. 2, even hypothetically, let alone in practice, that there are Gentiles who are not merely noble but who keep and fulfil God's Law without knowing it in its revealed form, and who are thus justified before God as its doers? Something is wrong here. In the context the statements of Paul in Rom. 2 are possible only if they refer to Gentiles whom Paul, his readers and the Jews may see in the Christian community, who, in contrast to Jews who persist in rejecting the Gospel, have let themselves be brought by God's goodness to conversion by obeying the summons to the obedience of faith. That the reference is indeed to Gentile Christians, and has nothing whatever to do with natural theology, is plain once one grasps the obvious point that Paul is here describing the strange fulfilment of the radiant Old Testament promise of the future establishment of a completely renewed Israel which is awakened to obedience to God and empowered and ready to keep His commandments.[9] Thus we read in Jer. 31.33f.: 'But this shall be the covenant that I shall make with the house of Israel after those days (the days of the breaking of the covenant and the ensuing rejection), saith Yahweh: I will put my law in their inward parts, and write it in their hearts; and will be their God, and they shall be my

9   Barth believes that Romans 2.13–14 refers to Gentile Christians and their graced lives, rather than to Gentile unbelievers and their natural lives. The ethical agent moves beyond her natural capacity solely owing to the grace of Christ (cf. III/2.165; III/4.473). The interpretation of Romans 2 (and its relationship to Romans 1.16–17 and 3.21ff.) remains hotly debated amongst New Testament scholars; one recent survey of literature finds 14 ways commonly employed to alleviate the tension between these verses and the broader Pauline teaching on justification by faith in Christ (Dane Ortlund, 'Justified By Faith, Judged According to Works: Another Look at a Pauline Paradox', Journal of the Evangelical Theological Society 52, no. 2 [2009], pp. 223–39). It should be noted that Barth's approach here is not the same as that found in his earlier The Epistle to the Romans (6th ed.; trans. Edwyn C. Hoskyns; New York: Oxford University Press, 1968), pp. 65–70.

people. And they shall teach no more every man his neighbour, and every man his brother, saying, Know the Lord: for they shall all know me, from the least of them unto the greatest of them, saith Yahweh.' In the decisive matter Jer. 32.39f. is even stronger: 'I will give them another heart and another way, that they may fear me for ever.' Stronger still is Ezek. 11.19f. (*see* 36.26f.); 'I will ... put a new spirit within you; and I will take the stony heart out of their flesh, and will give them an heart of flesh, that they may walk in my statutes, and keep mine ordinances, and do them.' Also Deut. 30.6 (*see* Jer. 4.4): 'Yahweh, thy God, will circumcise thine heart, and the heart of thy seed, to love Yahweh, thy God, with all thine heart, and with all thy soul, that thou mayest live.' Here are obviously the elements which go to make up the sayings in Rom. 2. The point of the contrast hazarded by Paul here is that now, in the Messianic age of fulfilment, the men intimated in Old Testament prophecy are to be found – unfortunately in only small numbers from among Israel, but in large numbers from among the Gentiles. According to biblical usage the heart denotes the centre of life in which a man is inwardly what he is, and from which he is also what he is outwardly, in all his acts and attitudes. If God's Law is written on his heart, if his heart is circumcised, if he acquires a new and different heart, this means that he himself, in so far as this has a decisive bearing on his whole being and act, becomes another man. According to Rom. 2 Gentile Christians have become other men, and consequently true Israelites before God. He contrasts them as such with the majority of God's ancient people who continue in their old ways. It is plain that in so doing he is describing the same process underlying the Christian life as is elsewhere represented as the putting on of a new garment, i.e., a new man.

In a third set of passages the same process, the divine establishing of the Christian life, is described as a new and second generation and birth which a man undergoes in sharp contrast to his natural genesis. In classification of these passages it should be noted that in the description of the process in Tit. 3.5 the same word is used (rebirth) as that which Mt. 19.28 employs for the renewal of the world on the appearance of Jesus Christ in judgment. When a man becomes a Christian, his natural origin in the procreative will of his human father is absolutely superseded and transcended (Jn. 1.13). 'That which is born of the flesh is flesh' (Jn. 3.6). The Christian, however, comes into being in a very different way, of incorruptible, not corruptible, seed (1 Pet. 1.23). Thus the question of Nicodemus (Jn. 3.4) how a grown man can return to his mother's womb and be born again, is quite pointless. Not *as* a child, but *like* a child (Mk. 10.15), beginning from the very beginning as is proper to 'new-born babes' (1 Pet. 2.2), a man comes to see the kingdom of

God, receives it, enters into it. For this he must be born from above / again, not on the horizontal plane of the sequence of generations, but on the vertical plane of direct divine fatherhood (Jn. 3.3). He must be begotten to a living hope, to a share in the heavenly inheritance (1 Pet. 1.3f.). To love God and to believe in Him he must be born of God (Jn. 1.13, 1 Jn. 4.7; 5.1). Christians are addressed in the New Testament as men who have their genesis in this event. They are begotten by God through the word of truth (Jas. 1.18). They are begotten again (ἀναγεγεννημένοι) through His word which lives and abides (1 Pet. 1.23). They are thus born of the Spirit, who as life-giving Spirit (Jn. 6.63, 1 Cor. 15.45) blows where He wills (Jn. 3.8). They are born of God, who both can and does raise up children to Abraham from these stones (Mt. 3.9). This is the mystery and miracle of divine sonship which Nicodemus, even though he is a 'master of Israel,' cannot grasp (Jn. 3.9f.). Paul obviously has the same point in view when, instead of speaking of a new begetting and birth, he refers to himself, and quite plainly to every Christian, as a new creature (Gal. 6.15, 2 Cor. 5.17), as a man for whom the old has passed away and the new has come, as a man who owes his existence, his knowledge, and the whole thought and volition grounded therein, to a new creation. Nor is it difficult to find in all this the same thought encountered already in sayings about the new clothing or the new heart. The Christian life begins with a change which cannot be understood or described radically enough, which God has the possibility of effecting in a man's life in a way which is decisive and basic for his whole being and action, and which He has in fact accomplished in the life of the man who becomes a Christian.

How sharp and inconceivable this change is may be seen finally in the (particularly Pauline) passages which describe the genesis and origin of the Christian as a transition through dying and death to a life which is visible and attainable beyond this pitilessly clear line of demarcation, and which is definitely promised and indeed opened to the dead man, but to him alone. This life of one who was dead but who is raised from the dead is the Christian life. Man died, but in so doing he began to live. The tension in this statement is almost unbearable. Yet this is what Paul meant and said. I was crucified and died; I no longer live (so far as my previous existence is concerned). This is what he says about himself in Gal. 2.19f. He can thus go on to speak of his whole continued existence as one in which he bears about this dying in this body, 2 Cor. 4.10. But Paul speaks to all Christians about this origin of their life which is so dark, and yet as bright as day in the light of what follows. They would not be what they are if they did not have crucifixion, dying and death behind them, if they did not have a future only on this basis (Rom. 6.2, 6, 8, 11; Col. 3.3; 2 Tim. 2.11). From this dreadful event, and from it alone, they can go forward. From it they do go forward and they should – on to the resurrection (Rom. 6.5), to newness of life (Rom. 6.4). From death they have passed to life (Jn. 5.24, 1 Jn. 3.14). If the old were not passed away and perished, they would have no future, and the new could not come (2 Cor. 5.17). Without passage through this narrow defile there would be no entrance into the beautiful open country beyond. But the old is indeed passed away. The Christian has gone through the narrow defile. The new comes; he can and may and should move forward into that land. Forward is his only option. This is the great change in the life of a man wherein he becomes a Christian – an astounding change which can be regarded only as divine. His Christian life begins with this beginning. Is this all metaphorical? In the immediate sense it is undoubtedly so; it seems to apply to this man only in a transferred sense. Nevertheless, in what is said about the dying and ensuing resurrection of this man there is concealed and declared already – we shall have to investigate this further – the true point at issue, the point in whose light the reality denoted by the figure may be seen in the figure. This being so, we have to ask in retrospect whether the reality described in these images is not concealed and declared already in what the New Testament says about the new garment, the new heart, the new generation and birth of man. In the description just given of the divine change which we are seeking to understand, we are already on the threshold of the statement in which the matter itself must be expressed and which will thus sum up and give meaning to all our deliberations thus far, and to all that has been adduced thus far from the New Testament.

We must pause for a moment at this juncture. Apart from the Christian view, there are other ideas, conceptions and doctrines of the divine change which sets a man's life on new ground and which consequently alters the man himself in a true and radical way. Restless human longing, inspired human hope, the boldest and most genuine striving, and the most incontrovertible individual and collective experiences have all combined in this matter to produce the most comprehensive theories and to give them concrete form in various more or less successful ways of life. The self-satisfaction with which man – slothful or diligent, cheerful or gloomily sceptical, rough and crude or refined and spiritual – seeks to affirm and express himself, is only a thin cover underneath which, constantly striving upwards, a restless disquiet and boundless discontent lies concealed. Always and everywhere there is as it were a repudiation of his present being and work, a final anxiety (we are not the first to live 'with the atom bomb') lest the paths which he thinks he can and should take will not lead to any good outcome, a dissatisfaction with what man is both in general and in detail, a desire to strike out for new shores, to conquer self and leave it behind, not merely to become different but to become another, and to be able to make a highly serious beginning as such. Always and everywhere the inescapable vision of the finitude of all human striving and the imperfection and transience of all human achievement and accomplishment, and the suppressible but ultimately irrepressible thought of ineluctably approaching death, have given man the prospect of a new beginning of this kind, tormenting him, yet also inspiring him, impelling him, keeping him on the alert. Always and everywhere there has herewith impressed itself on man the consideration and even the certainty that this new beginning implies a possibility which is not at man's disposal, which has first to liberate him for freedom, which is thus higher, transcendental, and in some sense divine. Always and everywhere man has dreamed, and written, and formed more or less clear conceptions, and claimed, not without cause, to have had convincing experiences, of a change from without which, whether as imparted gift or imposed disaster, summons him to personal decision, of the suprahuman coming of a very different humanity, of the miraculous investiture of man with a new nature, of a miraculous inner change, of a wonderful new birth, of the last thing, dying, being in some wonderful way that which is truly the first. Furthermore, ways which might lead in this direction have been shown to man, and opened up to him in practice, in no small measure.

What the Christian, whether in obscure conception or even in clear vision, knows in this respect as hope or even as the present, namely, the divine change which is his origin, might at first glance seem to be simply a particular instance of the general search for, or experience of, this final deepening, exalting, transcending and at the same time realising of human existence on the basis of its radical transforming from without. Hence it is apparently rivalled and relativised by so many similar and no less human strivings and experiences, theories and practices. Nothing is indeed more natural than that there should be a more or less considerable corner in its self-understanding where it, too, can regard itself as a participant in this general striving and experience, so that it hesitates to insist with final certainty that what it understands as the new beginning of human life is the only possible one, or even perhaps by far the best among many others.

It is no wonder that even in so-called Christianity there is so much Liberalism, i.e., so much scattered surmising, comparing and questioning whether that which, with so many others, the Christian also seeks and thinks he has may not be found and enjoyed equally well or even better, more radically, in a way which is more satisfying and liberating, in a way which gives greater happiness, with greater depth or

height, or simply, perhaps, more practicably, in some other form,[10] e.g.,
in the liturgico-sacramental or privately cultivated mysticism which so
quickly made its way as an alien body into Christianity, or in the distant
religions and philosophies of India or Japan, or in Dornach or Caux,
or in the concept of the new man proclaimed as the work of deity, i.e.,
the 'historical process,' by Moscow or even more wildly by Peking;
or whether it might not be worth while to snoop about a little in the
hereafter in a para-psychological institute, with the help of a medium
and for hard cash.

How is that which must be thought and said about the foundation of
the Christian life to conduct itself at the annual fair of philosophies and
panaceas, of disguised or undisguised religions, with the very different,
yet confusingly similar, foundations of life which they espouse and
proffer?

The answer to this vexed question can only be no less confusingly
simple. All these foundations of life which resemble the Christian view,
which use the same images, which are in many ways comparable, are
in fact unable to compete with it at the decisive point. Hence they can
be ignored or rejected, but are not in any event to be relativised or
regarded as comparable. It should not even occur to a Christian, who
knows whence as such he comes, to vacillate between his own and
other origins, or to regard another as possibly just as authentic as his
own, or even more so. The decisive point is the divine nature of the
change which is the start of the new life of a man in both cases. In all
non-Christian views of the matter this change consists in an event in the
context of the direct relation to a certain man of a godhead, variously
depicted, which exists, and is present and active, generally, i.e., outside
time and space. Or else it consists in an event in the framework of the
direct relation of a certain man to this godhead. Whatever their deities
be, all other bases of life are alike in this. But in this, too, they all differ
from the foundation of the Christian life. This has nothing whatever to
do with the being and work of a general deity outwith time and space.[11]

---

10   This small-print section offers a remarkably concise definition of liberal Protestantism or
      Neo-Protestantism, according to Barth, namely, an approach to Christianity as one instance
      of a wider reality. Thus, it is one path to a destination that may be reached in other ways (e.g.
      ecological shalom, international peace, psychological balance, racial reconciliation). Over against
      this universalizing tendency, Barth posits the need to listen to the particularism of the gospel of
      Jesus Christ. Barth wound up severing partnership with other so-called 'dialectical theologians'
      (especially Emil Brunner and Rudolf Bultmann) in the late 1920s and early 1930s over precisely
      this issue: the particularism intrinsic to the gospel and, thus, the dogmatic (and not correlationist
      or apologetic) shape of doctrine. For a helpful historical account of their partnership and eventual
      breakup, see Bruce L. McCormack, *Karl Barth's Critically Realistic Dialectical Theology: Its Genesis
      and Development, 1909–1936* (Oxford: Clarendon, 1995), pp. 391–411.
11   The notion of a 'general deity' is a projection of human progress and aspiration and one which

To be sure, the Christian does not dispute the existence and activity of a supposed power which pretends to be deity, which is honoured as such, and which exists, like God, outwith time and space. Hence he does not contest the possibility and actuality of a direct relation of this power to man, and of man to it, within which there may take place all kinds of incisive events which might seem quite seriously to be new beginnings. On the contrary, the existence and work of a supposed deity of this kind, and hence the possibility and actuality of a direct relation between it and man, will be presupposed by the Christian as a foil to the foundation of his Christian life. This is the being and occurrence, powerful in its own way, which was overcome and left behind as outdated by the Christian when the founding of his Christian life took place. What he must question is the true divinity of the general godhead which is reflected in the human striving for, and experiencing of, something new and different, and which confirms and fulfils itself in this striving and experience. What he must deny is the identity of this deity with the God whom he sees active and self-revealed in the origin of his Christian existence. The God whose work is the starting-point in his life is not this general deity. A direct relation between this God of his and himself, within which that event might one day take place, he must categorically repudiate. He cannot believe in the divine nature of the changes which are sought and experienced in the direct relation between that deity and man. Hence he cannot believe in the final relevance of the renewals which might well take place in a man's life in the course of dealings between that deity and man. He cannot believe in the genuineness of the difference, transcendence and otherworldliness which there breaks into the life of man and manifests itself therein. He cannot believe in the mystery, the true newness, of the phenomena which take place there. In spite of their claim and appearance, and the titles ascribed to them, he can regard and interpret them only as (perhaps highly significant) movements in the world, operating on the level of this-worldliness. Hence he cannot view them as events in the same category as that in which he himself has his origin. There can be for him no question of vacillation or choice between his own and these quite different origins. The true divinity of the change to which he owes his being as a Christian gives him clarity of vision in relation to these real changes, in their own way notable, but without

humans must 'categorically repudiate', precisely because the 'decisive point is the divine nature of the change which is the start of the new life'. An underdetermined theology – or anything other than a triune account of God – will fail to honour the gracious nature of salvation in its every aspect. Remember Barth's triune approach to revelation: God as Revealer (Father), Revelation (Son), and Revealedness (Spirit). The triune work arranges, accomplishes, and applies salvation; it is wholly grace, and only so is it possible.

doubt only ostensibly divine, which he sees at work in the philosophies, panaceas and religions of the market-place. It empowers him for,
and summons him to, a decision which, even if he wished, he could
not reverse. He understands their concerns, meanings and intentions;
how could he fail to do so? But there can be no question of his finally
taking them seriously, or even applauding them. For their part, they
themselves show how different they are, at least indirectly, by the fact
that the foundation of the Christian life can only seem to them obscure,
offensive and even absurd in its distinction from them, from new births
grounded in the work of that general godhead.

The freedom of God in which is grounded man's becoming free
to be faithful to God as God is faithful to him, the freedom in which
the Christian life thus has its absolutely unique origin, is the freedom
of which He, the God of Abraham, Isaac and Jacob, has made use
in supreme majesty and condescension in the history of Jesus Christ.
This history is the change, impossible with men but possible with
God, and indeed possible only by God's actual judgment, in which a
man becomes God's friend instead of His enemy, a man who lives for
Him instead of being dead for Him.[12] It is the divine change which
has been made for every man and which is valid for every man,
but which is thankfully acknowledged, recognised and confessed by
Christians. It is so as Jesus Christ is the One elected from eternity to
be the Head and Saviour of all men, who in time responded to God's
faithfullness with human faithfullness as the Representative of all men.
As and because He was this, as and because, in the name and stead
of all, He was born and suffered and died as the Man of God, as and
because He was manifested for all in His resurrection as the One who
did this for all, the change which took place in His history took place
for all. In it the turning of all from unfaithfullness to faithfullness took
place. In this history of His the Christian life became an event as the
life of all. A Christian, however, is a man from whom it is not hidden
that his own history took place along with the history of Jesus Christ.
As a word spoken to him and received by him in the living power of
the Holy Spirit, this has been disclosed to him as the decisive event
which establishes his existence as a Christian. He himself in the midst
of all other men can see himself as one of those for whom and in

12   The history of Jesus is the change of men. When Barth was asked once when he was saved, he
     pointed back to the year 33 A.D. Here he will speak of the birthday of the Christian as Christmas
     Day. He means to depict the objective nature of the work of Christ and its ongoing ripple effects
     throughout the centuries and across the globe. He can answer such, because he also says here that
     the Christian is 'a man whose acknowledged, recognized, and confessed Lord he has become. He
     is a man to whom Jesus Christ has given not just a potential but an actual share in that history of
     His.'

whose place Jesus Christ did what He did. The Christian is a man whose life Jesus Christ has entered as the subject of that history of His. He is a man whose acknowledged, recognised and confessed Lord He has become. He is a man to whom Jesus Christ has given not just a potential but an actual share in that history of His. Thus Jesus Christ, His history, became and is the foundation of Christian existence; this and this alone. The Christian comes from Him, from His history, from knowledge of it; he also looks back thereto. This is the ground on which he stands and walks. This is the air which he breathes. This is the word which he has in his ears before, above and after all other words. This is the light, the one light, the incomparably bright light, which illumines him.

This, the history of Jesus Christ, is the point of convergence for all the New Testament approximations, which, even though they are figurative, are ultimately more than figurative. This is the reality of the new beginning which is at issue in all of them.[13]

For what is the new garment which the Christian has put on – and must continually put on – and as the wearer of which he is a Christian? The new man? Yes, but any suggestion which might remain that this is only a self-made costume, or that it is a new costume in which the wearer is still the same, is dispelled when it is expressly stated in Gal. 3.27 and Rom. 13.14 that when a man puts on Christ he puts off the old man and puts on the new. Who other than this is the One who in 1 Cor. 15.47 is called the second or new Adam from heaven by whom the first and earthly Adam is done away, transcended, overcome? In His blood, the blood of the Lamb (in a bold combination of images), the garments of the elect and called (Rev. 7.14; 19.13) are made white. And it need hardly be said that only with reference to Him can a man be addressed seriously as a man of God (2 Tim. 3.17). Who is meant again when this new man is called the inner man is plain when Paul says in Gal. 2.20 that it is Christ who lives in him, or when Christians are summoned in 2 Cor. 13.5 to know themselves, and therewith to know Christ in them. Similarly, when there is reference to the new name of Christians which is written in the book of life, it is simplest and surest to think of the name Christians (which they were first given in Antioch, Acts 11.26), and thus to think once more of the name of Jesus Christ Himself.

---

13 Barth argues that the moral change in us and the conversion of us are founded on what is accomplished outside of us. The first strand of NT teaching grounds and sustains the other two strands: *extra nos* (outside us) founds and fuels what is *in nobis* (in us) and *pro nobis* (for us). Barth shows that Jesus Christ is the centre of moral change and the writing of the law upon the heart as well as the person in whom we experience death and new life.

Again it is only as His law (Gal. 6.2) that the work of the law, the fulfilling of what God requires, can be written in their hearts. The spiritual man is distinguished from the merely physical man by the fact that he has the mind of Christ (1 Cor. 2.16). By His circumcision (Col. 2.11) – the context shows clearly that the reference is to His death – these new hearts, in virtue of His dwelling in them in faith (Eph. 3.17), become and are the centres of a life which is to be lived anew.

It is exactly the same with what the New Testament says about the new birth and begetting in virtue of which alone, but assuredly, a man enters the kingdom of God. The authority with which men become the children of God does not fall on them from heaven, nor can it be mediated through other men, and they certainly cannot fashion it for themselves. It is given them by Him to whom John the Baptist could only bear witness, by Him who came into the world and to His own as the true light, by Him who was not received by His own. He gives it them as the freedom to believe on Him, on His name. Thus these men were born of God (Jn. 1.9–13). The completely unexpected christological turn of the conversation with Nicodemus points in this direction. In interpretation of 'from above' (Jn. 3.3) this points first to birth from the Spirit. But then quite suddenly (v. 13) the coming down of the Son of Man from heaven, and on earth His exaltation on the cross (compared to the lifting up of the brazen serpent), are described as the event, incomprehensible to Nicodemus, in virtue of which those who believe in Him will have eternal life in Him. Thus, as the first Adam became living soul, so the second and last Adam became life-giving Spirit (1 Cor. 15.45). Through His resurrection Christians were begotten again to a living hope (1 Pet. 1.3). The decisive statement of Paul in the account of his conversion in Gal. 1 is that it pleased God to reveal His Son in him ('in me,' v. 16). Conversely, but to the same effect, if a man is in Christ he is a new creature (2 Cor. 5.17). Through Him God has poured out the Spirit on us as 'the bath of regeneration and renewal' (Tit. 3.5f.). Nor is the meaning any different in other passages which speak of the new begetting and birth of man from God. It is true exegesis, not eisegesis, to say that the nativity of Christ is the nativity of the Christian man; Christmas Day is the birthday of every Christian.

Finally, the matter is plain when we think of passages which describe death as man's entry into life and consequently as the foundation of the Christian life. According to the New Testament, the death of man, whether literal or figurative, does not have as such any saving power for him. These passages, though often construed thus, have nothing whatever to do with a mysticism of physical or spiritual dying. When the extraordinary thing happens that a man (Mk. 8.35) loses his life in order that he may thus (only thus, but truly thus) save it or gain it, this takes place 'for my sake and the gospel's.' Nor does this mean in the first instance that he dies as a martyr or in some other self-sacrificial endeavour for Jesus and His cause. The saying may include this, but the decisive point is that this saving loss of life takes place for him as one of those who have a share in the life-saving and life-winning loss of life of Him who is the origin, content and proclaimer of the Gospel — as one of those who died in the death which He suffered in their place and for them, and who for this reason, again in fellowship with Him, may look and move forward to the resurrection and to life. Jesus spoke of this saving death of His for many, for all, when in Mt. 3.15 He gave the reason for commanding John the Baptist ('let it be done at once') to admit Him to the baptism of repentance in the Jordan along with all the people: 'For thus it becometh us (it is right) to fulfil all righteousness.' That is to say, Jesus must and will — and the Baptist must recognise this by admitting him to the baptism of repentance — subject Himself, in solidarity and even in identification with all, to the divine judgment proclaimed in the preaching of the Baptist, so that everything which is righteously demanded of all, and therewith the whole of God's righteous will, is fulfilled. As attested by His letting Himself be baptised with them and like them, He thus entered on His Messianic office. Indeed, He here began the discharge of this office which was completed on the cross of Golgotha. In this office the main concern will be, and already is, the justification, sanctification and vocation of this whole wretched people. Already, then, those who with Him and like Him are baptised by John are passive participants in His death, not in virtue of their own baptism, but in virtue of the fact that Jesus lets Himself be baptised with them and like them, and that He therewith enters upon, and begins to exercise, His saving office. How the event at the Jordan and the event at Golgotha are interrelated as beginning and end may be seen from the saying in Lk. 12.50 which describes the goal of the office of Jesus in His death as a baptism: 'I have a baptism to be baptised with; and how am I straitened till it be accomplished!' That this baptism of death includes within itself that of His disciples and therewith their death, that they, too, will die in and with Him, may be seen in Mk. 10.35–40. Here, when the sons of Zebedee ask that they may be allowed to sit on His right hand and His left hand in His future kingdom, He gives a threefold answer. First, He states: 'Ye know not what ye ask.' Then He puts the question whether they can drink the cup which He drinks (He is already doing this) or be baptised with the baptism with which He is baptised (the present tense again). Finally, when they boldly assure Him that they can, He surprisingly makes the positive statement: 'Ye shall indeed drink of the cup that I drink of; and with the baptism that I am baptised withal shall ye be baptised.' The question of the places of honour is left open; they will be given to those for whom they are appointed and prepared. Instead, a clear answer is given to a question which the disciples had not put and which they had obviously not considered, namely, how a man is to enter at all into that glory. The answer is that he enters into that glory, not as he 'can' participate in Jesus' baptism of death, but as his participation in it actually becomes an event.[14] If in passing – but only in passing – there is here perhaps a hint at the martyrdom which the disciples should suffer, the decisive reference of the prophecy is to the death of Jesus Himself, in which it is ordained that the disciples should participate. Jesus does not drink that cup for Himself alone. He is not baptised with that baptism in isolation. This all takes place in their stead and for them. Hence they, too, will die in His death, and therewith their entry into glory will be secured (no matter what places they occupy). Similarly, in other New Testament statements there is no crucifixion or death of a man which in itself and as such is of saving significance, or constitutes the foundation of his Christian life, or includes within it the hope of resurrection and eternal life, no matter whether it be death in the literal sense or in some transferred sense. Nor is there any begetting or birth of a man which is saving in itself and as such, even though it be understood as a kind of spiritual, moral, or religious regeneration. In itself and as such a man's death is the wages which sin pays him (Rom. 6.23). Death came into the world, and passed upon all men, through sin (Rom. 5.12, 17). Death is the sting of sin (1 Cor. 15.56). Sin reigns in death (Rom. 5.21) so long as it can and may. Man dies through sin (Rom. 7.10). Christian mysticism in every age, which has often, in pagan fashion, led to death mysticism, ought to have taken warning from these passages.[15] It leads into a blind alley. In itself and as such man's death is in no sense a transition to life. Death is destruction into which all the will of the flesh plunges as into a cataract. It is the evil fruit which man, having

---

14　Many theologians are debating the nature of 'participation' in the divine; Barth is not totally opposed to such a notion, but he wants to insist on (1) its Christocentric focus, and (2) its actual-istic nature as event and not as a possession or power. For further reflection on recent debates, see Bruce L. McCormack, 'Participation in God, Yes; Deification, No: Two Modern Protestant Responses to an Ancient Question', in *Orthodox and Modern: Studies in the Theology of Karl Barth* (Grand Rapids: Baker Academic, 2008), pp. 235–60. McCormack argues that the actualistic nature of this participation owes to its eschatological flavour.

15　Barth sketches a path from introspective mysticism to morbid focus on one's death and one's sin – he identifies this as a malady. He responds throughout this paragraph by pointing outside the self to the saviour, who has died and risen.

sown to the flesh, must reap (Gal. 6.8; Rom. 8.6). But Christ, according to so many New Testament sayings, died for our sins (1 Cor. 15.3). He bore our sins on the tree (1 Pet. 2.24). He was and is the Lamb of God which removes, bears and bears away the sin of the whole world (Jn. 1.29). In His death, therefore, He took the place of all men − the place where they all should have died a hopeless death as sinners. He gave His life a ransom for many slaves (Mk. 10.45 par.). He, the sinless One, who was made sin for us (2 Cor. 5.21), died this hopeless death, the accursed death of sinners on the cross (Gal. 3.13). He died this death for us (1 Thess. 5.10). Hence we ourselves neither must nor can die the death which we ought to die as sinners. We neither must nor can experience any more the dereliction of this death (Mk. 15.34). For He has 'tasted' death for us all (Heb. 2.9). Inasmuch as He died the death in our place, we have it absolutely behind us. In His death we who deserved to die as He died are already put to death. With Him Paul (Gal. 2.19) who was once Saul, and indeed each of us (as the old man we all were and are, Rom. 6.6), is crucified − with Him the two thieves, the impenitent no less than the penitent (Lk. 23.39ff.). What Paul carried about all his life in his body as his own dying was not really his own, but that of Jesus (2 Cor. 4.10). We are all 'planted together in the likeness of his death' (Rom. 6.5). We are all dead with Him. As the sinners we were and are, therefore, we are set aside, done away, no longer present in Him. 'One died for all − then all are dead' (2 Cor. 5.14). How is this? Because they have appropriated the crucifixion of Christ in the obedience of faith? (R. Bultmann) This is true; it is the necessary consequence of their dying with Him. They are to crucify the flesh with its affections and lusts (Gal. 5.24; see Col. 3.5). Nevertheless, their saving death, which promises new life and in which they become the Christians who do this, took place when Jesus Christ, in His death on the cross, at a time when they were still enemies (Rom. 5.10) and there could be no question of the obedience of faith, appropriated them and took them up into His death. Their saving death took place, not now and here, but in supreme actuality then and there, when they, too, were baptised in and with Jesus' baptism of death, when He 'was lifted up from the earth' ('he said this, signifying what death he should die') and drew 'all men unto him' (Jn. 12.32ff.). More accurately, it took place now and here inasmuch as it took place then and there.

In the history of Jesus Christ, then, is the origin and beginning of the Christian life, the divine change in which the impossible thing that there is movement from faithfullness, from the depth and power of the faithfullness of God, to faith, to the corresponding faithfullness of man

(Rom. 1.17), is not only possible but actual.[16] The witness of the New Testament is so definite in this respect that there can be no evading this statement, and it is so unequivocal that no demythologising or reinterpretation of the statement is possible. Many human events and developments may have other origins and beginnings; the Christian life, faithfullness to God as the free act and attitude of a man, begins with that which in the days of Augustus and Tiberius, on the way from the manger of Bethlehem to the cross of Golgotha, was actualised as that which is possible with God. The fact that the change in which a man becomes a Christian has its ground and commencement in the history of Jesus Christ characterises it as a divine happening, in distinction from all the other natural or supernatural changes which are notable enough in their own way. Any description of the Christian life which might seek to assign to it any other basis can only be the description of a tree hewn off from its root. Whatever may become of it, one can never again ascribe its own life to it. It can have its own life only in unity with the root. Similarly, man's own life as the Christian life is possible and actual only in unity with its origin in Jesus Christ. We speak of its mystery when we say that it has its origin there in Him, that it derives from the divine change which has taken place there in Him. What may be said in explanation of this statement cannot dispel the mystery. It can only make it greater, not smaller. Explanation of the statement will consist only in its confirmation, in giving it greater precision.

Let us consider at once the point at which the statement seems to place us before a riddle, so that one is naturally tempted either to evade it or to blunt its force by reinterpretation. With good reason we have had to begin this whole discussion by laying stress on the fact that, if it is to be possible for a man to be faithful to God instead of unfaithful, there must be a change which comes over this man himself. Nor may this change be simply an awakening of his natural powers, nor his endowment with supernatural powers, nor his placing by God under another light and judgment in which he may stand before God. It must be an inner change in virtue of which he himself becomes a different man, so that as this different man he freely, of himself, and by his own resolve, thinks and acts and conducts himself otherwise than he did before. Does, then, the unavoidable and unequivocal statement of the New Testament that the divine change effected in the history of Jesus

---

16   Barth is rendering Romans 1.17 – 'from faith to faith' – as reflecting, first, on divine faithfulness and, second, on a corresponding human faithfulness, made actual by the divine faithfulness as expressed in the proclamation of the gospel. Barth has already offered this reading in his *The Epistle to the Romans* (6th ed.; trans. Edwyn C. Hoskyns; New York: Oxford University Press, 1968), p. 41.

Christ is the origin and beginning of the Christian life, simply bring us back to the highly unsatisfactory view that this change does not affect the man himself, who is not Jesus Christ and whose history is not His history, that, while it might apply to him in some way, it does not really touch him, that it necessarily remains alien and external to him, that it neither is nor can be his own change from disobedience to obedience? If something took place outside us, it is an event which is not merely distant in time and space, but also completely different from all our own possibilities and actualities – the event of the obedience of Jesus Christ, of His birth, of His self-proclamation, of His crucifixion, of His whole being and work as very Son of God and Son of Man. What has this Other, who there and then was born in Bethlehem and died on Golgotha, what has He to do with me? What has the freedom of His life as very Son of God and Son of Man to do with my necessary liberation to be a child of God, and consequently with the humanity which is true because it corresponds to the will of this Father? And what have I to do with Him? How can it be that, as I grow out of Him as out of a root, He can be one with me and I with him, and in unity with Him my own life can begin as a Christian life, the life of a man who is faithful to God? How can that which He was and did outside us become an event in us? And if it does not, how is it that, in virtue of His existence and history, I can and should be faithful to God, becoming a friend instead of an enemy, one who moves on to life instead of being a victim of death, a member of the kingdom of God, a Christian? This is the question which we undoubtedly face and which we must undoubtedly accept and answer.

Now if on the one side we are not allowed to offer an artificial solution to the riddle presented by the situation, on the other we must pay heed to the natural solution which suggests itself (if only the facts are permitted to speak for themselves). It may be assumed that any solution is artificial in which the contrast in the unity between Christ and the man who becomes a Christian is eliminated, in which it is obscured or denied that the founding of the Christian life is an event in the genuine intercourse between God and man as two different partners. Anything of this kind involves a falsifying of the matter at issue.[17]

---

17 Change must come from God, yet be lived by the human. Thus Barth addresses two false paths to resolution, what he calls the christomonist and anthropomonist approaches. He believes that many heirs of the Reformation wrongly construed the legacy of Luther as a christomonist path, where God's grace is magnified but a real Christian humanism is not affirmed. He suggests that the Neo-Protestants take the anthropomonist path, along with the Roman Catholic Church, in affirming real moral change and yet failing to root it adequately in divine grace. He argues that both errors seek to do away with the mystery of the faith – both allow for an extraneous

Hence we have to describe as artificial what might be called a christomonist solution. On this view the 'in us,' the liberation of man himself, is simply an appendage, a mere reflection, of the act of liberation accomplished by Jesus Christ in His history, and hence outside us. Jesus Christ, then, is fundamentally alone as the only subject truly at work. The faithfullness of the man who is distinct from Him cannot be an answer to the word of divine faithfullness spoken in His history. It is not man's free action. It is simply an aspect or manifestation of the act of God fulfilled in Jesus Christ. It is not an act of grateful human obedience which, though awakened and empowered by God's grace, is still achieved by man himself. It is simply a passive participation of man in that which God alone did in Jesus Christ. It is itself a divine action, not a human action evoked by God and responsible to Him. The request or summons: 'Be ye reconciled to God' (2 Cor. 5.20) is rendered superfluous from the very first by the reconciliation of man with God which has been omnipotently effected in Jesus Christ. It thus seems to be a pointless summons to an act which is completely useless. The question of a human activity corresponding to the divine activity, the ethical problem of the genesis of the Christian life, is answered by its dismissal as irrelevant. All anthropology and soteriology are thus swallowed up in Christology. Even in their most far-reaching statements, however, the New Testament witnesses, including Paul in Gal. 2:19f., did not think or say this. They do not ask us to entertain any such 'subjectivism from above.' If we are to be true to their teaching, we must not be misled by even a sound christocentric intention into

solution to be imposed on the Scriptural data, rather than following the Scriptures to their own presentation (for this critique elsewhere, see I/2.124–125; IV/1.16–17). Over against a monist position (either in the christomonist or anthropomonist direction), Barth poses the option of 'Christocentricity', wherein the mystery of the Incarnation affirms the reality of divine and human life. The 'Chalcedonian pattern' that Hunsinger finds in Barth's theology certainly elucidates this claim. The divine and the human each have their own integrity (as divine or as human, respectively), even as they are related in the most intimate way (in the person of Jesus and, thus, in the lives of all those included in him); this can be so only because the divine precedes and produces the truly human (so that there is a fundamental asymmetry). See George Hunsinger, 'Double Agency as Test Case', in How to Read Karl Barth: The Shape of His Theology (New York: Oxford University Press, 1991), pp. 185–224. Later in his book Hunsinger argues that the Incarnation provides the pattern for understanding Christian fellowship with God in Christ: 'The Incarnation is the great mystery which grounds and patterns the mystery of fellowship in which the great mystery finds secondary reiteration. The great mystery is that of the objective enactment of divine self-revelation and human salvation. Its secondary reiteration is the mystery of the acknowledgment and personal reception of that which has been objectively enacted, and the mystery of fellowship with the absolute sovereign who enacted it' (p. 228). John Webster summarizes his ethics in this way: 'grace both accomplishes and ... elicits' ('The Christian in Revolt: Some Reflections on The Christian Life', in Reckoning with Barth: Essays in Commemoration of the Centenary of Karl Barth's Birth [ed. Nigel Biggar. London: Mowbray, 1988], p. 144).

thinking or speaking thus, or even in this direction.[18] Indeed, a true Christocentricity will strictly forbid us to do so.

An anthropomonist view, of course, is also artificial. On this view it is Jesus Christ, and what took place in His history, outside us, which is regarded as a mere predicate and instrument, cipher and symbol, of that which truly and properly took place only in us, the subject being none other than man himself. Now it is man who occupies the stage alone in his transformation into a Christian. His human change, his awakening, his inner compulsion, his resolving on faith and love and hope, his much-vaunted decision, is now as such the truly divine change. In its fulfilment the history of Jesus Christ perhaps serves as stimulation, instruction, or aid. Perhaps (but only perhaps) it is even indispensable as an example. But the first moving cause, the secret, of man's salvation history is man himself, his transition from unfaithfullness to faith-fullness, his free act of obedience. Act of obedience? Can it seriously be called this? This understanding allows no place for a concrete other which acts with power towards him and which speaks to him in the word of promise. Hence the change does not really have the character of a response to the action of another, of an answer to his word, of an act of gratitude. Here too, from the other side, by making man his own reconciler, teacher and master in the relation to God, the ethical problem of the genesis of the Christian life is solved by its dismissal as pointless. Christology is now swallowed up by a self-sufficient anthropology and soteriology. It need hardly be said that the New Testament witnesses, even when they appeal most strongly to man himself, even in their most urgent calls for repentance, decision, faith, patience and love, never think or speak thus. Once again therefore, if we are to be true to their teaching, we must not be seduced by this monism, which, in contrast to the first, might be called a 'subjectivism from below.'

Common to both these obvious but distorted solutions is the fact that they approach the data – this is why they are artificial – from outside and with the aid of an alien concept of unity. They do not allow the matter to be its own interpreter. Hence both of them conjure

---

18 The gospel for Barth brings with it a demand in its wake. He will say a few pages later that 'particular stress should be laid on the fact that it [the beginning of the Christian life] demands gratitude. It demands it by giving man what is necessary for it and what he could not have without it. Herewith it does truly demand it' (IV/4.35; cf. II/2.511–512; III/1.414; IV/2.504; IV/3.369–371; as well as his essay, 'Gospel and Law', in *Community, State, and Church* [trans. G. Ronald Howe; Garden City, NY: Anchor, 1960], pp. 71–100). For a helpful analysis of Barth's approach to the law and gospel, see Eberhard Jüngel, 'Gospel and Law: The Relationship of Dogmatics to Ethics', in *Karl Barth: A Theological Legacy* (trans. Garrett E. Paul; Philadelphia: Westminster, 1986), especially p. 117; Michael Allen, *The Christ's Faith: A Dogmatic Account* (T & T Clark Studies in Systematic Theology; London: T & T Clark, 2009), pp. 166–7.

away the mystery which confronts us in it. But if we conjure away the mystery and imprison it in one or other of the two monistic formulae (or perhaps alternately in both), we falsify the matter itself and let it slip from our gaze. Thus, no matter how successful the imprisonment (from above or from below) may be, we are really speaking about something else. But this is the very thing which must not be allowed to happen. One must accept the first riddle if one is to see how the matter interprets itself, how the riddle is solved from within.

If we follow the singular movement of New Testament thinking we must affirm on the one side that basically the enigma of the matter is posed quite simply by the mystery of the faithfullness of God which in the One affirms, rectifies, saves, gladdens and therewith summons to faithfullness each and every man. This is, then, the faithfullness in which God shows Himself to be the God of man by giving and interposing Himself to prosecute man's cause before Him, to make it a good cause instead of a bad one. He who may hear and follow the call of God sounded forth in this faithful work of God cannot take offence or start back; he can only worship and praise. Everything is well. The history of Jesus Christ is different from all other histories. In its particularity, singularity and uniqueness it cannot be compared or interchanged with any other. Different from all other histories, it demands the singular thinking of the New Testament witnesses (which we must accept if we are to understand) because, as the history of the salvation which God in His free grace has ascribed, addressed and granted to all men, it is from the very first a particular story with a universal goal and bias. In its very limitation it reaches beyond itself. It comprehends the world around, i.e., the whole world of mankind. Indeed, it comes with revolutionary force into the life of each and every man. As this individual history it is thus cosmic in origin and goal. As such it is not sterile. It is a fruitful history which newly shapes every human life. Having taken place outside us, it also works in us, introducing a new being of every man. It certainly took place outside us. Yet it took place, not for its own sake, but for us: who for us men and for our salvation descended from heaven. This 'for us' or 'on our account' is to be taken literally and strictly. As the true Son of God, and hence as the true Son of Man, Jesus Christ was not merely faithful to the faithful God; by being faithful to Him as His Father, and according to His righteous will, He was also faithful to us as His brethren (Heb. 2.17; 3.2, 6). He was faithful to us by being ready to give Himself, and by giving Himself, to fulfil the covenant between God and man in His own person, i.e., by being faithful to God in our place, in the place of those who previously were unfaithful to Him. In our place – even as He was there and then what only He could be, He was this in our here and now, in the weakness, ungodliness and enmity, the heart, the personal centre of the existence of every man. But if He acts outside us for us, and to that extent also in us, this necessarily implies that in spite of the unfaithfullness of every man He creates in the history of every man the beginning of his new history, the history of a man who has become faithful to God. All this is because it is God Himself who has taken man's cause in hand in His person. It was not a man who posited or made this new beginning. Not of himself did man become another man, faithful to God instead of unfaithful. Nevertheless, on the path from Bethlehem to Golgotha which Jesus Christ traversed for him as very Son of God and therefore as very Son of Man, the new beginning of his life was posited and made as that of a man who is faithful to God. On the ground of this beginning of his in the history of Jesus Christ he here and to-day can and should live his new Christian life which corresponds to, because it follows, the divine transformation of his heart and person which took place there and then. This is the self-explication of the matter as, with a primary reference to Jesus Christ, the New Testament witnesses render it in their admittedly singular thinking. It is surely clear that, if we follow them, the anthropomonism which we have called subjectivism from below is ruled out at once. The Christian life is founded, not when man takes the place of Jesus Christ as his own liberator, but when Jesus Christ takes the place of man to liberate him there.

To give the more place to its mystery, however, we must pursue the other aspect of this self-explication of the matter in which the enigma is resolved from within. The matter explains itself, not only from above downwards, but also from below upwards. Hence the New Testament witnesses of the self-explication, presenting it with reference to Jesus Christ, always present it also with reference to the Christian. As Jesus Christ takes the place of man, does there what he does not do, and is faithful to God in the stead of the unfaithful, He, or God through Him, liberates man for faithfullness to God on his own part. What, then, does it mean for us who are not Jesus Christ that His history, which took place outside us, took place for us, that this 'for us' is efficacious, and that it thus includes the fact that, as it took place then and there, as the history of that One, it also takes place here and now, in us, in the life of the many? Obviously, in fulfilment of the fullness of the divine possibility, it means that the God at work in that history, while He does not find and confirm a direct relation between Himself and us, does create and adopt this relation, which we could not create or adopt for ourselves, but which we cannot evade when He does so. Interceding for us in Jesus Christ, He is now present to us, not at a distance, but in the closest proximity, confronting us in our own being, thought and reflection. Since He is the righteous, merciful and as such almighty God working in the history of Jesus Christ, what takes place is thus quite simply that in us, in our heart, at the centre of our existence, there is set a contradiction of our unfaithfullness, a contradiction which we cannot escape, which we have to endorse, in face of which we cannot cling to our unfaithfullness, by which it is not merely forbidden but prevented and rendered impossible. Inasmuch as Jesus Christ is at work for us and in us, unfaithfullness to God is a disallowed possibility which can no longer be actualised. It is seen to be the wholly impossible possibility on which we can no longer count, which we see to be eliminated and taken from us by God's omnipotent contradiction set up in us. What then? We can will and do only one thing – the thing which is positively prefigured for us in the action of the true Son of God and Son of Man at work within us. The only possibility is to be faithful to God. This is our liberation through the divine change effected in the history of Jesus Christ. This change which God has made is in truth man's liberation. It comes upon him wholly from without, from God. Nevertheless, it is his liberation. The point is that here, as everywhere, the omnicausality of God must not be construed as His sole causality.[19] The divine change in whose accomplishment a man becomes a Christian is an event of true intercourse between God and man. If it undoubtedly has its origin in God's initiative, no less indisputably man is not ignored or passed over in it. He is taken seriously as an independent creature of God. He is not run down and overpowered, but set on his own feet. He is not put under tutelage, but addressed and treated as an adult. The history of Jesus Christ, then, does not destroy a man's own history. In virtue of it this history becomes a new history, but it is still his own new history. The faithfullness to God to which he is summoned is not, then, an emanation of God's faithfullness. It is truly his own faithfullness, decision and act. He could not achieve it if he were not liberated thereto. But being thus liberated, he does it as his own act, as his answer to the Word of God spoken to him in the history of Jesus Christ. As there must be in this matter no subjectivism from below, so there must be no subjectivism from above. As there must be no anthropomonism, so there must be no christomonism.[20]

---

19 Later in IV/4 Barth will deny the role of 'sacraments' in the life of the Christian community (IV/4.106, 134). John Webster has argued that some of this approach to divine and human action (seemingly at odds with his teaching on the *concursus Dei* here and elsewhere) is rooted in his early study of Zwingli ('The Theology of Zwingli', in *Barth's Earlier Theology: Four Studies* [London: T & T Clark, 2005], especially pp. 35–9). For sharp criticism of Barth's approach (from a former student and one of the editors of the English edition of his *Church Dogmatics*), see T. F. Torrance, 'The One Baptism Common to Christ and His Church', in *Theology in Reconciliation* (Grand Rapids: Eerdmans, 1976), pp. 82–105.

20 This section has been produced elsewhere as Karl Barth. 'Extra Nos – Pro Nobis – In Nobis', *The Thomist* 50, no. 4 (1986), pp. 497–511 (trans. George Hunsinger).

INDEX

Name index

Scripture index

Christology
140-206
Paradigmatic
16-56

Made in the USA
Middletown, DE
15 January 2019